WORKING WITH TRUMAN

Books by Ken Hechler

Insurgency: Personalities and Politics of the Taft Era

The Bridge at Remagen

West Virginia Memories of President Kennedy

Toward the Endless Frontier

The Endless Space Frontier (American Astronautical Society abridgement)

Working
with Truman

A PERSONAL MEMOIR OF

THE WHITE HOUSE YEARS

KEN HECHLER

G. P. PUTNAM'S SONS

New York

The author acknowledges permission from the following sources to reprint material in their
control:

Brandt & Brandt Literary Agents, Inc., for material from *The Man from Independence*
by Jonathan Daniels, copyright © 1950 by Jonathan Daniels, copyright renewed 1978 by
Jonathan Daniels, originally published by J. B. Lippincott Company.

Farrar, Straus and Giroux for material from *Mr. President* by William Hillman, copyright © 1952 by William Hillman and Alfred Wagg, published by Farrar, Straus and Young.

William Morrow & Company for material from *Harry S. Truman* by Margaret Truman,
copyright © 1972 by Margaret Truman Daniel.

The New York Times Company for the May 14, 1950, article by Anthony H. Leviero, ©
1950 by The New York Times Company.

W. W. Norton & Company, Inc., for material from *Conflict and Crisis* by Robert J.
Donovan, copyright © 1977 by Robert J. Donovan.

G. P. Putnam's Sons for material from *Plain Speaking* by Merle Miller, copyright ©
1973 by Merle Miller.

The Regents Press of Kansas for material from *The Truman White House*, edited by
Francis Heller, copyright © 1980 by The Regents Press of Kansas.

Russell & Volkening as agents of the author for material from *The Loneliest Campaign*
by Irwin Ross, copyright © 1968 by Irwin Ross.

Scripps-Howard News Service for April 4, 1950, article, copyright © 1950 by Scripps-
Howard Newspapers.

Ticknor & Fields for material from *Aspects of the Presidency* by John Hersey, copyright
© 1980 by John Hersey.

Time Inc. for material from *Memoirs of Harry S. Truman: Volume Two: Years of Trial
and Hope,* copyright © 1956 Time Inc., published by Doubleday & Company, Inc.

United Features Syndicate, Inc., for September 14, 1950, column from "The Washington Merry-Go-Round," by Drew Pearson, copyright © 1950 by The Bell Syndicate, Inc.

Library of Congress Cataloging in Publication Data

Hechler, Ken, date.
Working with Truman.

    Bibliography: p.
    Includes index.
    1. Truman, Harry S., 1884–1972. 2. Presidents—
United States—Biography. 3. Hechler, Ken,
date. 4. Presidents—United States—Staff—
Biography. I. Title.
E814.H377   973.918′092′4 [B]   82–7514
ISBN 0-399-12762-3   AACR2

To my fellow-members of the Truman White House staff

Contents

Acknowledgments

This book could not exist without the shared experiences of every man and woman who worked on the Truman White House staff. Beyond the White House, there were hundreds of people scattered throughout the federal departments and agencies, on Capitol Hill, in the news media, at all levels of officialdom down to the grass roots, and in countless private organizations in all walks of life who unknowingly helped provide the grist for this literary mill. I wish I could list them all.

Special thanks go to George M. Elsey and Charles S. Murphy for the many suggestions they made and the encouragement they gave me. Clark M. Clifford and James L. Sundquist were also extremely helpful. The late Judge Samuel I. Rosenman, who drilled me so successfully on the twin principles of truth and thoroughness, and tried his best to teach me clarity, is clearly a moving spirit behind this volume. My debt to Judge Rosenman and his widow, Mrs. Dorothy Rosenman, is considerable. That incomparable Indiana University history professor, Robert H. Ferrell, kindly read some of the manuscript and made a host of very useful suggestions. Professor Louise Bailey of Marshall University and my administrative assistant while serving in the U.S. House of Representatives, Dick Leonard, also suggested ways of improving my rough English.

Words can never express my enthusiasm for the entire staff at the Harry S. Truman Library in Independence, Missouri. Their friendly spirit of cooperation makes it a joy to delve into their rich collection of Truman documents. Elizabeth H. Safly, librarian, answered innumerable questions and gave me a lot of good sound advice, in addition to the tasty brown-bag lunch she once prepared. Life at Independence would certainly have been duller without the incredible speed and sunny smile of Tanya Paskowski at the Xerox machine. Director Benedict K. Zobrist, assistant director George Curtis and the truly great staff—people like Dennis E. Bilger, Erwin J. Mueller and all those other wonderful folks assisted above and beyond the call of duty. Dennis introduced me to what a good research archivist can find, and Erwin is a genius at spotting the bull's-eye of any research target.

Great home cooking and a friendly household characterize the bed and board provided by Mrs. Haroldine Helm—just the thing to put you in the mood for a full day's work at the Truman Library a few hundred yards across the fields from her home.

When others told me this book didn't have a chance, Julian Bach kept the faith. At G. P. Putnam's, I had the pleasure of working with a competent, responsive and speedy editor, Christine Schillig. Who could ask for anything more?

Foreword

During Harry Truman's presidency, he was assisted in the White House by a small staff that enjoyed extraordinarily high morale. This is the story of that staff and the problems they confronted and tackled, written from a personal point of view. This is not a complete biography of Truman, but a memoir of what I saw and experienced during some of the most exciting years of my life.

As a research assistant and protégé of Judge Samuel I. Rosenman, Franklin D. Roosevelt's key speech-writer over a seventeen-year period from the New York governorship through the presidency, I had been a frequent visitor to the White House. When Judge Rosenman continued to help President Truman, first on a full-time basis and later as a part-time speech draft contributor, I was lucky enough to realize a boyhood ambition to work at the pinnacle of government. Clark M.Clifford, President Truman's special counsel, recruited me late in 1949 on a temporary assignment. Early in 1950, this developed into full-time work on the Truman White House staff. Judge Rosenman and Clifford both left the White House to establish successful law practices, and in later years I worked most closely with Charles S. Murphy, who succeeded Clifford as Truman's special counsel.

Over the years the White House speech-writers—less than half a dozen eager and ambitious historians, political scientists, economists and lawyers—helped President Truman translate policies into action through the spoken word and also through direct negotiation with movers and shakers of public policy. We were united by a burning loyalty and tremendous personal admiration for a man thrust into the presidency against his will, who daily demonstrated a deep understanding of the constitutional power and leadership of this high office. At the same time, this outspoken group of dedicated White House assistants sounded off loud and clear when any staff member felt the President was wrongly advised or could benefit from a fresh viewpoint. Yet there was never any question that Harry S. Truman was in charge.

There wasn't much of a hierarchy in the Truman White House, but I guess I was somewhere in the middle—high enough to see the President frequently, and low enough to escape the glare of media notoriety. In my capacity as "special assistant," in charge of research and a contributor to the speech team, there were days when I saw the President three or four times, other periods when I holed up with a special writing project for a week at a time without much contact with the Oval Office. As the specialist in "local color" for all the "whistle stops" where the Truman train pulled in for a speech, I went on all the campaign trips after 1950, and during these periods I had frequent contact with the President. A trip to Key West for one of the semi-annual Truman vacations furnished my best opportunity for relaxed and extended conversation with one of the busiest men in the world.

In this volume I have tried to convey what it was like to be associated with President Truman. Readers who expect a deep analysis of modes of staff operation, or the basic theories that underlie presidential addresses, may find that this account does not fit their own formulae. I'm interested in telling what we all experienced in working with Harry Truman, and in chronicling the great moments in history in which I was privileged to participate.

WORKING WITH TRUMAN

1

"What Kind of a Person?"

Just outside the President's Oval Office, an expensively tailored visitor fidgeted and glanced at his watch. Winthrop W. Aldrich had been waiting well over half an hour beyond his scheduled appointment with President Truman. A Missouri couple, looking for all the world like tourists with little else to do, stuck their heads in the door and casually wondered if the President were busy. They were waved in, and emerged laughing.

Aldrich did a slow burn. Brother-in-law of John D. Rockefeller, Jr., chairman of the board of the powerful Chase National Bank, scion of a prominent family, he tried to appear unconcerned but his anger was apparent. A staff member, observing the thundercloud on Aldrich's face, sauntered in to get a paper signed by the President and remarked that the visitor in the outer office seemed agitated.

The man from Missouri chuckled and said bluntly: "He's got exactly twenty-two minutes more to wait!"

Not long after that incident, I was talking with the President during a brief interlude between speeches on his campaign train. Recalling Aldrich's visit, President Truman observed:

When I was head of the Senate War Investigating Committee, I was looking into a company with an account at the Chase Bank. I had to make a trip to New York. One of the many vice-presidents gave me the information I needed, and then he wanted me to meet their top man, Mr. Aldrich. Well, do you know that old S.O.B. made me wait for an hour, until I finally said they should tell him to go to hell that I didn't want to see him anyway.

"Do you think Mr. Aldrich ever got the point of why he had to wait for a solid hour?" I asked.

The President laughed uproariously and explained:

I have a pretty good Irishman named Matt Connelly who drew a picture for him. That's what an appointments secretary is for and Matt can do it without hurting anybody's feelings. I'll bet the great Mr. Aldrich never read Josh Billings.

Although I knew that Abraham Lincoln was fond of quoting Josh Billings (Henry Wheeler Shaw), I had to confess to the President that Mr. Aldrich and I were apparently in the same boat so far as understanding the reference.

He smiled tolerantly and added, "Josh Billings said: 'Always be nice to your poor relations—they may suddenly become rich someday and it will be hard to explain.' Now I doubt whether old Aldrich ever heard of Josh Billings."[1]

"Old Aldrich," a perpetually somber-looking man who once said, "I never smile south of Canal Street," must have been spurred by the incident. He went out and raised several million dollars for the Republican presidential nominee in 1952, General Dwight D. Eisenhower, who then named him to the prestigious post of ambassador to England in 1953.

Truman had a robust Jacksonian attitude toward people. Wealth and power never intimidated him. He had a healthy contempt for those he labeled "stuffed shirts" or "prima donnas." He could spot a hypocrite with lightning speed. A deeply religious person, he had little use for anyone who wrapped a sanctimonious mantle around himself and beat his own chest to proclaim superior piety.

Truman and His Staff

President Truman had principles and traits that made it not only easy, but also inspiring, to work for him. The famous sign on his desk proclaiming "The buck stops here," wasn't merely a slogan. He sensed better than any human being I have ever known precisely when to make a decision and make it stick. There was never any wavering or second-guessing. He was an excellent listener, an avid reader who understood and remembered most of what he read, and he had no patience with sycophants. At the same time, he would not tolerate staff members who tried to build themselves up or to throw their weight around. Several staff members were quickly escorted to the exit with footprints on the seat of their pants when they appeared to be using their positions in violation of these principles.

On the other hand, one of the Truman weaknesses was that occasionally—like many presidents—he kept some people on the White House staff who were clearly an embarrassment to the administration. Looking around the White House, you couldn't escape the conclusion that President Truman had a combination of extraordinarily competent people and only a few incompetent "cronies." Perhaps one measure of their ability is the post–White House careers of the Truman staff. George M. Elsey, an administrative assistant, became national president of the American Red Cross. Clark M. Clifford, special counsel, was President Johnson's secretary of defense, adviser to many Democratic presidents, and later one of the most successful lawyers in the nation's capital. Charles S. Murphy, special counsel, became undersecretary of agriculture and later chairman of the Civil Aeronautics Board. David H. Stowe, administrative assistant, was later named chairman of the National Mediation Board. David E. Bell, administrative assistant, was President Kennedy's director of the budget, head of the foreign aid program, and later executive vice-president of the Ford Foundation. Philleo Nash, administrative assistant, was elected lieutenant governor of Wisconsin and later was appointed U.S. commissioner of Indian affairs. Press secretary Roger W. Tubby became U.S. ambassador to the European office of the United Nations. Naval aide Rear Admiral Robert L. Dennison, holder of a doctor's degree in engineering, later was Supreme Allied Commander, Atlantic. Richard E. Neustadt, a special assistant, became professor of political science at Cornell, Columbia and Harvard and one of the nation's leading authorities on the presidency. Clayton Fritchey and John A. Carroll joined the Truman staff in its latter months, and Fritchey went on to become a nationally syndicated columnist, while Carroll was elected as U.S. senator from Colorado. I migrated to West Virginia in 1957, was elected to the U.S. House of Representatives in 1958, then served for eighteen years in Congress.

You almost had a gut feeling about where Truman would stand on the issues and how he would approach a problem. There was nothing devious about the way he operated. Unlike President Johnson, who loved to keep his staff guessing, Harry Truman "plowed a straight furrow" and rarely deviated from a few basic principles. That made it much easier to work for him. The Mark Twain quotation on his desk— "Always do right. This will gratify some of the people and astonish the rest"—sounded naive. But you soon learned that this was a principle which the President took very much to heart.

One of Truman's closest long-time personal friends, military aide Major General Harry H. Vaughan, received his comeuppance one day when he violated this simple rule. Admiral Dennison, the naval aide, tells it this way:

> Well, this was a painful experience. It was in the afternoon and I was alone with the President and Harry came bursting in, all enthusiastic, and he said, "Boss, I've got a great thing I want to tell you. If you'll make a statement about ownership of offshore oil rights, . . . we can get 'x' number of hundreds of thousands of dollars for the Democratic committee out of Louisiana and some other Southern states."
>
> This was one of the very, very few times that I've ever seen the President upset. I know he must have been upset a good many times, but he *never* showed it. But this time he said, "Harry, don't you *ever* say anything like that to me again." He said, "I'm the President of all the people and I don't give a damn whether I'm re-elected or whether any Democrat is *ever* elected, if we have to do it by doing something that is wrong."
>
> Now Vaughan was absolutely crushed. He thought he had *great* news. So he didn't say a word, just turned around and went out. I was embarrassed and kept my mouth shut.
>
> After a moment the President turned to me and said, "Bob, that really hurt me, but I just had to do it."[2]

The Truman ethical principle was not honored to the letter by every member of his staff. The overwhelming majority went about their work with a high dedication to the standards set by the President. There were a few incidents that, along with some corruption in the Department of Justice and Bureau of Internal Revenue, gave a little substance to partisan attacks on the "mess in Washington" in the later Truman years. These attacks focused on the acceptance of several deep freezes by General Vaughan and his friends, and of a mink coat by Mrs. E. Merl Young, a White House secretary and wife of an official of the Reconstruction Finance Corporation. The mink coat–deep freeze episodes were cleverly escalated by opposition leaders and by the press into what appeared to be a scandal, which embarrassed the President personally and politically.

Mrs. Young was summarily dismissed from her job. That Vaughan remained reveals one of President Truman's fundamental personality traits that both endeared him to his staff and occasionally got him into public difficulty. President Truman always gave his staff the benefit of the doubt, usually backed them up one hundred percent, and was

fiercely loyal to those who worked for him. If a staff member was subjected to public criticism, the President would frequently smile and tell
that person not to worry, that the attackers were merely "trying to get
at me and attack me through you." There were times when some of the
White House staff felt that those who had worked for Truman's senatorial office were too friendly with favor-seekers and were treating them
much as a senatorial office might. Federal agencies that were experienced at sidestepping senatorial office inquiries that could lead to im-
propriety found it difficult to resist a call from the White House, or from
a favor-seeker who claimed close White House contacts. Because of the
alacrity with which an agency responded to a White House request, staff
members working for the President had to be very sensitive concerning
the absolute propriety of an inquiry to anyone in or out of the government.

President Truman had a way of making every person working at the
White House feel he or she was part of a magnificent effort aimed toward achieving peace in the world and justice at home.

The staff meetings were clearly joint efforts to share information,
with the President conducting each one in a light and informal fashion.
Every morning he assembled about a dozen senior members of his staff
in a semicircle around his Oval Office desk and handed out key assignments. News of topics discussed and assignments made quickly spread to
all hands, and soon everybody felt a part of the unfolding drama. Many
presidents escape from their staff at vacation time, but Truman pointedly took his staff with him to Key West, Florida. To the great delight of
junior staffers like myself, we had a chance to enjoy the sun and surf and,
more important, to chat in relaxed circumstances with the President as
we sat on the beach or picnicked on the lawn. I also got a great kick out
of playing volleyball with Margaret Truman and the Secret Service
musclemen, as the President threw in jocular comments from the side-
lines. There were occasional yacht trips on the *Williamsburg.* The
hardest work, but also the most rewarding in personal contact with the
President, took place on the frequent whistle-stop train trips from coast
to coast. Here, as on other occasions, Truman always gave everybody
the feeling that the most minor functionary was a vital cog in the machine.

I had been aboard only a few days when I discovered something
about this President that made his stock soar in my book. I wandered
over to the South Lawn for one of the many receptions honoring a for-

eign leader paying a state visit. Spotting a friendly messenger, I asked: "Are you going to the ceremonies?"

He smiled a little self-consciously and answered: "Well, you know, I'm just sort of a flunky around here, I guess you would say."

I asked: "How often do you see President Truman?"

"Oh, I s'pose 'bout three or four times a day. I carry papers back and forth, see him out walking early in the morning, or going to the swimming pool, and sometimes over in the Mansion."

"Well, that's really something," I said. "I've been around just a little while. I met him at the White House Christmas party, saw him speak once, and went to one of his press conferences, but I really haven't gotten to know him real well yet. Just what kind of a person is he?"

"Well, the first thing you find out is that he calls you by name. You don't feel like some kind of a servant, but like a human being. One day he was walking along with General George C. Marshall, and I tried to slip by quickly, but he stopped and introduced me to General Marshall in a way that sounded like I was somebody who was real important. He has a kind word for everybody. Come to think of it, I guess that anybody who has a chance to work at the White House is just about the luckiest person in the world. I tell my family I'm not just working for the most important person in the country, but he's a real human being."

Those Earthy Remarks

I had heard about President Truman's earthy language, but was not exactly prepared for my first exposure to it. During the time when the White House was being reconstructed, between 1948 and 1952, the President lived across the street at Blair House. Several months after I joined his staff, I received an invitation, along with a half dozen staff members, to be his guest for dinner. Press secretary Charles G. Ross, boyhood friend and school classmate, was there, along with courtly Bill Hassett, the correspondence secretary, whom we all referred to as "the Bishop." Elsey, Murphy and a few others were there for a fairly intimate gathering of what the President called "my speechwriters."[3]

The President started out the evening by telling us in some detail how very lonely he was without Mrs. Truman and Margaret. He explained that they had gone back to Independence, which they enjoyed much more than Washington, and he complained about how difficult it was for him to "batch" it. The more he talked, the more I appreciated how deeply he loved his wife and daughter and how much he missed them if they were away even a short time.

We talked of many things, of the early history of the nation, of the days when the canal flowed through the area on which the Washington Monument was built. The President told us in detail of the landing pier on the banks of the canal at a spot called "Jefferson's Pier." He encouraged us to go out and find the stone near the Washington Monument marking Jefferson's Pier. (I did so the next day, and marveled at his accuracy.) We talked about some of his favorite characters in ancient Greek and Roman history. All in all, it was a stimulating and learned discussion.

" COME, CHILDREN, MR. TRUMAN IS TALKING TO REPORTERS! "

After dinner the President sat down at the piano. As his fingers began to roam across the keys with several Chopin selections, he seemed to get better and better and his touch surer. I was entranced. I pinched myself. Looking at the portraits of Thomas Jefferson and Andrew Jackson on the wall, I asked myself, "How lucky can you get?" As I soared higher and higher into the clouds, I was suddenly brought down to earth when the President chuckled: "If I hadn't become President, I sure would have made a helluva good piano player in a whorehouse!"[4]

The earthiness of Truman's language perhaps was a carryover from the days when as a young man he had been the timekeeper for a railroad construction company, and later from experience with his World War I field artillery battery.

In mixed company, Truman was scrupulously careful about his language. But in privacy with friends he sometimes lapsed into barnyard vernacular.

Truman loved his bourbon and branch water, in moderation, and the stag conviviality that accompanied the many late-afternoon sessions he enjoyed with his colleagues. It was at a similar session—one of the meetings of Speaker Sam Rayburn's "Board of Education" in a private room in the Capitol—that Vice-President Truman received his fateful summons to the White House on the day of Roosevelt's death, April 12, 1945.

Those Poker Games

Aside from his spirited morning walks and side-stroke swims in the White House pool or at Key West, President Truman loved to play poker for relaxation. After watching him play a number of times, I concluded that he really didn't care who won or lost, but mainly played for the light, bantering conversation of the game. In the early months of the first administration, there were a few games on the third floor of the White House, but this locale was suddenly abandoned, perhaps because of adverse public comment.[5] From then on, the games were either on the *Williamsburg*, at someone's home, or during the Key West vacations. Although the conversation was never very heavy, I did observe several occasions when the President sized up prospective appointees and other people by measuring how well they stood up to ribbing.

I was fascinated to sit close by as a silent kibitzer when Chief Justice Vinson joined the President at Key West late in November 1951 for a number of lively games. What I did not know at the time was that Truman had just told some of his senior staff of his decision not to run in 1952, and Vinson was there because Truman was trying to persuade him to be the 1952 Democratic presidential nominee. One afternoon the customary poker game started about four and was interrupted by dinner, after which the players reassembled around the table. In scooping up the cards for the next deal, someone inadvertently mixed up two decks. It wasn't long before it was discovered that there was one ace too many in the hands! Vinson puffed slowly on his pipe and leaned forward with a confidential tone: "What would the people of the United States of America think if they knew that the President and the Chief Justice were playing poker with five aces?"

Someone else at the table blurted out: "The President and the future . . ."

For reasons I could not understand at the time, the President quickly and deftly changed the subject.[6]

Truman and the National Interest

I never heard a stronger advocate of America's two-party system than President Truman. One of his most powerful arguments related to the need for the parties to pull together the competing claims of special interest pressure groups. He thoroughly understood James Madison's arguments in Number X of the *Federalist Papers,* that the proper role of government was to regulate and control "a landed interest, a manufacturing interest, a mercantile interest, a moneyed interest, with many lesser interests." Once, in a rambling conversation at the Truman Beach in Key West, I made some comment about Madison and was as surprised as most people were to discover that he knew far more about Madison and his beliefs than I remembered.

Truman sensed the strength of those forces which propelled pressure groups, and he was determined to use the full powers of the presidency to articulate the national interest. At the same time, as a master politician he capitalized fully on the strength of organized labor, farmers, consumers, small businessmen and minority groups and kept them loyal while he appealed to their pocketbooks to back the Democratic party. Sometimes it took some careful political toe-dancing to achieve these twin objectives. For example, the sudden upsurge of labor's restless demands after the end of World War II presented a difficult challenge, expressed in Truman's diary entry on September 20, 1945: "Like every 'new rich,' and person who comes into power suddenly, 'Labor' has gone off the beam. The job now is to bring them back. And it is going to take guts to do it."[7]

Dislike of Estes Kefauver

As a friend and admirer of Tennessee's Senator Estes Kefauver, whom I had known since his days in the House of Representatives, I found it puzzling that Truman so vehemently opposed Kefauver's efforts to fight organized crime and monopoly. He invariably referred to the Tennessee senator as "Cowfever," called him a "demagogic dumb bell,"[8] a "fakir," "intellectually dishonest," and in private used even stronger terms. In the early days of television, Kefauver's anticrime investigating committee gave the senator nationwide notoriety as the networks carried the drama of big-name criminals and big-city machine politicians testifying in the cavernous Senate caucus room. President Truman regarded these hearings as a direct contrast to the thorough, statistics-laden reports the Truman Committee had issued while probing fraud and mismanagement in government war procurement and construction. When Kefauver cleverly donned a coonskin cap to answer Memphis Boss Ed Crump's slur that he was like a raccoon caught with his paw in the drawer, Truman discounted this tactic as sheer gimmickry.

I soon discovered that it was highly unpopular around the White House to raise a peep in defense of Kefauver. The source of Truman's displeasure was that Kefauver's anticrime hearings concentrated on cities controlled by Democratic machines, while seeming to ignore cities like Philadelphia, where the Republicans were then in power. Reflecting on Kefauver's attempt to obtain the Democratic presidential nomination, Truman wrote this note to himself on Christmas Day, 1952:

> Philadelphia at the time had the rottenest Republican city machine since Quay, Penrose and Vare. Did the "able" Senator look into it? He did not.
>
> In Tennessee the county of Polk adjoining his home county is rotten to the core as is the city of Chattanooga. Did the "able" Senator look into conditions in his home state? He did not.
>
> He toured the country in 1952 after using the report of his crime committee as the basis for a book, which he sold at a long price. He also received fantastic fees to make speeches on his "crime crusade."

After all this counterfeit talk and campaign he had the nerve to ask the President to support him for the nomination for President! The country cannot afford an intellectually dishonest man for President. It should never have a man ignorant of the history of his country. So the Democratic Party turned Mr. Cow Fever of Tennessee out of the Convention.

I wonder how that great State could produce Andrew Jackson, James K. Polk and Sam Houston and then come up with Keufevor [sic] and McKeller [sic].[9]

Political Attitudes

For a man who could give the most rip-roaring, convincing stump speech on the superiority of the Democratic party, Truman had many close Republican friends. He had studied very carefully the tragic experience of Woodrow Wilson and Wilson's bitter fights with Massachusetts Senator Henry Cabot Lodge over the League of Nations. The strong bond of personal friendship that Truman developed with Senate Foreign Relations Committee Chairman Arthur H. Vandenberg had much to do with the landmark foreign-policy achievements between 1947 and 1949, when Congress was in Republican hands. The President encouraged his staff and cabinet to cultivate these bipartisan contacts, and they paid off in a remarkable string of successes, such as the Truman Doctrine, the Marshall Plan, the North Atlantic Treaty Organization, and containment of communist expansion.

Despite Truman's long association with the Pendergast machine and his tutelage in the uses of Democratic patronage, there never appeared to be any party loyalty test for White House staff members. Nobody seemed disturbed that I was a registered Republican when I went onto the White House payroll, and I was reasonably sure that my employers were aware of an article in *Time* magazine stating that I was a Republican.

The case of press secretary Roger Tubby is also interesting. On his first meeting with President Truman, Tubby commented that "in Vermont in the thirties, I had been on the Republican town committee and I had campaigned for a liberal Republican for Congress . . . and that I had been the one editor of a daily paper in the state who had supported George D. Aiken for the Republican nomination when he first ran for the Senate." According to Tubby, Truman replied, "Well, if you're okay with George Aiken, you're okay with me, and I understand you *are* okay with George Aiken."[10]

Lobbyist for the People

Some months after American military forces became engaged in Korea in 1950, Truman called Republican and Democratic Senate and House members to consider how to combat skyrocketing food prices. The group assembled in the Cabinet Room. The President crisply outlined the hardships being suffered by housewives and shoppers throughout the country. At that point, Indiana's corpulent Senator Homer Capehart shifted his ample bulk in his swivel chair and querulously interjected, "Mr. President, I don't understand all this talk about hardships. I see my mail every day, and I haven't been getting any complaints from consumers. What's all the pressure and excitement about?"

The President set his jaw and snapped: "I represent the consumers; that's why I called you here!"[11]

For those present in the Cabinet Room that day, it was a spine-tingling display of Harry Truman's personal definition of the role of the President as number one lobbyist for the people. It also showed his unique ability to cut through the thicket of debate and come to the heart of an issue.

As a lobbyist for all the people, Truman firmly believed that the Democratic party was the best vehicle to achieve peace in the world and a prosperous America. He exerted his leadership in the Jeffersonian and Jacksonian traditions—with policies that favored the average farmer, worker, small businessman and consumer. He stressed that these policies brought prosperity to the entire economy, thereby greatly benefiting producers, bankers, business and professional people and the nation as a whole. He fought what he regarded as the Hamiltonian approach of the Republican party, aiming to assist the upper levels of society with the hope that some of the prosperity would trickle down to the average people. He branded some would-be leaders in the Democratic party as "obstructionists" or worse because they were attempting to swing the Democratic party toward the "trickle-down" approach. On the world scene, Truman worked toward strengthening the United Nations, building collective security rather than isolationism, enabling the free nations of the world to resist aggressive communism by building their economies. In his approach to both domestic and international issues, he was attuned to the average human being in the United States and all over the world.

As leader of the Democratic party, President Truman had an approach to politics that was far more complex than it appeared on the surface. His loyalty to the basic principles of the Democratic party was deep and unquestionable. As a master politician, he nevertheless showed that the unique responsibilities of his office required him to take a national or world view of many issues. There were times when officials in the Truman administration, including members of the White House staff, overlooked this abiding principle in the President's decision-making process. Perhaps the best description of President Truman's view of the awesome power of his office is contained in this analysis by special counsel Murphy:

> He just flatly refused to do anything for political reasons that he didn't think ought to be done anyway. We learned that one way to make him skittish of a proposition was to put it up to him on a political basis. He'd be suspicious right away. This was not the best way to get him to agree to anything, which I expect would surprise a good many people. If you wanted to get him to agree with you about a matter down there, you subordinated the political angles.[12]

His Personal Approach to Official Duties

President Truman was very orderly, yet friendly and informal in his relationships with his staff. These qualities at times seemed inconsistent, but adjustments were easy. He had a sharply negative reaction to the casual administrative habits of his predecessor, Franklin D. Roosevelt. The staff, cabinet and officials in the Roosevelt administration were frequently confounded by presidential directives that conferred competing or overlapping assignments and responsibilities. It was also disconcerting when a Roosevelt cabinet member discovered that orders often came directly from the President or the White House staff to a subordinate official, as occurred when Roosevelt dealt with Undersecretary of State Sumner Welles instead of Secretary Cordell Hull. Truman's practice was to trust cabinet officers to run their own departments, without interference from the White House staff. But below the cabinet level, Truman encouraged personal contacts between the White House staff and agency personnel—so long as they did not undercut a top official.

Truman's work habits were regular and predictable. The staff meetings always started punctually and ended in less than thirty minutes. His

8:00 A.M. breakfast, 1:00 P.M. luncheon and 7:00 P.M. dinner were standard. The small size of the staff allowed easy access to the President, and appointments secretary Matt Connelly was a fairly liberal guardian of the gate to the Oval Office. In the west wing of the White House it was not unusual for the President to stick his head into a staff office to discuss a pending problem.

This friendly informality was displayed in countless ways. People were always sending him neckties, and he usually gave the staff a post-Christmas grab-bag pick of gifts. On other occasions, he gave presidential cuff links, place cards, special White House matches, and other special mementoes. Some fortunate staff members and close friends received silver dollars minted in the year of Truman's birth, 1884. I marveled at the consideration the President showed to the families of staff members. He distributed autographs and photos on many occasions.

When Joseph H. Short was sworn in as press secretary, as Mrs. Short (later correspondence secretary) relates:

> One of the boys had two front teeth out at the time—he was nine—and he said, "I won't go. I'm not going to go see the President of the United States with two front teeth out. The rest of you can go, but I won't go."
>
> We did finally get him into the President's office. Suddenly, after we had all spoken to the President, I looked around and he was not there any more and neither was my nine-year-old son. There were people waiting to greet the President, and Chief Justice Vinson was there to do the honors. Just about that time President Truman and Steve walked out from behind those circular curtains in the Oval Office, and the swearing in began.
>
> On the way home I asked Stephen, "What was going on when you and the President disappeared?" He said, "You know, Mother, now I don't mind having those two front teeth out. The President took me behind the curtain to show me that he had a tooth out, and the only difference is, he is going to have his capped today and I have to wait until mine grows in."[13]

The President had a knack for making the most tangled problems seem easier for the staff. Martin L. Friedman, a special assistant who worked with administrative assistant Donald S. Dawson on personnel policy, received a peremptory threat from a congressional committee one day. Angered at the refusal of the White House to turn over some very personal files, the Hill source indicated that as retaliation funds for the White House payroll would be cut off. According to Friedman:

> I got a little excited and I went down and slipped in to see the President. He was busy signing a lot of papers and I told him the story about this call, how they were going to cut off our money for all these people.

And he grinned and he said, "Well, you call him and tell him that we'll just use whatever money we've got and when we run out of that we'll close up." And I thought that was just a wonderful, Trumanesque response. He didn't worry about it at all. He kind of laughed and went on signing his papers.[14]

The Truman-Acheson Relationship

I always marveled at the magnificent relationship that President Truman maintained with Dean Acheson, who served as secretary of state through thick and thin during Truman's full term, starting in 1949. Truman made no secret of his contempt for some Ivy League types, whom he ridiculed as "Hah-vud" snobs. Although Acheson was a Yale man, he had a Harvard law degree, and he talked and dressed like the very modern model of an Eastern, elite, upper-class intellectual. Truman's rough-hewn, direct, unvarnished approach to problems and policies seemed on the surface to differ from the reasoned detachment Acheson displayed. The relationship is even more interesting when it is considered that Acheson was a political liability and a target at which not only McCarthy but also Taft, many Republicans, opposition newspapers and sizable groups in Congress were firing. Truman never wavered in his loyal support of Acheson. Their private correspondence reveals the remarkable mutual respect of these two individuals who came from such radically different backgrounds. At the same time, correspondence also shows the humor of both men when dealing with sober or trivial issues.

Shortly after Truman took office in 1945, London sources sought and obtained from the White House a detailed series of physical measurements and personal characteristics needed to prepare a likeness of the new President for Madame Tussaud's waxwork collection. Several years later, Truman was mildly irked by an obscure item he read in a British publication entitled "The Tailor and Cutter and Women's Wear," roundly criticizing his clothing and the necktie displayed on the wax model:

> One expects Americans to wear shocking ties, of course, but Mr. Truman's is not in the old Picassian tradition of the U.S.—it is a hideously striped affair which looks more like a bad English tie than a bad American one; if this is Lend-Lease in reverse then here is one Anglo-American tie we can do without.[15]

Truman promptly sent Acheson a little memo signed "H.S.T.":

Comment, not complimentary to the President, has been made in the British Press about a certain "wax" likeness of me in Madame Tussaud's Waxworks.

Please have our Ambassador to the Court of St. James send someone over to the "Waxworks," have him undress my supposed likeness and dispose of the clothes in such a way as they won't be seen again.

Then let the "Madame" whistle for cover for a naked statue![16]

Acheson had an order he could scarcely ignore. Always the perfect diplomat, the secretary of state sought to resolve the issue by a return salvo to the President:

I have your memorandum and instructions for action regarding the sartorial indignities committed by Madame Tussaud's establishment on the wax resemblance of the President of the United States.

Before carrying out the President's instructions, I wish to call the President's attention to the possibilities of revenge open to Madame Tussaud's staff. This might consist in leaving the wax figure in its stripped condition and placing under it a sign reading "The President as he appears after a poker game on *The Williamsburg.*"

I await your further instructions.[17]

Acheson's notes indicate that he felt his response would end the matter. Not so. The President fired back immediately:

Your memo of February 1, 1951 states that the "Madam" of the Waxworks in London may display a stripped likeness of the President after we get our clothes from the establishment—and I'll wager the clothes belong to me. Well let her do that. The burden of proof then would be on the English tailors to guess what I might use for covering if I were alive and not Wax.

As you know I've been stripped before both personally and politically, in campaigns and in poker games—but I still walk around "decently" clothed. So let's let the "Madam" do her damnedest.

H.S.T.[18]

From that point, Acheson concluded it was the better part of valor to instruct his functionaries to resolve the issue in London with minimum fanfare. The President, as usual, got the last word.

Truman, who loved to quote Puck, the mischievous sprite in Shakespeare's *Midsummer Night's Dream,* had a somewhat puckish sense of humor that occasionally surfaced in political jokes. Some years after the Potsdam Conference, he related to Acheson an incident that occurred while he was holding a strategy meeting with America's military leaders in between the Big Three sessions. Jim Blair, at that time lieutenant colonel in military government and later governor of Missouri, joined the President at Potsdam, even though he still called Mr. Truman "Senator" at that late date. As Truman wrote to Acheson:

> When Jim arrived at the Little White House I was having a conference with all the high military—five star generals and admirals not one there with less than three stars. I invited Jim in and introduced him to Marshall, Leahy, Eisenhower, King, Patton and the rest and while that was going on I told him that I'd just appointed his pet political enemy to a job back in Missouri. He stopped and ripped out a paragraph of swear words (no one has a better vocabulary) and wound up by saying:
> "For God's sake Senator what in hell did you do that for."
> The high brass almost fainted. I knew what Jim would do and I told him that good lie so he'd blow his top.[19]

Truman confided many of his feelings to Acheson, in a fashion he would not have dreamed of adopting with other members of his cabinet. On one occasion after leaving the White House, Truman erupted with an extemporaneous lecture to fellow Democrats at a dinner honoring House Speaker Sam Rayburn in 1955. "Now I'm feeling much better after exploding at Rayburn's dinner," he confided in a letter to Acheson. He added:

> Of course I'll catch hell for that and be right in my element. I don't want to be an "elder statesman" politician. I like being a nose buster and an ass kicker much better and reserve my serious statements for committees and schools.[20]

Mrs. Truman and Margaret

At Key West and on campaign trips, I got to know the Truman family better than in the rarefied atmosphere of the White House or Blair House. Mrs. Truman and Margaret were tremendous crowd-pleasers on the whistle-stop trips, even though they never made any campaign remarks and merely smiled and waved when introduced. I soon discovered the firm but subtle influence they both had in convincing Mr. Truman he should not run again in 1952. One afternoon at Key West I had a long conversation with Mrs. Truman in the sitting room of the "Little White House" at Key West. Mrs. Truman loved biographies. She paused in her reading of the autobiography of James A. Farley,[21] Franklin D. Roosevelt's national political chairman, to discuss Farley's adamant opposition to a third term for Roosevelt in 1940. She voiced her strong support for Farley's view as a matter of sound national policy in a republic, and went on to describe in sentimental fashion her conviction that far too many people in public life refuse to admit when it is time to quit. Mrs. Truman commented with some feeling on the selfish "hangers-on" who are constantly importuning public officials to stay in office one more term so these self-seekers can continue to bask in the glory of the boss. I came away from that conversation with the distinct feeling that Mrs. Truman was a major force in convincing the President to stick to his decision to retire in 1952.

During the period I worked at the White House, Margaret was in her twenties and was just embarking on her singing career. On the first day I visited Key West, the Truman family had a roast corn and hamburger picnic in the garden of the Little White House. I was a few steps behind Margaret in the chow line, and once I had filled my buffet plate, I glanced over at where she was sitting. She quickly melted my hesitant look by singing out a then-popular song: "C'mon-a my house, my house-a come on!" It was easy to tell that, like her mother, she tolerated the trappings of public life with some amusement. But Margaret was a real trouper on our whistle-stop trips. Somehow she managed to squeeze in enough time away from her concert tours to endure the endless appearances, the crush of the crowds, and the pressure to get up early, which she detested. It was on one of the 1952 trips that she coined a phrase the President plagiarized and quickly adopted as his own.

In 1948 and 1950, all of Truman's crowds were warm and friendly. The occasional interruptions were of the "Give 'em hell, Harry" character. But every now and then in 1952 there were organized blocs of teenagers who sometimes chanted "We like Ike," perhaps with the encouragement of local partisan organizers. This did not happen often, but it disturbed the President's composure when the heckling interrupted his speeches, as it did on one occasion in rural Pennsylvania. After the incident, I was bringing a speech draft back to the President's railroad car at the rear of the train. The President was talking earnestly with Margaret, and as I approached she looked around. She had a mischievous glint in her eye that I sensed always preceded one of her sure laugh-provokers. As I came closer, Margaret said: "Dad, did you know that ours is the only campaign train which carries its own heckler right aboard?"

2

Truman Selects His Staff, 1945–1948

Early on the morning of April 13, 1945, a heavy-set man rang the door-bell of the upper Connecticut Avenue apartment of the new President of the United States. Hugh Fulton had every reason to believe he would be the most powerful man in the Truman administration. After all, he had done a good job as staff director of the Truman Committee investigating military procurement and construction. Attorney General Robert H. Jackson had recommended him to Senator Truman, and the senator liked the fact that he was a take-charge guy. It did not hurt their relationship that Fulton loved to get up early, like Truman. They always got a head start on the day's planning before any of the rest of the staff arrived on Capitol Hill.

After breakfast, Fulton waited around with the Secret Service men until the new President was ready to drive downtown for his first full day in his new White House office.[1] This was the best way to get in on the ground floor, before others pressed in to get the President's ear. Fulton squeezed his bulky frame into the President's automobile and shared the Boss's most intimate thoughts as they made their way down Connecticut Avenue. At the White House, Fulton joined Edward D. McKim and J. Leonard Reinsch for President Truman's first appointment in the Oval Office. McKim had been a close friend since their days together in Truman's World War I field artillery battery. Reinsch, an experienced radio adviser, working with the Democratic National Committee, had helped numerous Democratic speakers improve their radio performance.

Of the three men who felt they had the "inside track," McKim stayed only a few months as "chief administrative assistant," Reinsch remained a few days, and Fulton was not appointed at all. At his first news conference, on April 17, 1945, the President announced: "Mr. Reinsch is going to help me with press and radio affairs."[2] The newsprint journalists raised a storm of jealous objection to having a radio man handle the press. Truman then decided to bring in his old school classmate, Charles G. Ross, as press secretary. At his second news conference, on April 20, 1945, the President read what sounded like a carefully contrived letter from the head of the Cox Broadcasting System, explaining the "tremendous tasks" that made it imperative for Reinsch to return to their employ.[3] In subsequent years, Reinsch dispatched a number of analytical memoranda to the President, making suggestions on Truman's oratorical style, pronunciation, emphasis, and the dramatic qualities of the presidential addresses. There is little evidence that his advice was followed.

McKim, a forty-nine-year-old Omaha insurance executive, had been through the political wars with Truman since the early days. In 1922, when Truman first ran for county judge, McKim persuaded a local pilot to take Truman up to bombard a farmers' picnic with campaign pamphlets. Landing in a nearby pasture, the pilot nearly lost a future president as they wound up about three feet from a barbed-wire fence. McKim was on hand to accompany Truman on his cross-country vice-presidential campaign in 1944. And on the day Roosevelt died, McKim had everything in readiness at his suite at the Hotel Statler, waiting for the Vice-President to show up for a planned poker session. The new President, of course, had to call it off when the news of Roosevelt's death arrived.

Despite all this intimate background, McKim could not survive the pressure at the White House. He drew up several fancy charts showing White House lines of authority, only to discover that Truman preferred to hand out assignments informally rather than follow rigid administrative boxes on charts. Just two months after taking office, the President explained at a news conference that his old friend would be leaving the White House: "John Snyder put a draft on Ed McKim to get him away from me for a special job, and I guess I'll have to let him go for the time being."[4] Truman hated to hurt an old friend, so he just sent him over to work for another old Missouri friend—the federal loan administrator.

What happened to Fulton after his auspicious start on the Truman Committee, and his early-bird bid for glory on April 13? Truman was fond of quoting Woodrow Wilson on the effect that Washington, D.C.,

has on people: "Some people grow, while others simply swell up."
There is little doubt that Margaret was accurately reflecting her father's
views when she wrote:

> Poor Mr. Fulton was suffering from what Dad calls "Potomac fever." Basi-
> cally, this very common Washington disease involves delusions of grandeur
> and an itch for power and publicity. The news that my father had become
> President had aroused the virus in Mr. Fulton, in its most acute form. Dad
> soon learned from friends that Mr. Fulton was telling everyone in Washing-
> ton that he was going to be the acting President—the implication being
> that Harry S. Truman did not have the talent to do the job. Although they
> parted amicably enough that morning, Mr. Fulton was never offered an of-
> ficial post in the White House.[5]

Luck seems to play a big part in getting assigned to the White House
staff. Still, one can make generalizations that apply in any administration. A president surrounds himself with people whom he trusts. They
share his goals, or are flexible enough to embrace and enthusiastically
support them. They are on the staff to help the president in his job,
rather than grind personal axes for themselves. They should have a point
of view broader than the executive departments and agencies or special
interests. They must be able to see beyond the water's edge.

Every president—and Truman was no exception—appoints people
from his home state whom he has known a long time. Thus he tries to
insure there is mutual trust and loyalty between the president and staff
members. Doing so does not always insure competence and ethical behavior. There is a tendency to keep and defend friends beyond the point
of usefulness if they should get into difficulties. President Truman's
deep-seated loyalty was an admirable trait during a difficult period
when Wisconsin Senator Joseph McCarthy was slandering innocent
people—including members of Truman's White House staff. Opposition
newspapers and columnists roused Truman's anger by what he considered unfair attacks on his friends. Indeed, the *Kansas City Star* and the
St. Louis Post-Dispatch (which he dubbed the "Post-Disgrace") had been
misconstruing and twisting his actions long before he reached the presidency. These factors caused him to draw his wagons into a circle when
his staff came under attack.

When a president succeeds to office after an election, he has advantages over a president who moves up from the vice-presidency after the
death of a president. He has many weeks in which to choose his White
House staff and cabinet members, and can make other appointments

after thorough advance checks. Second, the new president's appointees have an opportunity to meet the president and their counterparts, get oriented and fully briefed by the people they are replacing, and move easily into their new assignments. Third, a president who has been elected has had an opportunity to test the administrative and political skills of numerous individuals during the heat of a campaign. Truman had none of these advantages, and was beset by other staffing handicaps peculiar to the situation produced by Franklin D. Roosevelt's death.

Unlike Lyndon B. Johnson, who had been thoroughly briefed on all major decisions made by President Kennedy, Truman had almost no opportunity to become oriented to the problems and challenges of the presidency. During the eighty-two days he served as vice-president, Truman saw Roosevelt only a few times, and the latter was out of the country at the Yalta Conference or vacationing at Warm Springs, Georgia, for much of the period. He could not help but recall that Roosevelt had opposed him in the 1940 Democratic senatorial primary. Roosevelt had even tried to appoint Truman to the Interstate Commerce Commission to clear the way for Roosevelt's favorite Senate candidate, Missouri Governor Lloyd Stark. As vice-president, Truman had been assigned the unpleasantly messy task of twisting Senate arms to obtain the confirmation of the politically unpopular former vice-president, Henry A. Wallace, as secretary of commerce. The assignment was disagreeable, but Truman's reaction might have improved had he detected any sign of subsequent gratitude by the ailing Roosevelt.

Although he believed that Roosevelt had a number of "crackpot liberals" with fixed ideologies in his administration, Truman was filled with admiration for Roosevelt as a national leader and pragmatic politician. He also had a deep, genuine loyalty to New Deal principles. He disapproved of some of Roosevelt's tactics, such as the heavy-handed pressure he used on Congress and the subtle, devious manner in which he supervised his cabinet and the executive branch. Thus it was with ambivalent feelings toward his predecessor that Truman built his White House staff and cabinet from Roosevelt holdovers, his old Senate staff, Missouri friends, and those who were available on short notice. However, Truman knew that he was serving out an unexpired term for which Roosevelt had been elected, and he was therefore determined to carry out Roosevelt's policies. In foreign policy, he welcomed the crash course provided by such men as Harry Hopkins, Averell Harriman and James F. Byrnes, which enabled him to carry on Roosevelt's policies within the framework of America's national interest.

Truman tried to preserve continuity while winding up the war in Europe and the Far East and during the establishment of the United Nations. He told the Roosevelt White House staff and cabinet that they could stay as long as they wanted. This policy quickly changed. Some, like Secretary of Labor Frances Perkins and Agriculture Secretary Claude Wickard, departed quickly. A few more decibels of protest surrounded the forced resignations of Secretary of State Edward R. Stettinius Jr. and Attorney General Francis Biddle. Treasury Secretary Henry Morgenthau was downright obnoxious. Author of the Morgenthau Plan to strip Germany of her industrial resources and reduce the nation to an economically crippled pastoral land, Morgenthau became very agitated when he was not included on Truman's list to attend the forthcoming Potsdam Conference. He stormed over to the White House to lay down the ultimatum that either he be included in the trip to Potsdam or he would resign. Truman's decision was made easier because he wanted to appoint Fred Vinson as secretary of the treasury, but he bluntly surprised Morgenthau by responding: "All right, if that is the way you feel, I'll accept your resignation right now."[6]

Charles G. Ross

Charles G. Ross, who took over as press secretary when J. Leonard Reinsch departed, had good credentials as a Pulitzer-prize-winning journalist for the *St. Louis Post-Dispatch*. His intimate, long friendship with Truman helped make him a very special policy adviser. Early on, Ross started the practice of staff skull sessions prior to news conferences, at which he would take the lead in firing the most challenging and insulting questions to try to soften the bursts of Truman temper when newsmen later shot their real queries. Beyond that, Ross was always on hand for occasional strategy meetings, relaxed chit-chat when it could be squeezed in late in the day, and presidential poker games and Key West vacations.

I always got a kick out of Ross, who had droopy eyelids and huge pouches under his eyes, which gave him the appearance of a sleepy, friendly dog with a perpetually sad expression. Like many Missouri associates of the President, Ross was very adept at gentle ribbing, and was also one of those sharply alert staffers who thoroughly enjoyed the discussions of ancient history the President frequently initiated.

In December 1950, on the eve of Truman's explosive letter to *Washington Post* music critic Paul Hume for his "lousy" review of Margaret's

Constitution Hall concert, Ross suffered a heart attack and died in his office. It was a grievous personal and official loss for Truman. The several press secretaries who followed Ross were more aggressive in organizing the press operation, and they were all given higher marks by the newsmen. Yet none would be on as intimate a basis with Truman.

John W. Snyder

John W. Snyder of St. Louis was successively federal loan administrator, head of the Office of War Mobilization and Reconversion, and secretary of the treasury, but should properly be classified as an "intimate old friend and Missouri adviser."

Truman drafted Snyder a few days after he took office, although he was scheduled to head a bank in St. Louis. He slipped in and out of the White House at will, frequently came over for a swim with the President, joined the poker sessions and Key West vacations, and caused no end of difficulty for the liberal advisers at the White House. As Snyder put it:

> I am perfectly satisfied to say that I was a conservative. We must remember that a president has a large group of counselors and advisers; and he is entitled to have at least one or two on the conservative side when there is always such a willing and anxious group on the progressive or liberal side.[7]

Matthew J. Connelly

In the waning twilight hours of October 16, 1952, the Truman campaign train paused in Clinton, Massachusetts, the hometown of Matthew J. Connelly, one of the few White House staff members who served from start to finish of the Truman years. From the rear platform of the train, the President cast aside his prepared notes, and delivered a sentimental, emotional address about Connelly, who served as his appointments secretary from 1945 to 1953. Truman added accolades about others on his staff and in his cabinet, but especially wanted the people of Connelly's hometown to know how highly he valued Connelly's loyalty and service. He told the people of Clinton that Connelly had been able and efficient and was a "tower of strength."

When President Truman made these remarks, Connelly was already under fire, and the Eisenhower administration subsequently prosecuted him in connection with a tax-fixing case. There is reason to suspect that the attack against Connelly was at least partially inspired by a desire to prove that "corruption" existed in the highest circles of the Truman White House. Characteristically Truman never wavered in his loyalty to Connelly. But Connelly was convicted and served time in federal prison.

After watching Connelly operate in a wide variety of situations, I concluded that he was extraordinarily successful at controlling the President's schedule. Connelly was smooth, slender, handsome, adroit, fast on the phone, incredibly patient, charming but firm, never losing his cool, shuttling big and little shots in and out of the Oval Office, always mindful of whom it was necessary to slip in to see the President. At the end of a long day, he would give the White House telephone operators twenty or thirty numbers to reach. With a reassuring word and a boost, he would spend a minute or two on each call to explain why these people could not be squeezed into the schedule that day; invariably he left everybody happy.

Connelly seemed to know, during a ten-minute whistle stop, who was important enough to board and ride the train, who deserved a few minutes in a quick group meeting with the President, and who could be satisfied with a quick handshake. And if there were the slightest hint of puzzlement on Truman's face, Matt was always at his elbow to say: "You remember County Chairman Joe Doakes who carried Podunk County for the first time this century, don't you, Mr. President?"

Never a policy-maker, Connelly nevertheless put in his two cents when he had a chance. He usually supported John W. Snyder on issues that were resolved on conservative versus liberal lines.[8] As if Connelly didn't have enough responsibility to keep him busy, the President assigned him to take notes of discussions and decisions at cabinet meetings.

Judge Samuel I. Rosenman

On the day that memorial services were held for Franklin D. Roosevelt in the White House—April 14, 1945—one of Roosevelt's closest friends and advisers, Judge Samuel I. Rosenman, submitted his formal resignation to President Truman. Slightly rotund, scholarly-looking, Rosenman had been a familiar figure around the White House for many years as a Roosevelt speech-writer. Courteous, even-tempered and unassuming, he had undertaken numerous trouble-shooting assignments for Roosevelt, including reorganization of executive agencies in such areas as war production, information and intelligence, and housing. Now he was resigning as special counsel, not only because he desperately wanted to return to private life, but also because an eye ailment had seriously impaired his vision several years before.

When Truman was catapulted into office, there was simply nobody at the White House who had Rosenman's superlative writing ability or the clarity and fluency of his style. At Truman's urging, he agreed to stay on for a few weeks to help the new administration get organized.

Rosenman had survived some pretty bloody battles in the arena of "palace politics" and intrigue at the highest level during some seventeen years of association with Roosevelt as governor and President. So he was not being simply oversensitive when he recollected: "I am sure that his [Truman's] staff started out with great hostility toward me, not as a personal matter, but because they knew I had been closely associated with Roosevelt."[9]

Despite this feeling of some staff members, Truman left no doubt about his own personal trust in the mild-mannered jurist. A few days after turning down Rosenman's resignation, the President pointedly included Rosenman in a private luncheon at the Mansion. Only two others were present, both old Missouri friends. Truman confided to his diary:

> Took Ross, Snyder and Rosenman to the "House" for lunch. Had 'em upstairs in my so called "Study" and gave them a libation before we went to the family dining room for lunch. Told the three of them that they were most in my confidence and that I wanted frank and unadulterated statements of fact to me from them—and that when they couldn't treat me on that basis, they'd be of no use to me.[10]

This was no news to Rosenman, who always had dealt with Roosevelt on that basis. He emerged from the luncheon with the knowledge that even if there might be backbiting from other staff members, he had Truman's support.

When Roosevelt died, Rosenman was in London on a double-barreled mission: to head a delegation assessing the critical food shortages in war-devastated Western Europe and to negotiate with Allied governments on the trial of war criminals. Truman directed him to resume both assignments, insisting that the war criminals be tried rather than executed summarily as advocated by Churchill. Rosenman successfully negotiated the basis for the Nuremburg trials. His report on the food crisis went to Truman on April 30, 1945. These were just two of the many tasks Rosenman undertook, plus a flood of administrative duties.

While Truman was at the Potsdam Conference in July and early August of 1945, he asked Rosenman to fly over and help him prepare the public report on the Big Three Conference. Sailing home with the President on the U.S.S. *Augusta,* Rosenman received another big assignment—to draft a major message to the Congress outlining Truman's postwar policies. Rosenman was delighted to learn directly from Truman that he wanted the message to be a hard-hitting liberal statement that went beyond even the New Deal.

After returning home, Rosenman found that many Truman advisers were leery of making the September 6 message a liberal document. Some White House staff members argued heatedly that Rosenman's hard-hitting liberal language "was ruinous for the country as well as for the President."[11] He noted that Snyder, Connelly and James K. Vardaman, Jr., were most insistent that Truman should rest on his oars and not stir up the waters with New Deal language. Working for Roosevelt had usually involved a speech-writing team of Robert E. Sherwood, Harry Hopkins and Rosenman himself, but in the autumn of 1945, Rosenman said, "I found that I was trying to write a speech in the presence of a convention! There must have been fourteen people around the table, all of Truman's old friends." He bemoaned the fact that "it takes five times as long to write a sentence with fourteen people around as it does to be alone with him [the President] and one or two others." He tried the technique of saying to all those who were making gratuitous suggestions: "Now that sounds fine. I wish you would take this yellow pad and go into the other room and write five paragraphs on it."[12]

Eventually, the message was sent to Congress. It included a twenty-one-point program, a repetition of Roosevelt's Economic Bill of Rights, and a clear signal that Truman intended to press forward beyond the New Deal in the vigorously liberal tradition of the Democratic party.

Early in 1946, Judge Rosenman concluded that the time had come to think about his own future and the means to educate his children. He left the White House to head a new law firm in New York, after Truman awarded him a Medal for Merit in a sentimental White House ceremony. In telling a news conference of Rosenman's departure, Truman accurately characterized him as "able, devoted and self-effacing." After his departure, Rosenman continued his warm friendship with Truman, helped him with his acceptance speech at the 1948 Democratic national convention, visited the White House frequently, prepared Truman's will, and along with Mrs. Rosenman, accompanied Mr. and Mrs. Truman on an enjoyable European trip in 1958.

Clark M. Clifford

Rosenman's most famous successor, Clark M. Clifford, came to the White House by chance, then used his talents and seized the opportunity to work his way up. It all started back in St. Louis, where Clifford was serving as the lawyer for a shoe company headed by James K. Vardaman, Jr. Truman tapped Vardaman as his first naval aide, and Vardaman in turn induced Clifford to join the White House staff as assistant naval aide.

Tall, strikingly handsome, articulate and effective, Clifford made an immediately favorable impression at the White House.

Things went along swimmingly for Vardaman and Clifford for a few months, with Clifford finding his new surroundings exciting, challenging and glamorous—adjectives that well describe Clifford's own sparkling personality. Meanwhile, Vardaman was promoted from captain to commodore, accompanied President Truman to the Potsdam Conference and on trips down the Potomac on the *Williamsburg*, and took part in the President's regular morning staff conferences. What went wrong in the autumn of 1945 is best described by Margaret, who noted that Vardaman "immediately acquired an acute case of Potomac fever." She added:

> In the White House Mr. Vardaman proceeded to stick his nose into almost every office and tell them how it should be run. Then he made the blunder of all blunders. He descended upon Mother's side of the White House and started telling *them* how to do the job. That was the end of Mr. Vardaman as naval aide. Dad elevated him to the Federal Reserve Board, and he repaid him for his kindness by voting against every Truman policy for the next seven years. He also went around Washington spreading the nasty story that he was kicked out of the White House because he did not drink or play cards.[13]

While Vardaman was at Potsdam, as well as later, Clifford took magnificent advantage of his opportunities. He did not relish spending his career standing around like a "potted plant," simply looking glamorous at White House social affairs—though he was resplendent in his dress uniform with the gold braid. He looked around and discovered that a fellow lawyer, Judge Rosenman, was tremendously overworked with all the speeches, messages, executive orders and agency contacts with which he was burdened. "I had an enormous interest in what Judge Rosenman was doing," related Clifford.[14] He volunteered to help, and soon Rosenman was turning over some of his work to Clifford. When Vardaman left in January 1946, President Truman named Clifford his naval aide. Before long, Clifford found he could accomplish his naval aide's work in twenty percent of his time, which left the remaining eighty percent for helping Judge Rosenman.

When Rosenman left in February 1946, Clifford moved easily into the vacuum. It was a difficult testing period, but Clifford rose to the challenge magnificently. He tackled such diverse issues as universal military training, unification of the armed services, full employment, atomic energy, railroad and other strikes, and a wide variety of other domestic and international problems. Clifford brought to his job a zestful, fresh enthusiasm, tempered with an ability to stand back and assess the long-range implications of presidential decisions. He gave the President a crisply confident, objective summary of arguments, which included just the right dash of imagery. Although a Missourian himself, Clifford stirred jealousies from many of Truman's old Missouri friends like Snyder and Vaughan, as well as former Senate staffer Connelly. There was some resentment because Clifford's star was clearly rising. He could sense that his standing in the White House was improving and by the spring of 1946 Clifford knew that "I had developed a relationship with President Truman where we understood each other and were getting along well."[15]

George M. Elsey

The rise and fall of Vardaman, which brought Clifford to a position of great power and influence, also gave another able staff assistant the chance to rise through the White House hierarchy. In April of 1942 a young naval ensign named George M. Elsey was assigned by the Office of Naval Intelligence to work in the White House map room. Located next door to the oval reception room where President Roosevelt delivered his fireside chats, the heavily guarded map room was an intelligence and communications center that handled the latest top-secret cables and posted current war information on huge display maps. For a bright and eager young history major, scarcely twenty-four years old, this was a chance in a million to be front and center while history was in the making.

During the war years, Elsey polished his natural talents by putting into clear and understandable form the massive amounts of intelligence material that poured into the map room. The ability to summarize and express complex ideas in simple form served him well in his later responsibilities as a speech-writer.[16]

Like Clifford, Elsey made himself useful and proved his value and competence. While Rosenman was still special counsel, Elsey indicated, "He frequently wanted background information on military events or military happenings to help him better understand how to write some of the material he was working on."[17]

As assistant naval aide under Vardaman, and as naval aide when Vardaman left in January 1946, Clifford helped supervise the map room and quickly learned that Elsey's talents went far beyond the ability to stick flags onto maps and decode cables. And just as Clifford pitched in to help Rosenman, Elsey tried to help both men. By the spring of 1946, he was in effect the assistant naval aide, although the President did not formally announce it.

The lack of formal status did not embarrass or deter Elsey in the least. He continued to help Clifford with the increasing burdens he shouldered. In July 1946, the President asked Clifford to compile a list of agreements the Russians had broken. When Clifford asked Elsey to undertake the assignment, Elsey quite typically raised the point that a simple list provided far too narrow a basis. After lengthy discussion, Clifford acknowledged it would be useful to develop a comprehensive report on the totality of United States–Soviet relations, including the goals and specific Soviet actions that affected world peace and international order. According to Elsey, "I tackled it with great zeal because I felt very deeply the necessity of this kind of thing."[18] The Elsey report was not written in an ivory tower. He interviewed top officials at the State, War and Navy Departments and the new Central Intelligence Agency, carefully weighing the facts and assessing the future. Elsey's study concluded that the Soviet Union could only be persuaded to arrive at some accommodation "when they realize that we are too strong to be beaten and too determined to be frightened."

Clifford was out of the country when much of the Elsey report was being written, and forwarded the final product to the President over his signature on September 24, 1946. The President immediately realized its importance, as indicated in the following account by Margaret:

Clark Clifford handed this report to my father one evening around five o'clock. He stayed up most of the night reading it, and early the next morning he called Mr. Clifford at his home. "How many copies of this report do you have?" he asked.

"Ten," Mr. Clifford said.

"I want the other nine," Dad said. "Get them right in here."

Mr. Clifford put the other nine on his desk within the hour. "This has got to be put under lock and key," Dad said. "This is so hot, if this should come out now it could have an exceedingly unfortunate impact on our efforts to try to develop some relationship with the Soviet Union."[19]

The document helped lay the foundation for Truman's major foreign policy decisions.The Truman Doctrine, Marshall Plan, North Atlantic Treaty Organization and containment of aggressive communism were rooted in the analysis developed in the Elsey report.

Dr. John R. Steelman

One day early in the Roosevelt administration, Secretary of Labor Frances Perkins paid a visit to Alabama College in Montevallo, Alabama, to make a commencement address. There she was impressed with a huge, open-faced, smiling man who taught economics but talked like a down-to-earth fellow and had a sensible comment on any topic that came into the conversation. He seemed to know what he was talking about on all the labor issues that interested Secretary Perkins. Dr. John R. Steelman, Arkansas-bred and possessing a Ph. D. from the University of North Carolina, so impressed her that she offered him a job in the United States Conciliation Service. He rose to become head of the Conciliation Service and quickly gained a reputation as an effective negotiator of labor disputes.

Truman discovered that his secretary of labor, former Senator Lewis Schwellenbach, was ineffective in dealing with the nationwide walkouts in steel, coal, railroads and other industries. This situation prompted the President to appoint Steelman on October 25, 1945, as special assistant to the President, "to act in any field in which I want to use him."[20] Steelman was in the eye of the hurricane to advise the President, to assist in negotiations, and to report and recommend necessary courses of action. Dramatic confrontations occurred. When the President ordered a federal takeover of the coal mines and, in the face of intransigent railway brotherhood leadership, prepared to order the Army to operate the railroads and draft strikers into the Army, Steelman shuttled from one crisis meeting to another. His dramatic telephone call from the Hotel Statler to Clifford, waiting off the House floor at the Capitol while Truman was addressing Congress with his proposal to draft strikers, enabled Clifford to pass a quick note so the President could announce to Congress that the railroad strike was over. The nation breathed easier over the weekend of May 25, 1946.

A new game of musical chairs affected Steelman's position in June 1946. Fred Vinson went from treasury secretary to chief justice. John Snyder went from director of the Office of War Mobilization and Reconversion to treasury secretary. And Steelman took over Snyder's job as OWMR head in addition to his White House duties as labor adviser.

As problems piled up in the early days of the Truman administration, arguments erupted among cabinet departments and agencies, and knotty situations developed on Capitol Hill. Steelman cheerfully moved in as a problem-solver. Many of these problems arose from jurisdictional squabbles over turf. Steelman understood very clearly how the President operated. He knew that his own job was simply to investigate the facts, after which the President made the ultimate decisions, quickly and crisply.

Steelman played his role carefully, keeping the minor "cats and dogs" away from the President's desk, briefing the President fully, insuring that cabinet members never felt he was keeping them away from the Oval Office, and sensing which issues had to be decided topside. Steelman eagerly picked up other assignments, such as liaison between the executive agencies and the President's Commission on Higher Education and the chairmanship of the President's Scientific Research Board. In the latter role, he beefed up the government's scientific research programs (this role was later undertaken by the National Science Foundation, and in future administrations it was filled by a presidential scientific advisory apparatus). In July 1946 the President transferred yet another function to Steelman and OWMR—the Office of Economic Stabilization, charged with leadership in the war against inflation.

At his December 12, 1946, news conference, the President announced: "I have today appointed John R. Steelman as Assistant to the President, to continue to aid me in coordinating Federal agency programs and policies."[21]

A very interesting thing happened when Steelman's charter of operation was being drawn up, with the assistance of the Bureau of the Budget. According to Elmer B. Staats of the Bureau staff (who later became comptroller general of the United States), Steelman took the initiative to write his own ticket:

> We worked up a draft based on conversations with various people in the White House, including the President. I went over one day to check out the draft with John; I had written on it, "assistant to the President." He looked it over and said he thought the substance was pretty good, but he penciled in the word *the* in front of *assistant*. He said, "My understanding is that I am supposed to be the chief of staff of the White House." I said, "Well, that's news to me, but I am afraid I cannot really make that judgment." But President Truman allowed it to stand.[22]

However, Steelman was not a chief of staff as Sherman Adams was for President Eisenhower. Truman always had been, and remained, his own chief of staff. Steelman never issued orders or directives to others beyond his own personal staff. But the magic and prestigious word "the" stuck, was printed at the top of Steelman's stationery and enhanced his prestige when talking with cabinet members, executive agencies, House and Senate members and outside interests. Although the President continued to refer to Steelman simply as "assistant to the President," other White House staff members bridled at the definite article preceding the title "assistant." They joked or grumbled about it in private, but so long as Steelman did not invade their turf, they did not make a major issue out of it.

Steelman and his staff had their offices in the east wing of the White House, that appendage to the Mansion (presidential family quarters) which had been built in 1934. Clifford was in the busy west wing, constructed in Theodore Roosevelt's time, which placed the special counsel closer to the center of power. The Oval Office, appointments secretary, correspondence and press secretaries and other top assistants were also in the west wing. This division prompted the inevitable comment that "east is east and west is west, and never the twain shall meet." Clifford was far more assertive and combative than Steelman, and some spirited arguments developed. The general lines of demarcation—that Clifford should handle policy and planning, and Steelman operations—shifted with the ebb and flow of the work at hand. Steelman rarely touched foreign policy and military matters; he concentrated on housing, education, surplus property disposal, synthetic rubber, strategic materials stockpiling, manpower and related issues. He attended most cabinet meetings as a silent partner and generated a vast flow of business from cabinet members "pre-testing" ideas.

Truman often asked Steelman to talk with House and Senate members who asked for favors or projects that affected their districts. The President described Steelman's role this way: "If what they were asking for was a legitimate proposition, we would try to accommodate them. John was very helpful in finding out how far it was necessary to go and if what these chaps were asking for was in the public interest."[23] Truman added, "It's been said that if you have two bureaus in disagreement in the same Cabinet member's office, sometimes the President can get an agreement, but if they are in different departments, such as Interior and Commerce, God himself couldn't get it settled."[24]

Steelman felt that it was a great morale builder for cabinet staff members to present their views firsthand to a White House official. This stimulated spirited enthusiasm for a White House decision, rather than grudging compliance down the line.

In addition to occasional tensions between Steelman and Clifford, there was no love lost between Steelman and Leon H. Keyserling, chairman of the President's Council of Economic Advisers from 1949 to 1953. While he was vice-chairman from 1947 to 1949, Keyserling related that "Steelman, in my view, sort of tried to take over the council and subordinate it to the Steelman operation." Keyserling noted: "When our Economic Report went over to the White House, it was thoroughly rewritten—mangled—by the Steelman office. But we succeeded in getting it brought back to the council through meetings in the council offices, which I recall very well."[25] Keyserling also aired his feelings in these comments:

> My contacts with John Steelman, the assistant to the president, were inconsequential during my years on the CEA, except that he contacted me and had (or claimed to have) considerable influence in the selection of the CEA members. I should mention, however, that Steelman could well have been a thorn in the side of the CEA, primarily because of his "conservative" views and alliances and also because of his aggrandizing tendencies. But the actions of President Truman himself and the great influence with the president of other members of the White House staff, especially Clifford, prevented it from happening.[26]

Steelman's many responsibilities were augmented by his supervision of a small staff, which had been inherited from the OWMR. The OWMR had kept in touch with public service organizations of the advertising and motion picture industries. This small liaison staff had nowhere else to go when OWMR was abolished, so Steelman took it under his wing at the White House. Its work remained a mystery because it did not relate to anything that the rest of the White House staff was doing.

Charles S. Murphy

The date was February 10, 1941.

As two swinging doors opened, Senator Harry S. Truman briskly walked into the long, narrow lobby back of the Vice-President's desk just off the floor of the Senate. There he spotted a methodical, precise, bespectacled, slightly balding man who had frequently helped him draft legislation.

"Murphy, I just made a speech in there on the Senate floor," the senator said. He pointed out that during a thirty-thousand-mile inspection tour of defense installations he had observed a great deal of waste and mismanagement. He asked his friend to read the speech and then draft a resolution to set up a special Senate investigating committee to review procurement, construction and other aspects of the defense program.[27]

Charles S. Murphy got right to work and drafted what became Senate Resolution 71 to establish the Truman Committee. This subsequently brought national attention to a senator whose main claim to fame had been his election by the Kansas City Pendergast machine. Although the senator had worked before with this very thorough draftsman in the Senate's legislative counsel office, in 1941 he had not yet gotten around to calling him "Murph" as he later did at the White House.

Murphy had come to Washington in 1934 and worked his way up in the esoteric field of legislative bill drafting. It was an area that did not require eloquence so much as clarity and the ability to absorb a vast storehouse of information on public policy. Before the days of computers, it necessitated speedy, accurate research on the legal and statutory precedents. Senator Truman was pleased with the caliber of Murphy's work.

When Truman became President, most knowledgeable insiders figured that his old friend Leslie Biffle, the ubiquitous secretary of the Senate, would be asked to join the new White House staff. Murphy asked Biffle one day whether the rumors were true. Biffle immediately answered: "No, but you're going."[28]

This news delighted Murphy, who felt he was reaching a dead end in the legislative counsel's office. Unfortunately, Senate Majority Leader Alben W. Barkley had other ideas. For some strange reason, he decided that Murphy was so essential to the operation of the Senate that he refused to release him. Not until the roof fell in on the Democrats in the 1946 elections and Barkley was demoted to minority leader did he finally consent to let Murphy join Truman, in January of 1947.

The President instructed Murphy to report directly to him, as administrative assistant, but left his assignments flexible. With typical modesty, Murphy subsequently stated: "I soon found out the kind of work that Clifford did. It was the kind of work I wanted to do, and so I went and asked if I could help, and he said he would be glad to have me."[29]

Murphy not only made himself useful around the White House, but also built friendly relationships with all the White House personnel. For example, he received Steelman's permission to attend his regular morning staff meetings. This eased the conflict that had frequently occurred between the special counsel and Steelman's office.

For the most part, Murphy assisted Clifford with his tremendous work load. Murphy even tried to persuade Clifford to expand his staff, but Clifford preferred to continue with only one assistant, George Elsey.[30] Not until the 1948 campaign and its aftermath did Murphy succeed in increasing the staff. But Murphy would have been horrified at suggestions that a Truman White House staff of twenty to twenty-five professionals should balloon to many times that size, as occurred in the 1970s and 1980s.

As administrative assistant, Murphy also forged stronger ties with the Bureau of the Budget. He encouraged the bureau's Legislative Reference Division to expand its analysis of how legislation conformed to programs of the President. Murphy found this bureau assistance of prime importance, not only in suggesting the bills to sign or veto, but also in helping to formulate the President's legislative program.

Murphy rather modestly confesses that although administrative management "was not particularly my cup of tea,"[31] he consistently encouraged the Bureau of the Budget in its efforts along this line.

Whether or not Murphy was personally enthusiastic about a particular job, he shared Truman's sense of responsibility toward any necessary task. There was little difference in Murphy's approach to a job he genuinely liked and his approach to those somewhat messy, tangled problems that were constantly thrown into his lap. He was equable and even-tempered. Unlike Truman, he never blew his cool.

David E. Bell

Murphy worked closely with James E. Webb, director of the budget. Webb's able assistants often back-stopped the work at the White House. Murphy was impressed by a tall, young ex-Marine named David E. Bell, who worked on labor and welfare matters for the Bureau of the Budget. Webb wanted to help Murphy and also cement relationships between the bureau and the White House. So he offered to give Murphy any assistant from the bureau he wanted. Without hesitation, Murphy answered: "I will take David Bell."[32] At age twenty-eight, Bell became the youngest member of the White House staff—a year younger than Elsey.

Bell shouldered the major load of speeches and messages dealing with economics, international trade, labor, natural resources or Western development. He helped draft presidential reports on the budget and the state of the economy, and in 1948 returned to the Bureau of the Budget to help on the annual budget message.

A tall man who was a terror on the tennis court, Bell had a fresh, independent view on most issues. Like many other White House staffers, he had a good share of contacts in and out of the government off whom he could bounce new ideas. He worked well with Steelman's staff, thus helping to bridge the gap between the east wing and the west wing. He retained his close contacts with many of the Budget Bureau personnel, and it came as no surprise when President Kennedy named him budget director in 1961.

In 1952, Bell received the physically exhausting assignment of working for Adlai Stevenson's campaign and maintaining liaison with Truman. Given the differences in temperament of Truman and Stevenson, this was almost a no-win assignment for Bell. Later, after Bell had been running the foreign aid program, he experienced some of the differences between the leadership of Presidents Truman and Johnson. As he put it:

> One of Mr. Truman's most characteristic attitudes was that he wanted to place responsibility clearly on an individual, to give him leeway and opportunity to function to carry out that responsibility. . . . Johnson was the kind of man who would give you a job at 3 o'clock, call at 3:30 and ask if you had finished yet, and at 4 he would call up and say: "Good Lord, haven't you done it yet?"[33]

David D. Lloyd

Murphy's small stable of speech-writers also included David D. Lloyd, a lawyer with two minor novels among his credits. Truman had some uneasiness about Lloyd at the start because he had served as research director of the liberal Americans for Democratic Action—an organization that took some pot shots at Truman prior to the 1948 campaign on the grounds he wasn't liberal enough. But Truman's trust in Lloyd grew steadily. Soon he emerged as the point man on major speeches, as well as handling a number of special assignments in such fields as housing, immigration, displaced persons and constitutional issues involving the President's war powers.

Lloyd had an off-beat sense of humor, which he used to good effect in poking fun at the glittering generalities used by Dewey in the 1948 campaign. In 1951, both Bell and Lloyd were promoted to administrative assistants and they remained with the Truman White House until the end of his term. Truman then entrusted Lloyd with the assignment of executive director of his proposed library in Independence.

Rear Admiral Robert L. Dennison

Admiral Dennison, who served as naval aide from early 1948 until Truman left office in 1953, was one of Truman's superior appointees. His duties went beyond those usually assigned to a naval aide. He helped screen some of the information flowing to the White House from the Joint Chiefs of Staff, Atomic Energy Commission, Department of State and other agencies. He coordinated federal maritime affairs and looked into claims of overpayment of ship construction subsidies. As time went on, Truman gave him a series of increasingly responsible special assignments.

When Truman and his family went to Brazil in 1947 to sign the Treaty of Rio de Janeiro, they had an enjoyable return trip on the battleship *Missouri*, commanded by Dennison. It wasn't long before the President had Dennison transferred to the White House.

When our White House troupe went to Key West, Admiral Dennison was the official host, because the vacation resort was on the naval base. Whenever a political subject arose, and this was frequently, I was struck by the sage and thorough understanding of democratic institutions and human nature that Dennison displayed. I concluded that he would have been equally at home as a political leader, had fate thrust him into that role. In carrying out his maritime responsibilities, he dealt frequently and effectively with members of Congress and officials in the Justice, Commerce, Labor, State and Defense departments.

Admiral Dennison learned early that Truman had a "shell" around him that sometimes gave the impression that he was a simple, poorly educated man trying to do a job. The admiral observed:

> He wasn't a simple man. He was the most complex individual I ever knew. He *was* well educated . . . Anybody who was stupid enough to question anything he had to say about personalities or American history had better look out, because he knew.[34]

The admiral learned about Truman's bluntness and penchant for colorful language even before he came to the White House. One day during their voyage on the *Missouri*, when Tito was massing Yugoslav troops on his northern border, which threatened Trieste, Dennison brought the President a critical message about the situation. As the President and his staff were sitting around playing poker, Dennison silently handed the message to the President. Without telling anyone at the poker table what was in the message, Truman calmly handed it back with this simple comment: "Tell the son of a bitch he'll have to shoot his way in." Dennison said, "Aye, aye, sir," and left, recalling that he "probably sent back exactly what he said because there wasn't any way to paraphrase that."[35] In any event, it stopped the rumblings from Yugoslavia.

Dennison also recognized Truman's weaknesses. For example, Truman's memory and interpretation of conversations he had had with those with whom he disagreed frequently did not square with the recollections of others who were present. Dennison explains it this way:

> I have been with the President on occasions when he had what appeared to me to be a perfectly normal and amiable conversation with a caller. After the caller left, he would say to me, in effect, "I certainly set him straight," or, "I let him have it." The President's remarks seemed to me to have no conceivable relation to the conversation I had just heard. He may have been commenting on what he wished he had said or perhaps his words were too subtle for me to understand.[36]

Late one afternoon, about six o'clock, Dennison was briefing the President on a critical situation in Korea that he had to absorb for an address that evening. Appointments secretary Connelly interrupted the conversation by asking whether the President could see four Iowans who did not have an appointment. Truman asked them to come in and sit down, whereupon they explained a complex road and bridge problem for which the President had no responsibility. But he took considerable time making various suggestions to his visitors, all in a patient and friendly fashion. They came in looking dejected, but they left as changed people. Dennison related this aftermath:

> It was all too much for me and I said, "Mr. President, if you'll forgive me, I know what's on your mind. I know the decision you've got to make right now. How could you have the patience to listen to these people? This is not a problem that you can solve."
>
> And he said, "Bob, I'll tell you something. Sure it's not a problem I can solve. It isn't a national problem, and maybe to *you* it isn't a problem, but believe me to these people it's a problem." He said, "I'm the President of the United States and I should listen to people like that who are in trouble, even if that's all I can do."
>
> So I just shut my mouth and learned something.[37]

Major General Harry H. Vaughan

One spring day in 1952, after having lunch with General Vaughan in that small room in the White House west wing that we dubbed "the real mess in Washington," I penned these notes: "He is quick, sharply perceptive, and with a prodigious memory. I wonder if he realizes what a political handicap he really is to the President. As a human being, he is tops, however."[38]

Press secretary Ross coined the expression "cherchez le Vaughan" when some gaffe reflecting on the President was traceable to the blustery military aide. Vaughan caused the President no end of political difficulty, capped by his receipt of a cut-rate deep freeze, which became one of the symbols of the Democratic downfall in 1952.

Laughter was a great and necessary tonic for Harry Truman. Offstage, when he shucked the serious or boring routines to which he was daily subjected, he loved the company of Vaughan, who knew how to light the fuse that caused an explosion of hearty laughs. Nobody could equal Vaughan as a Falstaffian court jester.

Their friendship dated back to World War I days when they commanded field artillery batteries, blossomed during reserve training after the war, and was cemented as Vaughan played a leading role in Truman's senatorial campaigns and Senate committee staff. After serving as military aide when Truman was Vice-President, Vaughan moved into the same position in the White House.

It wasn't long before he got himself into hot water. A few days after Truman became President, reporters discovered that Vaughan planned to have an FBI investigation of every member of the White House press corps.[39] From that point on, Vaughan became the butt of many attacks by columnists and commentators. He welcomed everyone, like a friendly puppy, and many lobbyists and favor-seekers took advantage of his friendliness. One of these was John Maragon, onetime Kansas City shoeshine boy and Capitol Hill railroad ticket agent. North Carolina Senator Clyde Hoey brought out embarrassing details of Maragon's influence-peddling, and the connections he claimed with the White House through Vaughan. Maragon was subsequently convicted and served a jail term for perjury and failure to disclose truthfully some of the shady business dealings in which he had been engaged.

As early as 1946, press secretary Ross recognized the potential damage that Maragon was causing the President through Vaughan. Ross wrote in his diary:

> I thought I had him killed off, but John Maragon popped up again. A query came to us from the Overseas News Agency regarding his activities in Athens, where he seems to have been throwing his weight around. The message said he had "terrorized" members of the Henry Grady mission (the Mission to Observe the Greek Elections) by talking to correspondents. It was the first word we had had that Maragon was attached to the Mission. Some weeks ago at the suggestion of Matt Connelly and myself, the President had ordered the State Department to strike Maragon's name off the list of members of the Mission, where it had been placed on the recommendation of Ed Pauley and General Vaughan. It now develops that after this order was given, the Department talked again about the matter with General Vaughan, with the result that Maragon was left on the list in a "minor capacity."
>
> I took the matter up again with the President. It was the first he knew about it. Matt and I then talked to Loy Henderson and Donald Russell of the State Department and they both agreed with us that Maragon's name should be immediately stricken and he should be brought back to the United States as rapidly as possible. He is a dangerous man to have loose in a foreign country. Russell later read me a copy of a very explicit directive to Grady for the separation of Maragon from the Mission. I hope to God that this is the end of Maragon so far as the White House is concerned.[40]

Unfortunately, despite the concern of Ross, this was not the end of Maragon. Vaughan failed to realize the embarrassment he caused the President by continuing to ask for special treatment for Maragon.

Truman steadfastly defended Vaughan against his critics, not only because Vaughan had helped him when times were tough, but also because Truman liked a companion who treated him without the artificial deference displayed by many. Once when Vaughan tried to resign, Truman answered: "Harry, you and I came in here together and we're going to leave together and I don't want to hear any more of this damned foolishness about you wanting to resign."[41]

Sparks frequently flew between Vaughan and other staff members, despite the knowledge that Truman insisted on keeping him. Just after lunch one afternoon, Vaughan held an informal press conference in the west wing lobby to announce he would henceforth be the top defense aide to the President, superior to the naval and air force aides. Naval aide Dennison reacted immediately. He recalls:

> Well, that just infuriated me, and so I talked to Charlie Ross and Matt Connelly and said, "I don't want to get the President upset, but I was ordered here as a naval aide and I reported as a naval aide, and nobody ever told me about any arrangement such as this, and if it goes through I'm going to ask to be detached."
>
> Well, Ross got madder than hell about Harry having the nerve to hold a press conference, and Matt Connelly was real upset about it. So they went in to talk to the President and told him this was really going to raise hell. So he just said, "Well, forget the whole thing."[42]

Columnist Drew Pearson made Vaughan his favorite whipping boy. In a radio broadcast early in 1949, Pearson called on Truman to fire Vaughan because he had received a decoration from Argentine dictator Juan Peron. Incensed by Pearson's remarks, Truman ripped into Pearson at a dinner of the Reserve Officers Association honoring Vaughan on February 22, 1949: "I want you to distinctly understand that any S.O.B. who thinks he can cause any of those people to be discharged by me, by some smart aleck statement over the air or in the paper, he has got another think coming."[43]

Like Ross, Clifford winced at Vaughan's antics but never voiced his disapproval to the President. Nevertheless, Vaughan, like Connelly, was jealous of Clifford's obvious influence. Long after the end of the Truman administration, Vaughan was still jealous. When President Johnson appointed Clifford secretary of defense, Vaughan penned this note to Mr. Truman:

The Vietnam situation should improve very shortly with Ambassador Clark Clifford on hand.

A man who could originate the Marshall Plan, perfect the Truman Doctrine and re-elect you in 1948 all without you realizing it should find Vietnam a pushover.[44]

As the 1952 campaign approached, other Truman staff members tried their diplomatic best to convince the Boss that he was carrying a dangerous liability. One day assistant press secretary Roger Tubby told Truman that the people of his native Vermont supported the President, but always challenged, "What about Harry Vaughan?" Tubby noted, "As I recall, he stood up and walked over to one of the long windows and looked out towards the Washington Monument with his hands behind his back, and I knew I was dismissed."[45]

Through it all, Vaughan remained his ebullient self. He seemed to thrive on public criticism, and even joked about himself. One day at lunch in the west wing, I was sitting next to him as he regaled us with the roasting he had received at New York's Saints and Sinners Club. Vaughan described with vivid imagery the first skit:

When the curtain went up, Mrs. Robert A. Taft was sitting in a rocking chair, knitting away. And then there was a knock on the door, and this character came in with medals hanging down to his knees. The funny thing was that he not only looked like me, but he really *sounded* like me.

Then Mrs. Taft looks up and says: "Why, hello there, General Vaughan, how are you?"

And this character says: "Well, Mrs. Taft, I understand you're real anxious to move into the White House after the next election, and I just wanted to make sure you had everything you needed. Have you got your deep freeze?"

So Mrs. Taft turns around and says: "Oh yes, General Vaughan. I have a husband for a deep freeze!"[46]

On another occasion, I was declaiming about an inspiring address by Secretary of State Acheson, when he called for "the peace which passeth all understanding." Vaughan chomped on his cigar, poked me in the ribs and noted, "You know, Dean would get along a lot better if he spent less time with the Sermon on the Mount and more time with the Boys on the Hill."

Even old army buddies did not escape Vaughan's barbs. While Secretary of Defense Louis Johnson, a former national commander of the American Legion, was feuding with Acheson, Vaughan blurted one day,

"Louis Johnson is the only bull I know who carries his own china shop right along with him."

I shared the feeling of many Truman staff members that the presence of Vaughan was a handicap of the worst sort. How could the principles of the Marshall Plan, NATO, Point Four and the Truman Doctrine be sponsored by the same President who tolerated Vaughan? He just seemed to lack the "class" that most other Truman staffers possessed. Yet I realized his presence was a blind spot in Truman's vision.

Through the turmoil swirling around him, Vaughan always seemed to get the last word. On September 26, 1951, Truman accompanied the prime minister of Italy out to the Lincoln Memorial and to the Washington side of the Memorial Bridge over the Potomac River. There the President was to dedicate four attractive statues of gold-colored horses, presented by the people of Italy in appreciation of American economic aid to Italy. As we rounded the corner of the Lincoln Memorial, we could see a small crowd assembled. The equestrian statues were covered with huge sheets and there was a long piece of thin rope attached for the unveiling ceremony. The President fingered a delightful little speech Murphy had prepared for the occasion, then contemplated the scene a bit grimly as he asked his military aide, "What do you suppose I should say when I pull that string?" Vaughan took a quick glance and immediately shot back: "That's easy, Boss. You say, 'They're off!' "[47]

3

Planning the 1948 Campaign Strategy

Although I did not join the White House staff until 1949, several conversations with President Truman gave me an insight into how he planned the 1948 strategy and instilled in his supporters the extra determination that carried him to victory. The development of the strategy was not smooth and logical, there were many desperate crises, unforeseen events forced the abandonment of some plans, but through it all Truman's political instincts always came to the rescue.

Nationwide strikes, inflation, the meat shortage in 1946, the worsening international situation, and the weakening of the old Roosevelt coalition of farmers, workers, minorities and urban political machines made Truman's chances look bleak as 1948 approached. The nation had demonstrated its desire to return to normalcy in giving a resounding victory to the Republicans in the 1946 mid-term elections. The 1946 defeat appeared to be a personal repudiation of Truman.

By 1946, the last two Roosevelt holdovers in Truman's cabinet, Henry Wallace and Harold Ickes, had departed with well-publicized blasts against the new administration. Liberal supporters of Roosevelt deserted in droves. Organized labor was bitter at Truman's actions in seizing industries where strikes were occurring. The Democratic leadership in the Solid South was splitting up in the face of Truman's decision to push his civil rights program. Disenfranchised minorities in the South had no voice, and Northern blacks saw the civil rights program stymied by conservative Democrats controlling Congressional committees. The Democrats were being portrayed as flabby and helpless after sixteen years in office.

At the start, there were discordant notes among Truman's advisers, and his own attitudes wavered. Snyder and Steelman continued to push Truman toward a more conservative approach to issues, and they found an ally in Connelly. Truman himself still had reservations about New Dealers who seemed ideologically rigid. On May 22, 1945, he wrote in his diary that he considered a professional liberal "the lowest form of politician."[1] To his mother and sister, he wrote early in 1946 that "people are somewhat befuddled and want to take time out to get a nerve rest."[2]

The 1946 defeat, instead of discouraging Truman, seemed to toughen his determination to fight for the average people he felt obligated to lead. Facing an opposition Congress, he was enough of a politician to understand that great strides toward peace and security could only be achieved through a bipartisan foreign policy. The strategy proved to be a brilliant success in the waning months of 1946 and in the bold initiatives of 1947, which produced the Truman Doctrine and the Marshall Plan, followed by the dramatic Berlin airlift and the establishment of the North Atlantic Treaty Organization. Vacationing at Key West after the mid-term election debacle in 1946, Truman, along with Clifford, helped formulate the strategy that challenged Mine Workers' Union President John L. Lewis after Lewis broke his contract and struck the coal mines then being worked under federal seizure orders. The ultimate victory over Lewis, won through a court-imposed fine, dramatically boosted the President's prestige. It also sharply increased Clifford's standing at the White House.

Still another development in which Clifford was prominently involved resulted in furthering the successful strategy for the 1948 campaign. Oscar "Jack" Ewing, vice-chairman of the Democratic National Committee, organized a group of liberals throughout the federal government committed to a fighting program that was issue-oriented. Starting early in January 1947, the group met on Monday evenings for dinner and a free-wheeling discussion of issues and strategy. Ewing's apartment at the old Wardman Park Hotel was the site of the meetings, in which both Clifford and Murphy participated. Among other regulars at these sessions were Leon Keyserling of the Council of Economic Advisers, Assistant Secretary of Agriculture Charles F. Brannan, Assistant Secretary of the Interior C. Girard "Jebby" Davidson, and Assistant Secretary of Labor David A. Morse. According to Clifford:

> The group was very valuable to me. I was dealing with problems on behalf of the President, week in and week out, and to have a group with whom I could discuss these problems in complete confidentiality, and in the knowl-

edge that they were working toward the same goal that I was, made it *very* valuable.[3]

This combined strategy board and think tank fed a remarkable series of useful materials through Clifford and Murphy for use in presidential speeches and messages during 1947 and 1948. The high caliber of the data not only helped Clifford in his major responsibility of preparing Truman's statements, but it also served to strengthen Truman's increasing inclination to take an aggressively liberal approach to public issues. In August 1947, when Ewing became federal security administrator, he continued to serve as a catalytic agent for the group, which won increasing favor with Truman for its ideas and initiative. Drawing on all agencies of the federal government, this group bolstered Clifford and was a precursor to the research division set up at the Democratic National Committee in 1948.

On May 19, 1947, the President sent a strong message to Congress urging a national health insurance program. On June 7, he blasted the House of Representatives for cuts in conservation, reclamation, and power programs and called for greater soil conservation support as well as raising the minimum wage and enacting housing legislation. These statements were followed by the June 20 veto of the Taft-Hartley Act, which had a dramatic effect in winning back the support of the disaffected labor ranks.

In the fall of 1947, Clifford was involved in a major outline of political strategy that, in retrospect, seemed to blueprint the future with uncanny prescience. In August, Elsey proposed that the 1948 State of the Union Message "must be controversial as hell, must state the issues of the election, must draw the line sharply between Republicans and Democrats. The Democratic platform will stem from it, and the election will be fought on the issues it presents."[4] Agreeing with this analysis, Clifford proceeded to solicit additional details for a 1948 strategy memorandum. Meanwhile, James H. Rowe, Jr., a politically astute Washington lawyer who had served as one of Roosevelt's administrative assistants, distilled the results of a number of conversations with labor leaders, professional politicians and others, producing a thirty-three-page, fact-filled plan of action for 1948. Rowe dated his memorandum September 18, 1947, and he sent a carbon copy to Budget Director Webb with this notation:

Here is the memo; the alert and astute Brother Neustadt has galloped off with the original to Clifford. . . .

I do not know whether Mr. Truman would be elected if everything
done in this memo were done to perfection. But I *do know* that if no attempt is made to do the major suggestions, us Democrats ain't got a chance
in hell![5]

Neustadt, one of Webb's young assistants, who carried the Rowe memorandum to Clifford, joined the White House staff some three years later.
Neustadt feels that the Rowe memorandum was crucial in outlining the
1948 campaign.

Rowe's hypothesis predicted the Republican nomination of Dewey,
the formation of a Wallace third party, the loss of some Northeastern
states, and the creation of a successful coalition of labor, farmers, blacks,
westerners, moderate liberals and consumers. These remarkably accurate predictions were flawed in only one respect: It was also stated that
the Democrats could win the Solid South (actually, four states went for
States Rights candidate Thurmond). A preconvention inspection tour
was urged. The campaigning technique stressed a vigorous attack on the
Republican Eightieth Congress, with a conscious effort to put the Republicans on the spot on the issues of housing, inflation, farm supports,
civil rights and tax revision for low-income groups. To head off liberal
support for Wallace, Rowe recommended a strongly liberal program. At
the same time, to reassure Catholic voters, he underlined the anticom-
munist record of the President. There were other recommendations that
involved strengthening Democratic party organization and improving
Truman's image by inviting world-famous leaders like Albert Einstein
and Henry Ford for well-publicized social and political discussions at
the White House. (Truman put his foot down against the latter idea, on
the grounds that it was a transparently fake gimmick.)

Having some useful ideas of his own and fearful that Truman's strong
dislike for Rowe's law partner (Roosevelt confidant Thomas G. Corcoran, Jr.) would prejudice the President against the Rowe memo, Clifford decided to redraft it. The thirty-three-page document was increased to forty-three pages, without many substantive changes but with
some alterations in phraseology. Clifford then sent the important document on to the President on November 19, 1947. For academic historians attempting to pinpoint the origin of ideas, this process might seem
unusual, but in practice the White House staff would not be serving the
President best if outside suggestions were overlooked. As the screener of
a multitude of good and bad ideas, Clifford had the good sense to recognize an excellent memorandum, dress it up for presentation and insure it

got into the President's hands. In 1980, Rowe noted: "I was irritated at the time. I thought I was writing the memo for Truman. Clark [Clifford] has since gone out of his way to rectify the misunderstanding."[6]

Charles S. Murphy, who shared with Clifford the central responsibility for the speech-writing operation in the 1948 campaign, and who succeeded Clifford as special counsel, feels that this famous memorandum had little bearing on the 1948 strategy.[7] Murphy told me that he had not even seen the memo during the 1948 campaign, nor did he ever hear it discussed. He contends that the President would have adopted a fighting liberal approach to issues whether or not the memo was written, because that was his natural inclination. Murphy also concluded that a rallying of the traditional labor-farmer-minorities-small-business-consumer coalition, along with an aggressive attack on the Republican Eightieth Congress, was already very much in tune with Truman's basic philosophy and approach and therefore did not need a memorandum to put it into action.

Whether or not the Rowe-Clifford memorandum was significant in blueprinting the 1948 strategy, it is interesting to note the remarkable parallels between the memorandum's suggestions and the campaign itself. The 1947 memo advocated a nonpolitical inspection trip of the type Roosevelt had taken to look at defense plants, and such a nonpolitical trip was cooked up in June 1948. It also suggested a sharpening of the attacks on the Republican-controlled Congress, an emphasis on pocketbook issues, and stress on the "winning of the West"—all of which were successfully carried out. Rowe, the author of the first draft, insists: "Webb told me once, whether he was being kind or not I don't know, that the President told him that he kept [the memorandum] in a drawer of his desk and kept looking at it."[8]

In 1948, Truman's most painful and frustrating experiences involved the Roosevelt family. He desperately tried to extend the New Deal policies, yet became angered when Roosevelt's oldest son, James, led a California movement to replace Truman as the 1948 Democratic nominee. Both Truman and Johnson resented the unfavorable contrasts between their speaking styles and the eloquence of Presidents Roosevelt and Kennedy.

In his program, Truman charted a course that went beyond the New Deal, and he could not understand why the Roosevelts and their circle would not rally enthusiastically to his banner. The relationship with James Roosevelt, state Democratic chairman in California, became further embittered in the fall of 1947 as the result of a long-standing feud between California oilman Edwin W. Pauley and onetime Roosevelt and Truman Secretary of the Interior Harold L. Ickes. Young Roosevelt had no use for Pauley, a Truman political friend of long standing who was struggling with Roosevelt for control of the badly split California Democratic party. In October 1947, Roosevelt complained to Democratic National Chairman J. Howard McGrath that Pauley was maneuvering to send an anti-Truman California delegation to the 1948 national convention.[9]

McGrath trotted over to the White House and showed Truman the Roosevelt letter, whereupon Truman hit the ceiling. He blasted Roosevelt with one of those stinging responses that blew off steam and then was never mailed. Among Truman's unsent prose were these sentiments:

> I read with a great deal of interest your letter of October 29 addressed to Howard McGrath.
>
> As you know I have a very strong fondness for Ed Pauley—in spite of his "oil" connections to which you refer. When your great father insisted over the telephone that I become the candidate for Vice President in 1944, Ed Pauley went along with the Boss one hundred percent. So did I much against my own ideas.
>
> Most of the crackpots in California went with "honest?" Harold—and Harold owed his whole national career to President Roosevelt.
>
> I'm not particularly interested in what California or any other state does about the 1948 Democratic Convention. The only thing I'm working for is a peace, based on your father's four freedoms. If we had that now I wouldn't give a damn who the next President is, just so it isn't Henry or Taft.[10]

The involvement of the Roosevelt family in the establishment of the liberal Americans for Democratic Action in 1946 also irked Truman, who observed that the ADA was the hotbed of opposition to his nomination in 1948. Although Truman appointed Mrs. Roosevelt as a delegate to the United Nations, he felt privately that she was encouraging some of the anti-Truman sentiment in her family. As these reports filtered back to Mrs. Roosevelt, she felt obliged to write Truman a frank letter on March 26, 1948:

> There is without any question among the younger Democrats a feeling that the party as at present constituted is going down to serious defeat and may not be able to survive as the liberal party. Whether they are right or wrong, I do not know. I made up my mind long ago that working on the United

Nations meant, as far as possible, putting aside partisan political activity and I would not presume to dictate to my children or to any one else what their actions should be. I have not and I do not intend to have any part in pre-convention activities.[11]

To many liberal Democrats, enchanted by Roosevelt's commanding personality and sonorous voice, Truman seemed like a bumbler who couldn't even read a speech well and perhaps was in a job that was just too big for him to handle. In the spring of 1948 the ADA liberal Democrats, led by James Roosevelt and Florida Senator Claude Pepper, talked openly of dumping Truman in favor of General Dwight D. Eisenhower. The anti-Truman Democrats were so desperate for a candidate that they

Cy Hungerford, Pittsburgh *Post-Gazette*

did not even bother to find out whether Eisenhower was a Republican or a Democrat, or where he stood on the issues that concerned them.

Truman and his staff realized that the 1948 campaign strategy would be pointless unless something dramatic was done to weld together the disintegrating Democratic coalition. Clifford was the chief spokesman for those who felt that Truman should stop trying to live up to Roosevelt's rhetoric, and start a new form of off-the-cuff speech. This was not an overnight development, and the process emerged after a vast amount of soul-searching. Everybody on the White House staff recognized that the President was a poor speaker and that something was lacking in his ability to communicate. His eyesight was so bad that when he leaned over to read his manuscript more closely, all you could see was the top of his head. Lots of suggestions came from both inside and outside the staff, but nobody hit on the right formula for improving Truman's speech delivery. In 1945, during J. Leonard Reinsch's short-lived service as a press and radio adviser, he supplied a wire recorder for the President to do an advance reading of his speech draft, to play back for improvements in diction. This did not seem to help.

Elsey confesses that, in retrospect, the White House staff may have hindered the President by being slow to recognize the superior quality of his off-the-cuff speeches. He explains that the staff was "a little too nervous and a little too jittery" about possible mistakes in extemporaneous speeches. The staff keenly felt their solemn responsibility, for every word uttered by a president of the United States has an awesome effect around the world. On several occasions, Truman demonstrated that shooting from the hip was a dangerous practice.

Clifford, Ross and Murphy advocated a format that would enable Truman to project as interestingly in public as he did in the informal privacy of personal conversation.

A turning point was reached in Truman's appearance before the American Society of Newspaper Editors on April 17, 1948. Murphy conceived the idea of preparing an outline that the President could use as a springboard for extemporaneous remarks, or that he could simply read if he felt comfortable with it. On this occasion, the President started out with a series of prepared remarks, then he launched into an off-the-cuff address along the lines of the outline. Polite applause followed the prepared remarks. But, according to the usually phlegmatic Ross, after the extemporaneous remarks, "the audience went wild." Jonathan Daniels described the difference in audience reaction to what were essentially two different speeches. The carefully polished prepared speech on the evils of inflation and the dangers to the American economy contained "neither meat nor juices nor votes." Daniels observed: "Before he finished there was a perceptible movement among the molders of public opinion at the back tables from the banquet room to the bars."

What subsequently happened was unusual. Daniels wrote:

> He began an entirely different, extemporaneous, and off-the-record speech of his own, in his own vocabulary, out of his own humor and his own heart. . . . He made the story of his own problems seem one told in earnestness and almost intimacy with each man in the hall. He was suddenly a very interesting man of great candor who discussed the problems of American leadership with men as neighbors. He spoke the language of them all out of traditions common to them all.[12]

Truman himself was elated with the results. He recollected in his *Memoirs:* "I was surprised to get the most enthusiastic applause that I have ever received from a group made up mainly of Republicans." The ASNE appearance was followed by similar successes. On May 1, he addressed the National Health Assembly dinner, and wrote in his diary:

> Attend a health meeting and speak extemporaneously. Seemed to go over big. . . . Suppose I am in for a lot of work now getting my head full of facts before each public appearance. If it must be done, I will have to do it. Comes of poor ability to read a speech and put feeling into it.[13]

The President was reluctant to try the same technique in a May 6 address to the National Conference on Family Life because his remarks were being carried live over a radio network. Clifford and Ross finally persuaded him to follow his off-the-cuff style, and once again all hands were pleased with the results. Elsey noted that in thirteen and a half minutes the speech had been interrupted eight times for applause or laughter.[14] There followed still another extemporaneous triumph before a thousand Young Democrats at Washington's Mayflower Hotel on May 14, with the memorable line: "I want to say to you that for the next four years there will be a Democrat in the White House, and you are looking at him!"[15] Roars of applause greeted the new, pugnacious Truman, much preferred to the halting humility that many Democrats had found disconcerting.

From the time he had first campaigned for Jackson County judge, Truman emphasized the value of accurate facts and figures in his speeches. He could make the dullest statistics sing. Now, in 1948, he recognized that the Democratic National Committee, grown complacent through four Roosevelt victories, was ill-equipped to provide the ammunition necessary for the hustings. Over the objections of many of the older hands at the National Committee, the White House staff engineered the establishment of an independent research division, headed by William L. Batt, Jr. and nominally attached to the committee. A seven-man staff assembled a remarkable amount of useful background data on major issues such as human resources, labor, housing, agriculture, education, veterans, health, loyalty, foreign policy, social security, civil rights and inflation. This stockpile of information, including "local color" on key areas where Truman planned to visit, was an invaluable feature of the master plan outlined for 1948.

By June 1948, it was time to test the strategy by putting the show on the road.

4

The "Nonpolitical" Tour

Truman decided early in May that he would go over the heads of the opposition press and take his program directly to the people in a coast-to-coast train trip. He considered this a shakedown cruise to prepare for the 1948 campaign.

He was deeply concerned about the pessimism of state and local Democratic leaders. In several conversations in later years, Truman told me that the down-in-the-mouth attitude of most Democratic leaders was simply a natural reaction to the drumfire of criticism by the opposition press, the dismal figures published by the polls, and the evidence that the old Roosevelt coalition was breaking apart. He said he felt he could take steps to repair the coalition, but that the more immediate task was to rally the flagging spirits of Democratic leaders and average people through personal contact in their hometowns.

Truman told me that his central aim on the June trip, and subsequent trips, was to convince the people that their self-interest was bound up with Democratic success, and to persuade the political leaders that the only way they could elect their favorite local candidates was to build up stronger support for the presidential ticket. He also cited the examples of Andrew Johnson and Woodrow Wilson, who had undertaken similar swings around the country to explain Reconstruction policies and the League of Nations. When I pointed out that both Johnson and Wilson had failed, Truman snorted that Johnson should have covered more territory, and only Wilson's illness ruined his effectiveness.

The Democratic National Committee was virtually broke when Truman decided to launch his June 1948 trip. He steadfastly insisted that the trip was to be billed as "nonpolitical." In this way, the taxpayers had to foot the bill, rather than the financially strapped Democratic National Committee. The President had been invited to deliver the commencement address at the University of California at Berkeley on June 19. Undersecretary of the Interior Oscar L. Chapman telephoned and arranged to have the President awarded an honorary degree. Then a deal was made to switch the date to June 12 to allow the President to fit it into his schedule. Chapman single-handedly attempted the back-breaking job of acting as "advance man" for the eighteen-state trip, which covered over ninety-five hundred miles and included the delivery of seventy-six speeches.

On the evening of June 3, the President and a large party of reporters, photographers, staff and Signal Corps functionaries boarded a seventeen-car train at Union Station in Washington. Clifford and Murphy came aboard from the special counsel's office; Elsey and Bell remained behind to back up the entourage from their headquarters in the White House. Ross handled the press, and Connelly screened out local leaders eager to meet the President. The three military aides and Dr. Wallace Graham, Truman's personal physician, were also on the train. To preserve the fiction that the trip was nonpolitical, officials from the Democratic National Committee and other political leaders were scrupulously excluded.

The President's railroad car, the *Ferdinand Magellan*, was a marvel to behold. This two-hundred-eighty-five-thousand-pound behemoth carried a heavy base of concrete, reinforced by steel track, which could withstand a bomb placed on the railroad tracks. Bulletproof windows and three inches of armor plate transformed it into a rolling fortress. The Association of American Railroads had sold it to the United States Government for one dollar during the Roosevelt administration, because Roosevelt loved to travel by train. The car included comfortable living quarters for the President and his family, a galley and a spacious dining room, staterooms that could be transformed into private offices, a sitting room with a sofa and comfortable chairs, and at the rear of the train a platform that was ideally rigged for speeches. The presidential seal was emblazoned beneath a lectern on the rear platform, where it was an impressive and sobering source of pride. Blue velvet curtains furnished an attractive background as the President addressed the crowds at railroad stations. Overhead loudspeakers were directly connected to the lectern on the back railing, so that the visiting President never had to depend on faulty local equipment.

The other cars of the seventeen-car train provided sleeping and working space for the White House staff, Secret Service, Western Union, and Signal Corps with cryptographic equipment and radio. Dining cars had been converted into working office space for the White House staff, with another car toward the front of the train provided for the news media. Jack Romagna, a speedy stenographer and lightning typist, had his hands full squiggling away pothooks at a frantic rate while the President spoke, then typing onto a stencil for mimeographing the speeches as delivered. British-born, Jack was remarkably accurate in transcribing what the President said, but occasionally his ear was not attuned to every Trumanism. Once, when the President referred to recalcitrant Republicans as "mossbacks," Jack's mimeographed report of the speech interpreted Truman's epithet as "moth bags."

The *Ferdinand Magellan* had one of the most envied facilities on the entire train: a shower. Although it was rumored that there was another shower near the press car, none of the White House staff could ever locate it, so there were times when many of the hundred-plus riders on the train smelled somewhat gamey.

Truman ran into early trouble maintaining the fiction that the June Western trip was nonpolitical. At his first stop at noon on June 4 in Crestline, Ohio, he chuckled as he mentioned that "on this nonpartisan, bipartisan trip that we are taking here, I understand there are a whole lot of Democrats present, too."[1] He took great delight in introducing former Ohio Governor Frank J. Lausche, with the prediction, "I know he is going to be the next Governor of Ohio." Before the end of the first day on the road, Truman was lambasting the Eightieth Congress for listening to the National Association of Manufacturers and Chamber of Commerce of the United States instead of fighting for price controls to protect the people. He told a crowd at Gary, Indiana, that he hoped he would get a new Congress in the next election, and "maybe we'll get one that will work in the interests of the common people and not the interests of the men who have all the money."[2]

Responsibility for providing material for the shorter speeches on this first Western trip fell to Murphy. He relates: "This material was ordinarily furnished in the form of a brief outline. Sometimes it was only a few rough pencil notes which I wrote early in the morning and handed to the President before most of the people on the train had gotten up."[3]

It wasn't long before the Republicans, stung by Truman's jabs, began to counterattack. The chairman of the Republican National Committee,

B. Carroll Reece, dubbed the trip as "nonpolitical as the Pendergast machine." The reaction of the crowds was so positive that Clifford and Murphy decided that the tone of the trip should continue to get stronger, because the Republicans would scream in any event. The more candid members of the staff confessed that the trip was in effect very political. After the campaign, Elsey stated: "The trip was advertised as being nonpolitical, but anything the President does in a political year is very closely watched."[4]

Elsey also indicated that the reason Truman stepped up his attacks on the Eightieth Congress was that he discovered many people in the West were holding him responsible for lack of action on housing, high prices and slashes in funds for flood control and rural electrification. "When he realized that the sins of the 80th Congress were being blamed on him, he began giving a new kind of speech and he took a new approach. He began a series of open, blunt attacks on Congress, calling it the worst in American history."[5]

An incredible series of blunders beset the Truman trip, commencing on the second day of the speech schedule, in Chicago. With an eye on the upcoming national convention and an effort to save the South for the Democratic column, some Truman advisers favored soft-pedaling the civil rights issue. Bell and Elsey took the opposite position, urging that a clear-cut statement be made to pin on Congress the failure to pass a single piece of civil rights legislation.[6] They were over-ruled, resulting in a weak speech at Chicago, which was the first of several blunders on the trip.

There were twenty thousand people in the Chicago Stadium, but they barely responded during Truman's learned essay on how to strengthen democracy and fight communism by fulfilling the promise of democracy. Although Truman's February 2 message to Congress called for a specific, far-reaching civil rights program, at Chicago he failed to mention the subject, except for the bland statement that there should be legislation to extend "the full rights of citizenship."[7] It seemed almost like a retreat from the ringing phrases of his February civil rights message.

The cool reception in Chicago was followed by more horrendous developments during the next few days. June 5 started out as a fine day for the President in Omaha. It was reunion time for the President's World War I outfit, the Thirty-fifth Division. They paraded through most of Omaha's downtown streets, and Truman delighted the crowds by jumping out of his automobile to march briskly and jauntily with his buddies. Anybody who had the desire to see the President had a chance to do so at any street corner in Omaha. That afternoon, at the request of his old friend McKim, he dedicated Omaha's War Memorial, paying special honor in his remarks to Edward D. McKim, Jr., who had been killed in action in World War II. At McKim's suggestion, he then drove out to Boys' Town for a tribute to its founder, the late Father Flanagan. Up to this point, the day was a huge success for Truman. Then the roof fell in.

McKim had handled advance arrangements for what was to have been a huge rally at the Ak-Sar-Ben (Nebraska spelled backwards) Coliseum some miles outside of downtown Omaha. It was billed as an address to the Thirty-fifth Division reunion. McKim figured it would need the Coliseum, which seated ten thousand, to accommodate the hordes of people who would certainly want to see his old friend. Arrangements were also made to carry the speech on nationwide radio. When most people hear the phrase "the public is invited," it doesn't mean much if they have already seen the President on any street corner. There was also a natural disinclination to intrude on what was represented as a Thirty-fifth Division reunion meeting. And the Thirty-fifth Division members themselves felt more like drinking beer and swapping stories than driving miles out into the boondocks to hear a speech. In the cavernous auditorium, only a handful of people were assembled in the front. Photographers had a field day snapping telling shots of the seemingly endless rows of empty seats at the rear of the auditorium. The photos, which circulated throughout the nation, completely overshadowed Truman's major farm speech. But more serious blunders lay ahead.

The Nebraska state Democratic chairman, and later the Montana state chairman, complained they had been pushed aside, ostensibly to avoid violating the "nonpolitical" sanctity of the trip. *Time* magazine, ever ready to take a swipe at Truman, quoted the Nebraska chairman as saying Truman couldn't be elected, because "he seems to prefer his so-called buddies to the persons who have done the work and put up the money for the party."

Early on the morning of June 7, the Truman campaign train stopped at Pocatello, Idaho. There the President first used a technique that he later developed very effectively in subsequent campaign appearances— a "prop" to display and reinforce his point with the crowd. He held up a copy of a Bureau of Reclamation report on the Columbia River Basin to

drive home his strong support of Western power and reclamation projects, an issue that clearly helped in the winning of the West. Unfortunately, this point was somewhat overshadowed by an ad lib at the end of
his Pocatello speech. The President was trying to point out that the
press was constantly throwing false accusations at him, but he worded
his remarks this way: "I have been in politics a long time, and it makes
no difference what they say about you, if it isn't so. If they can prove it
on you, you are in a bad fix indeed. They have never been able to prove
it on me."[8] The opposition press had a field day with that remark, which
seemed to link Truman with the graft of the Pendergast machine—or so
it was interpreted. In the press car, the reporters, who liked Truman
personally, nevertheless guffawed among themselves about the gaffe.

Later in the trip, Truman joked to a folksy crowd at Davis, California: "I am going down here to Berkeley to get me a degree."[9] After a
few drinks, newsmen in the press car began to sing an original ditty, to
the tune "Oh, Susannah!"

> They can't prove nothing
> They ain't got a thing on me
> I'm going down to Berkeley
> To get me a degree[10]

The rest of the day after the Pocatello speech was pleasant and relaxing. The train moved northwest out of the lushly irrigated Snake
River Valley and arrived at Ketchum, Idaho, at 1:30 P.M. Everybody
piled off the train in this picturesque old mining town, with its mounted-
cowboy policemen and wooden sidewalks, where Ernest Hemingway once
shot at coyotes from a low-flying Piper Cub, spent the last years of his
life and later died by his own hand in 1961. It took quite a bit of extra
maneuvering to get more than one hundred people off the train and into
cars for the brief trip north to Sun Valley. Truman complained that it
was easier to move a Barnum and Bailey Circus cross-country than for a
United States president to travel. But everybody was happy to get to
Sun Valley, where they were personal guests of Averell Harriman, who
had built the resort some years before while board chairman of the
Union Pacific Railroad. The President had a good time trying his hand
with a fishing rod at a nearby stream and getting photographed on the
ski lift, and the staff and press had little else to do but enjoy themselves.
The schedule for the next day called for a 9:00 A.M. departure for a
cross-country motor trip to pick up the train at Idaho Falls. Word was

around that there would be a sumptuous six-course breakfast, with pheasant and other delicacies. Ross and his friends in the press corps spent a most enjoyable evening together and closed the bar in the wee hours of the morning, anticipating that they would have plenty of time to sleep and enjoy a good breakfast. Little did they realize what was in store.

There is some disagreement about what actually happened early on the morning of June 8. The President arose about six, his customary hour, enjoyed his usual brisk walk in the crisp mountain air and had a leisurely breakfast. He received word through the Secret Service and Vaughan that the mayor of Carey, Idaho, had telephoned asking if the President would make a little detour on his motor trip to Idaho Falls to say a few words to help dedicate an airport. Apparently, Ross was still asleep when the phone rang, so the call was taken hurriedly by a Secret Service agent, and then it was relayed through Vaughan that the airport would be named in honor of "Wilmer Coates." When it was agreed that the President would make an unscheduled stop, a cardinal rule of presidential appearances was violated: Never allow an appearance without thoroughly researching the background, circumstances and precise names of the principal participants. Neither Clifford nor Murphy, who ordinarily handled such matters, had any inkling that the President had agreed to speak, or what the occasion required.

Robert G. Nixon, the International News Service correspondent, recalls that he had just sat down for breakfast sometime after 7:30 A.M.— supposedly in plenty of time to enjoy a leisurely meal—when "Bill Simmons, the White House receptionist, came tearing down the hallway into the breakfast room shouting, 'Everybody leave, everybody leave, the President's ready to go.' "[11] Nixon hadn't even been able to get a crust of bread or place his breakfast order when, along with other correspondents, he was herded out and shoved into one of the waiting cars. Ross was not quite as fortunate; he was routed out of bed, made the mistake of believing he had time to shave, and was peremptorily dragged out to the motorcade with shaving cream still on his face. Murphy had gotten to the third course of his breakfast when the sudden order came to leave in a split second or not go with the President. He recalls: "So no one finished his breakfast or his coffee. The crowd got out in considerable disarray, and with somewhat irritable feelings all around, I guess. . . . I literally knew nothing about it until the motorcade stopped."[12]

Carey, a little crossroads hamlet with a population of only several hundred at the most, was thirty or forty miles southeast of Sun Valley in the center of an irrigated area on a plateau of volcanic waste. Close by was "Craters of the Moon National Monument," which looked like an eerie scene from a barren planet. Murphy, who was riding a few cars back of the President, looked up ahead to see a line of automobiles parked on the side of the road. Over to the left was what looked like a cow pasture with a mountain on the far side of it. The "cow pasture" turned out to be an airstrip.

When the President's open car stopped, someone immediately thrust a microphone into his hand. He didn't even have an opportunity to ask any of the local residents about the apparently elaborate ceremony that had been planned. He looked around and saw legionnaires and other veterans lined up as an honor guard and had only a second or two to conclude that perhaps a war hero was involved. In the confusion of the hurried departure, nobody had bothered to inform Jack Romagna, so no transcript was made of the President's remarks. The situation invited disaster, which is what actually occurred.

The President started by expressing his pride in the honor he was able to pay to a native son. There was immediate consternation in the crowd; someone pulled on the President's coattails and whispered in his ear that the airport was being dedicated to a young woman. Apparently, the telephone message had referred to "Wilma Coates" and not "Wilmer Coates," as it was relayed second- or third-hand to the President.

But the embarrassment did not end there. Clearing his throat, the President started again. He referred to the fact that the young woman, whom he now assumed was a WAC, WAVE or WAF, had bravely sacrificed her life for her country. Else why were the veterans all lined up? There was another interruption as more whispering and coattail tugging ensued. Apparently, Wilma Coates had been killed hedge-hopping with her boy friend, and she was a teenager without any military service. The President extended his profuse apologies to the father and mother of the young lady in whose honor the airport was being named. The entire experience was most disconcerting.

Because of some of these difficulties and delays, the train, which was scheduled to depart Idaho Falls at one minute after noon, was already nearly forty-five minutes late. Murphy recalls that the President then decided that his staff work was not what it should be, so he asked the staff to meet with him in the dining section of the *Ferdinand Magellan*. "He called the meeting, I'm sure, for the purpose of dressing the staff down, but when the time came for him to do that, he couldn't quite manage to scold us," Murphy recalls. At Omaha, Carey and other places, most of the fundamental rules of good advance work and staff research had been violated. It was fortunate that these boo-boos happened early in the year, because every member of the staff could now appreciate the horrendous results of approaching a presidential speech without preparation or full communication with those responsible in the special counsel's office. The President gave specific assignments to each staff member, to head off any repetition of the blunders.

Balm for the President's injured feelings came that night at a big stadium in Butte, Montana, where he received a boisterous welcome. Once again he lambasted Congress, and he attacked Ohio's Senator Taft, who had urged people to fight inflation by eating less. "I guess he would let you starve, I don't know," the President said. Stung by the criticism, Taft made a nationwide radio address to counterattack. On June 11, he made a speech at the Union League Club in Philadelphia, which accused Truman of "blackguarding Congress at every whistle station in the West." Truman and his staff loved it. In Los Angeles, when the President blasted Congress again, he jokingly referred to the fact that Los Angeles was the biggest whistle stop he had visited. The crowd roared its approval. The Democratic National Committee picked up the bait, and telegraphed thirty-five cities and towns along Truman's route to ask the mayors how they liked to be referred to as whistle stops—stations where you had to pull the cord on the train to make it stop. It must have chagrined Senator Taft to learn that when he referred to a "whistle station," the President edited his phrase to read "whistle stop," and then the Truman phrase not only stuck in the public mind but also became one of the accepted political descriptions of the Truman style of campaigning.[13]

The President visited the Northwest at a time when floods had caused great damage. Before he left, he persuaded a lot of his listeners that the Republican Congress was at fault for failing to appropriate sufficient money for flood control. His informal, folksy approach appealed to the friendly crowds that appeared at the railroad stations. Clifford and Murphy found the universal reaction was that people felt the President "wasn't nearly like the bad person the newspapers made him out to be."

"Give 'em hell, Harry!" or "Pour it on, Harry!" frequently reverberated from the growing crowds. Clifford was not averse to occasionally starting one of those cries himself. The President always answered a
shout from the crowd. Later he refined his answer to something like this:
"I'm only telling the truth on them, but they think it's hell." From very
early in the morning until way after bedtime, he was always out there on
the rear platform, pugnacious, peppery, down-to-earth, even getting up
to appear twice in his pajamas and bathrobe after he had gone to bed.
Between stops, his staff marveled at his ability to drop off and take a
sound nap as though he didn't have a care in the world.

When he finally arrived in Berkeley to get the honorary degree and
deliver the commencement address that was the original excuse for the
June trip, the President shifted gears and surprised many observers by
delivering an unusually sober, thoughtful and dignified oration on foreign policy. The outdoor stadium at the University of California was
jammed with fifty-five thousand people. Appropriate to the academic
occasion, he made none of the roundhouse swings so characteristic of the
speeches at other stops. Extremely careful work had preceded the
speech, which went through many drafts. It may not have roused whistles, cheers and roars, but it was praised editorially around the country.

Then it was back on the stump again. Close to a million people saw
the President in downtown Los Angeles as he paraded through the
streets and savored the plaudits of a friendly crowd. The warmth of the
reception must have surprised even Jimmy Roosevelt, who was still trying to figure out a way to dump Truman at the upcoming Democratic
convention. In a fighting address at the Ambassador Hotel, the President
threw down the gauntlet and challenged Congress to pass eight measures dealing with housing, labor, social security, health, education,
agriculture, economic controls, reclamation and public power.

Despite some of the boners that occurred on the trip, the net effect
was a whopping success for the President. Even though the polls and
newspapers still indicated that he didn't have a chance, everyone who
saw and heard the President was impressed. He scored some telling
points, roused his audiences to high pitches of enthusiasm, and came
across as a President who would be difficult to challenge. In fact, he had
seized the initiative and placed the Republican Congress clearly on the
defensive on this "nonpolitical" trip.

5

The 1948 Convention

Arriving back in Washington on June 18, Truman had less than a month before the Democratic national convention assembled in Philadelphia. He was very concerned about two aspects of the forthcoming convention: heading off the abortive effort of Roosevelt, Pepper and the liberals to dump him in favor of Eisenhower or someone else, and the vice-presidential nominee. National Chairman McGrath urged Truman to persuade a younger man with a liberal reputation to go on the ticket with him. The obvious choice was Supreme Court Justice William O. Douglas, who had previously declined a Truman effort to name him secretary of the interior. Although the President talked with Douglas twice by telephone, urging him to accept a vice-presidential nomination, Douglas answered: "I do not think I should use the Court as a stepping-stone."[1] Truman's reaction was caustic: "He owes it to the country to accept. He belongs to that crowd of Tommy Corcoran, Harold Ickes, Claude Pepper crackpots whose word is worth less than Jimmy Roosevelt's."[2]

Truman was not enthusiastic about aged Senator Alben W. Barkley as his running mate, as the convention approached. "Call old man Barkley and smooth his feathers so he'll go ahead and make the keynote speech," the President reported in his diary.[3] The Barkley effort was one of his best oratorical masterpieces—so good, in fact, that it roused a new attempt to dump Truman in favor of Barkley. Truman suspected that there was some dirty work at the crossroads. "My 'good' friend, Leslie Biffle, spends all his time as sergeant-at-arms of the Convention running Barkley for President," he wrote.[4] In 1944, Roosevelt had ruled out Barkley as too old to be his running mate. A Missouri-Kentucky combination was unattractive politically against a Republican ticket drawn from New York and California. But the circumstances almost forced Truman to maneuver toward grudging acceptance of Barkley as the vice-presidential nominee, so effective was Barkley's oratory.

The detailed entries in Truman's diary on July 12, 13, and 14 indicate that he was preoccupied with the composition of the ticket and the staff did the platform. Judge Rosenman had prepared a preliminary draft of the platform, and a task force headed by Clifford, including Murphy, Bell and Elsey, revised it.[5] Input was also received from the Batt research group at the National Committee. Elsey went to Philadelphia as a personal emissary, slipping this White House version of the platform to Biffle, who then forwarded it to the regular resolutions committee of the convention, as though it had been delivered by a stork rather than dictated by the White House. The most important element in the White House–drafted platform was a careful phrasing of the civil rights plank. It was clearly a straddle, in keeping with Truman's silence on the issue during his June "nonpolitical" trip. The strategy was obviously designed to prevent a Southern walkout at the convention. David K. Niles, White House minorities specialist, who was also present at the convention, lobbied hard to tone down inflammatory references to civil rights in the platform. Clifford also went to Philadelphia to confer with the chairman of the resolutions committee, Pennsylvania Senator Francis Myers. The White House desperately attempted to preserve unity by keeping the same civil rights language as the 1944 platform. The strategy was to dampen the controversy, keep the South in line until after the election, and then proceed to enact the much stronger program the President had enunciated in his February message to Congress.

But neither the President nor the White House staff reckoned with the emotional power of the liberals at the convention. Frustrated in their efforts to dump Truman, the ADA liberals were now joined by a wide spectrum of delegates who believed that the time had come to stop shilly-shallying on a moral issue and stand up for this righteous cause. Washington activist lawyer Joseph L. Rauh, Jr., drafted a minority civil rights plank that came out four-square for equal political and employment opportunity and carried out the spirit of Truman's own Civil Rights Committee. A young Minneapolis mayor named Hubert H. Humphrey, running for the United States Senate for the first time in 1948, electrified the convention with his memorable phrase: "The time has arrived for the Democratic party to get out of the shadow of states' rights and walk forthrightly into the bright sunshine of human rights."

The convention was in a turmoil. A Truman loyalist who had ridden on the train in the early stages of the June trip, Illinois Senator Scott Lucas, referred to Humphrey as a "pip-squeak," and warned Joe Rauh against meddling by the ADA. Niles tried to head off the uprising by telling Rauh that the fight would scar Humphrey's career; "You'll ruin the chances of the best political talent to come along in years," cried Niles.[6] But the liberals won.

President Truman's attitude was that the first priority was to win the election. He did not think the platform fight as important as did the convention battlers. He confided to his diary: "Platform fight in dead earnest. Crackpot Biemiller from Wisconsin offers a minority report on civil rights. . . . The Convention votes down States Rights and votes for the crackpot amendment to the Civil Rights Plank."[7]

By a fairly narrow vote of 651–582, plus a few fractions, the mavericks carried their cause against the wishes of the President and the lobbying of his staff. As good politicians, the President and his allies proceeded to transform what they felt would be a handicap into a great asset during the campaign. Now the once dispirited liberals and the urban minorities came out fighting for those principles to which they were emotionally dedicated.

The President and his party arrived at the convention hall before 10:00 P.M. on a steamy July evening. Without air-conditioning, the delegates were in a soggy condition, groggy from lack of sleep, and not too perked up about the future of their prospective ticket. By now, word had come down that the ticket would certainly be a sixty-four-year-old veteran from Missouri and a seventy-year-old warhorse from Kentucky. With the civil rights plank in the platform, there seemed to be no chance of holding the South. The more militant southerners walked out; those who remained prepared for their last struggle—to garner as many convention votes as possible for the candidacy of Georgia Senator Richard B. Russell. Foregone conclusions mean nothing to Democrats. They need time to fight among themselves about something. So it took four hours for the convention to nominate Truman and Barkley, and the expected Southern bolt occurred. In the face of this undignified thrashing around on the convention floor, Truman remained calm and unruffled. He chatted for a while with Barkley on an outdoor balcony, in the muggy July air, as more and more Americans turned off their television sets or radios and gave up to go to bed. The Democrats never seemed to learn that 2:00 A.M. is not the best time for an acceptance speech; they made the same mistake in 1952 and 1972.

There was more confusion when Truman mounted the rostrum after a mercifully brief acceptance speech by Barkley. When elderly Pennsylvania committeewoman Emma Guffey Miller decided she wanted to do something, neither hell nor high temperature could stop her. She presented the puzzled President with a giant floral Liberty Bell and triggered the release of a flock of white pigeons that flopped around aimlessly. One almost perched atop convention chairman Sam Rayburn's bald pate. Another had to be shooed away from the rostrum from which the President was to speak. Dressed in a crisp and gleaming white linen suit, Truman looked cool in the midst of all this sweaty confusion. After a few preliminaries, he brought the tired delegates roaring to their feet with this Trumanesque jab: "Senator Barkley and I will win this election and make these Republicans like it—don't you forget that!"[8]

Truman then threw back at the Republicans the platform they had just adopted at their own convention, and challenged the Republican-controlled Congress to enact the necessary measures to carry it out. He went one step further by suggesting that Congress be called back into special session to act on these necessary measures.[9] Truman relished this idea, and had told his staff meeting on the morning of July 13 that he planned to tell the Republicans: "Now, you sons of bitches, come and do your God damnedest."[10]

Although the basic idea was clear both in the speech outline and in his mind, the President expressed it at the convention in memorable Truman fashion: "On the 26th day of July, which out in Missouri we call 'Turnip Day,' I am going to call Congress back and ask them to pass laws to halt rising prices, to meet the housing crisis—which they are saying they are for in their platform."[11]

Very few people had heard of "Turnip Day," but it was the kind of expression that caught the fancy of those who were fed up with high-flown generalities like "the promise of American life." It was later explained that the expression came from an old Missouri saying that "on the twenty-sixth day of July, sow your turnips, wet or dry." It brought a glow of friendly satisfaction to millions of average people who heard their scrappy President use the vernacular. To Clifford, a master of imagery no matter how close he might be to a subject, the acceptance speech exceeded his expectations. He reflected some years later: "His sincerity and his courage shone through so clearly that he lifted that convention right up off the seats of their pants."[12]

One of the highly effective techniques that the President used was to tick off every issue in the Republican platform, repeating the litany and ending in the phrase "which they say they are for in their platform." He repeatedly challenged the Republicans to use the opportunity he was affording them in the special session to act on education, health, civil rights, social security coverage and all the other issues "which they say they are for." According to Elsey, "The manner in which he repeatedly jabbed the Republicans with that line caused wilder and wilder enthusiasm from his audience."[13]

The President was delighted with the response to his convention address. He gleefully recorded the reactions, as well as his own feelings the morning after:

> Arrived in Washington at the White House at 5:30 A.M., my usual getting up time. But I go to bed at 6:00 and listen to the news. Sleep until 9:15, order breakfast and go to the office at 10:00. I called a special session of the Congress. My, how the opposition screams. I'm going to attempt to make them meet their platform promises before the election. That is, according to the "kept" press and the opposition leadership, "cheap politics." I wonder what "expensive politics" will be like! We'll see.[14]

On the next day, he felt even better about what he had wrought:

> Editorials, columns and cartoons are gasping and wondering. None of the smart folks thought I would call the Congress. I called 'em for July 26, turnip day at home. Dewey synthetically milks cows and pitches hay for the cameras just as that other fakir, Teddy Roosevelt, did—but he'd never heard of "turnip day." I don't believe the USA wants any more fakirs— Teddy and Franklin are enough. So I'm going to make a common sense, intellectually honest campaign. It will be a novelty—and it will win.[15]

The maneuver took the initiative away from the Republicans. Dewey had hoped to interpret the Republican platform himself in a series of measured addresses, logically developed. Now the Republican majority in Congress was being forced in the white glare of publicity to act on the platform, and the Republican majority, led by Taft, was Old Guard to the core. Thus Truman had cleverly driven a deep wedge into the Republican party, which more than matched the split in his own party. Numerous Republican leaders prevailed upon Dewey to persuade

Taft to pass at least some of the legislation the platform called for. But Taft, who was just about as stubborn as Truman, refused to bow to what he felt was a slick political maneuver on Truman's part. As a result, Dewey remained silent and noncommittal, following the advice of some short-sighted aides who felt that since he was going to win anyway he had better not rock the boat.

The President and his aides decided on another bold step: to address the special session of Congress in person. Once again he set forth his anti-inflation program, and called for consumer credit controls, an excess profits tax, strengthening of rent controls, and comprehensive housing, education, civil rights and health legislation. He also asked for an increase in the minimum wage, an extension of Social Security, liberalization of the Displaced Persons Act, a loan to the United Nations to build its headquarters in New York, and appropriation for a TVA steam plant. He made no direct reference to the "do-nothing" Congress or the "special interest" Congress, nor did he give them a taste of his whistle-stop folksiness. About the closest he came was when he addressed the predominantly male legislators in this fashion: "All you need do is just go home and ask your wife how living costs are now, as compared to what they were January 1st, 1947."[16]

On August 12, the President released a detailed statement indicating that all the special session had accomplished was to pass the loan to build the UN headquarters. The same day he blasted Congress for the "do-nothing session." In addition to sharpening the image of the President as the friend of farmers, workers, consumers and average people, the special session succeeded in demonstrating Dewey's lack of leadership in his own party. One new issue that highlighted this was the Displaced Persons Bill sponsored by West Virginia's Republican Senator Chapman Revercomb. Dewey tried to persuade the Republican Congress to amend the bill by removing certain provisions which were anti-Catholic and anti-Semitic. This unsuccessful attempt not only played an important part in the presidential campaign, but also helped the Democrats in states like West Virginia, where Revercomb was being challenged by Representative Matthew M. Neely.

In summary, the convention and its aftermath provided a boost for Truman's campaign. To be sure, he was far from out of the woods. But those dispirited delegates who had sported "I'm Just Mild About Harry" signs had to eat them after Truman's dramatic acceptance speech. The frustrated liberals who had tried to dump Truman emerged from the convention with pride in their exciting victory for a stronger civil rights plank. The old Roosevelt coalition started to reassemble as its components began to appreciate that their best interest was in Truman's candidacy. The Southern bolt was serious, yet it rendered Wallace's Progressive party less of a threat to Truman's strength. To cap it all, the "Turnip Day" special session of Congress that followed the convention gave millions of people a well-publicized picture of the difference between the two political parties.

6
The Greatest Political Upset of All Time

Labor Day was not a holiday for Truman or his staff. Seven speeches were delivered in Michigan and Ohio, with the major effort concentrated on the big rally in Cadillac Square, Detroit. The planning and implementation of this trip were a ten-strike for Truman's bid to stimulate organized labor to greater campaign activity, as recommended in the November 1947 Rowe-Clifford memorandum. Clifford met with James B. Carey, secretary-treasurer of the CIO, on August 13 and received the good news that the President's convention speech and the sorry record of the Republican Congress in the special session had switched labor from grudging to enthusiastic support.[1] This development was doubly sweet because Carey had flirted with Wallace's candidacy and also was part of the abortive effort to dump Truman in favor of Eisenhower. Clifford next brought Assistant Secretary of Labor John Gibson to the White House to pick his brains for the Labor Day trip, with particular attention to the Cadillac Square address.

The outlines by this time had become fairly well standardized. In fact, one memorandum was entitled "Suggestions for Preparing Outlines for Brief Platform Speeches."[2] The outline started with a friendly local reference, drawn from material supplied by the Batt research group. It was then demonstrated that a vote for Wallace or Thurmond was really a vote for the Republican ticket, and the real choice was between the Democrats and Republicans. From there, the outline documented the concept that Republicans serve the rich and Democrats serve all the people. Finally, the point of the whole campaign was brought home by indicating that "It's a question of whether you'll have enough to eat and to wear. It virtually affects your chance for living in a world at peace."

A few days before the big show got on the road for Labor Day's strenuous schedule, Truman invited David M. Noyes and Albert Z. (Bob) Carr to the White House. Noyes and Carr were not White House staff members, although Carr had been a writer for the Roosevelt White House and stayed over briefly after Truman took office. Truman had met Noyes while he was in the Senate, and the friendship had blossomed since. Noyes recruited Carr and the two customarily moved together. Both considered themselves more liberal than most members of the White House staff, and friction often resulted as Clifford and Murphy found them infringing on their responsibilities.

The Labor Day Speeches and Other Early Campaign Activities

On Sunday afternoon, September 5, the President and his party boarded the campaign train bound for Michigan. Grand Rapids was the first stop, at 8:15 on Labor Day morning, where twenty thousand people greeted him. He charged twice during the speech that Senator Taft, an original cosponsor of the Wagner-Ellender-Taft housing bill, "ran out on his own bill." He blasted the record of "the worst Congress, except one, this country has ever had." The President suggested that history would indicate that the Thaddeus Stevens Reconstruction Congress was actually the worst. In Detroit, crowd estimates ranged from one hundred thousand to one hundred twenty-five thousand, and Truman pulled out all stops. He charged that the Eightieth Congress, instead of cracking down on high prices, had cracked down on labor. He scored the Taft-Hartley Act as a "body blow" to labor and warned of more serious setbacks unless they went to the polls to change the reactionary Congress. He charged that "the reactionary of today . . . is a man with a calculating machine where his heart ought to be."[3] Unfortunately, the President's delivery was not up to par at Detroit. National Committee publicity director Jack Redding had repeatedly pointed out that he had to finish within the time allotted for a national radio network broadcast. Like many politicians, the introductory speakers got carried away by the sounds of their own voices and the size of the crowd, and took longer than they were supposed to, thereby forcing the President to rush through the last part of his text.[4]

One of the most successful Labor Day speeches was at Flint, Michigan, before a trainside crowd of thirty-five thousand. Murphy handed the President a copy of "The Republican News," published by the Republican National Committee. Truman noted with great glee that after Congress had overridden his veto of a Republican-sponsored tax bill, the Republican National Committee appealed to those who had benefited from these tax cuts to kick in with contributions for the GOP. "I think that is plain, outright bribery," Truman charged, to the cheers of the big crowd. On the way back to Washington, the train stopped at Toledo, and Truman asked them how they liked Taft's characterization of Toledo as a whistle stop.

Less than two weeks remained after the Labor Day swing before the President took off again for a two-week whistle-stop tour of the Far West, the first extended major trip. This necessitated not only frantic advance preparations, but an important change in the speech-writing team. Charlie and Kate Murphy were expecting the arrival of another addition to their family at the end of September, and Charlie obtained the President's permission to remain in the Executive Office Building as the key Washington source for speech materials needed on the train. Elsey then went on the campaign train and assumed central responsibility for the whistle-stop outlines. Murphy later concluded: "As things developed later on, it became clear that it was very fortunate that I had stayed at home because the work which I did here in collecting materials for the speeches could not possibly have been done on the train."[5]

It had been planned to "freeze" the major speech drafts (have them read aloud and cleared by the President, thus put to bed) prior to the September 17 departure date. This meant a target of at least five major addresses through the drafting and polishing process. But for reasons that will be explained, the President left Washington with only one draft—albeit an important one—the address at the National Plowing Contest in Dexter, Iowa, which played a major role in swinging the farm vote in 1948.

Shortly after Labor Day, Clifford, Murphy and the rest of the speech-writing group started a draft for Dexter. This work began with a White House luncheon conference attended by Secretary of Agriculture Brannan and Wesley McCune and Duke DuMars of Brannan's staff. Murphy and Bell tackled the preliminary work on the speech, and churned through about five drafts.

At this point, the President indicated that the regular White House group should work with Noyes and Carr on the Dexter speech and that they were going to be with the President on a *Williamsburg* cruise down the Potomac on the weekend before the whistle-stop train left for the

Far West. Somewhat circumspectly, Murphy subsequently wrote about the problem that faced the White House staff: "We had not up until this time established any working relationship [with Noyes and Carr] for reasons which I did not fully understand then and certainly could not explain now."[6]

On Sunday, September 12, in order to carry out the President's instructions and move the Dexter draft toward a freezing session, Murphy boarded a seaplane and flew down the Potomac, landing on the river in a big wave of spray near the *Williamsburg.* Clifford and several members of the staff read Murphy's latest draft, which he handed to the President, but Truman was otherwise occupied that Sunday, resting for the strenuous weeks ahead. The uninterruptible poker game was also in progress. One can only conjecture what happened next, but it seems from the President's comments on September 13 that Clifford must have raised a strong protest against the confusion created by having competing drafts prepared by the regular White House speech team and by Noyes and Carr. The President noted in his diary on September 13:

> My staff is in a turmoil. Clifford has gone prima donna on me. So has Howard McGrath. It's hell but a part of the game. Have had to force McGrath to behave and Clifford too. But I get a headache over it. But a good night's sleep will cure it.[7]

When the President returned Murphy's draft of the Dexter speech, he gave him a copy of the Carr draft and asked him to merge them into one speech. "Being somewhat prejudiced in the matter, I think that the composite draft turned up about two-thirds from my earlier draft and one-third from Carr's draft," Murphy recalled.[8]

A new problem arose when the Department of Agriculture sadly passed on its opinion that the new Murphy-Carr effort was a distinct step backward. Brannan, McCune and DuMars were just about the most agreeable, cooperative, prompt and discerning people with whom the White House dealt. You could phone them at office or home any time of the day or night and they always came through with speedy and accurate information on anything connected with agricultural activities. Unlike many bureaucratic agencies, which sometimes labored long like a mountain to produce a mouse, you could always count on Secretary Brannan's people to deliver superior goods on time. Their objections to the new Dexter draft made the situation very difficult for Murphy, and things went from bad to worse when he tried to get the Noyes-Carr team to concur on the new effort. With his dry Southern humor, Murphy summarized: "This concurrence was given very readily—after they had made some slight changes, which consisted for the most part of taking out everything I had put in their draft and putting back everything I had taken out of their draft."[9]

The final compromise produced a speech that was based on the original material obtained from the Department of Agriculture, with the style and tone being primarily Carr's. Murphy was well satisfied with the final draft that the President took with him. The problem was that so much time had been spent on the Dexter speech that it was the only draft completed by the time the President left on September 17.

Two developments on which the White House staff capitalized just happened to fit into the Dexter speech and make it one of the most effective of the campaign. On September 2, Minnesota's Harold Stassen visited Dewey, and attacked the Department of Agriculture for purchasing grain for export, which Stassen contended was increasing consumer food prices. Secretary Brannan acted with lightning speed and sharply criticized the Republicans for trying to scuttle farm price supports. The counterattack reverberated throughout the Farm Belt, and made more hay for the Democrats as farmers began to worry about slipping prices.

A second big break came when James M. Cox, the Democratic candidate for president in 1920, assigned a reporter named W. McNeil Lowry to write a story for the *Dayton Daily News* and other Cox newspapers. It seems that in extending the charter for the Commodity Credit Corporation the Republican Congress in June had included an obscure provision that prohibited the CCC from acquiring new storage bins. Since 1948 was a bumper-crop year, the shortage of storage bins became immediately apparent. Clifford received copies of the Lowry news story, and it wasn't too long before the whole episode was portrayed as a Republican plot dreamed up by the big grain dealers' lobby in league with the GOP. Few people would have paid attention to this issue had not the President highlighted it in his Dexter speech and hammered it home thereafter during the campaign.

Of course, the problems of the world did not go away while the President and his staff prepared for the big push ahead. Russian troops were blockading the *autobahn* to Berlin, and Truman had to decide whether to allow American troops to shoot their way through. Ultimately, he ordered the Berlin Airlift, which remained freedom's beacon. On September 13, in addition to worrying about the internal turmoil in his staff, the President mentioned that he had "a terrific day"—meaning an extremely busy and worrisome one. After conferring with Secretary of Defense Forrestal, the Joint Chiefs of Staff and Secretary of the Air Force Stuart Symington about Berlin, the President noted, "I have a terrible feeling afterward that we are very close to war. I hope not."[10] Following a luncheon discussion with Secretary of State Marshall on the Berlin crisis and the customary postprandial nap, there was more hassling about the Dexter speech and the perennial problem of how to raise funds for the staggering expenses of the campaign. That evening the President went over to Constitution Hall where, with the drafting help of Steelman and his staff, he delivered a brilliant address before the American Association for the Advancement of Science. He enthralled his listeners, who had shuddered at the thought of hearing a political speech, with his deep understanding of the necessity for more basic research to enrich the wellsprings of the nation's strength.

"Pure research is arduous, demanding, and difficult," he told his rapt listeners. "It requires unusual intellectual powers. It requires extensive and specialized training."[11] His peroration lifted the scientists to accord the President the bursts of applause usually reserved for the emotional oratory of the stump:

> Science means a method of thought. That method is characterized by open-mindedness, honesty, perseverance, and above all, by an unflinching passion for knowledge and truth. When more of the peoples of the world have learned the ways of thought of the scientist, we shall have better reason to expect lasting peace and a fuller life for all.[12]

The President was well pleased with the address and its effects. It had been a busy day, and he had little time for reflection at the end of a long evening. But he took a moment to record in his diary: "Spoke to the scientists and knocked them for a goal."[13] He added the next day: "Papers gave science speech good coverage. Hope it does some good."[14]

The reaction of his listeners was typical for those who had formed their impressions of Truman from news accounts. They had wondered whether this crude, uneducated "Missouri clodhopper" could really contribute anything to their distinguished gathering, beyond a few gauche remarks. The scientists came away believers. They had seen a Truman they never dreamed existed.

The Winning of the West

The next day, the President finally nailed down the selection of a campaign treasurer. Rebuffed by Jesse H. Jones and Bernard M. Baruch, he finally persuaded a West Virginia–born corporate lawyer and former national commander of the American Legion, Louis A. Johnson, to undertake the onerous task. Truman was grateful and in 1949 he appointed Johnson to succeed the ailing James Forrestal as secretary of defense. Johnson worked tirelessly to raise funds for a candidate whom nobody expected to have a chance. The Western trip itself was in jeopardy until it could be funded. According to Margaret Truman:

> In mid-September, as we were packing to board the campaign train for our first national swing, party treasurer Louis Johnson called a group of wealthy Democrats to the White House and Dad got up on a chair in the Red Room to inform them that if they did not come through with $25,000, the "Truman Special" would not get beyond Pittsburgh. Two men immediately pledged $10,000, and that is how we got rolling.[15]

A smattering of Democratic loyalists assembled at Union Station when Truman left on September 17, accompanied by two of his most effective political assets, Mrs. Truman and Margaret. Barkley then provoked what became the battle cry of the campaign. " 'Go out there and mow 'em down,' Barkley cried. 'I'll mow 'em down, Alben,' Truman shot back, 'and I'll give 'em hell.' "

Despite the condescending way in which the President was treated as a sure loser, the press couldn't help but allow a sympathetic note to creep into their dispatches portraying the scrappy fight of an underdog. Margaret's tut-tut reaction to her father's language also made good copy.

The first two days of the Western trip were so taxing that they nearly hospitalized the President. On his way west, he stopped in Pittsburgh to help celebrate the first anniversary of the Freedom Train, carrying original copies of the Declaration of Independence, Constitution, Gettysburg Address and other treasures. After speaking in Pittsburgh, he gave a 10:30 P.M. whistle-stop talk at Crestline, Ohio, and was awakened at 2:15 A.M. in Chicago to exchange pleasantries with Chicago Democratic leader Jake Arvey and a coterie of Cook County politicos. His Crestline speech was sobered by the news of the assassination of United Nations mediator Count Bernadotte in war-torn Israel. The September 18 schedule was bone tiring. Starting at Rock Island, Illinois, at 5:45 A.M., Truman delivered five speeches from the rear platform before 9:00 A.M. as the train snaked through Iowa. Including his most important speech of all, at the National Plowing Match in Dexter, Iowa, the President spoke thirteen times on that hectic day, winding up at 8:10 P.M. whistle-stopping at Polo, Missouri.

More than eighty thousand people heard the President's address at the Plowing Match. Hot, humid weather greeted him. The plowing and the trampling feet stirred up huge clouds of dust on Mrs. T. R. Agg's model farm. It was just after noon, and the oppressive heat and windless atmosphere forced everyone to breathe the choking dust. Lack of sleep and the strenuous morning schedule aggravated a sore throat that Truman had when he reached Dexter. But he put everything he had into a rip-roaring attack on the GOP as "gluttons of privilege" who had "stuck a pitchfork in the farmer's back." Some years later, Clifford cringed at these colorful phrases from the pen of Bob Carr, and confessed: "I think if we had it to do again, we might have written it a little differently."[16] Truman plunged on with a slashing attack on the lobbyists representing the speculative grain traders who had "persuaded the Congress not to provide the storage bins for the farmers," playing on Midwestern fears of Wall Street. As in Vachel Lindsay's description of William Jennings Bryan, he was "smashing Plymouth Rock with his boulders from the West." Avoiding the time-honored political cliché, "vote for whom you please but vote," Truman went straight for the pocketbook nerve: "I'm not asking you just to vote for me. Vote for yourselves! Vote for your farms! Vote for the standard of living that you have won under a Democratic administration! Get out there on election day, and vote for your future!"[17]

Truman was in some pain after the Dexter speech. Margaret wrote that "Dad gave a rousing, scorching speech, which almost tore his throat apart. For at least a week, Dr. Wallace Graham, his personal physician, had to spray his throat before every speech."[18] The President took the whole thing rather casually. Reflecting on his discomfort following the Dexter effort, he wrote: "Dr. Graham just sprayed, mopped and caused me to gargle bad tasting liquids until the throat gave up and got well."[19]

As he roared west, the President's informal style at each whistle stop improved, thanks to the information relayed to the train by the Batt group and fashioned into simple and direct outlines by Elsey. Local candidates always received good plugs, and the President usually had a nice word to say for products of the area—many of which were presented to him by local citizens. Never before had so many high school bands practiced for weeks on "Hail to the Chief," and they were honored when the object of their attention complimented them before he flailed away at the "do-nothing, good for nothing" Eightieth Congress. Local residents gaped in surprise because their distinguished visitor seemed to know a great deal about their town, or had even visited the area as a representative of the National Old Trails Association, or his grandfather had driven through on an ox-train. Keys to the city, baskets of peaches, spurs and cowboy boots—gifts galore were presented to the President and Mrs. Truman, as well as to Margaret. At every stop, he left the people prouder of themselves and their community and injected adrenaline into the local Democrats, at the same time he was hammering home his repeated theme of the failures of the Republican Eightieth Congress and the consistent record of the Democrats on behalf of average people.

There were agonizing moments, but careful advance work under the direction of Chapman, later with the assistance of Donald Dawson, avoided a repetition of the June disaster at Omaha. And never again did anything like the embarrassment at Carey, Idaho, recur. Some reporters complained that since they were banned from the last three cars on the train, they missed the first and last portions of some speeches because they had to run along the tracks for several hundred feet. This inconvenience was alleviated to some extent when Ross arranged for a loudspeaker to pipe the President's speeches into the press car. Reporters protested they weren't getting advance texts of speeches on time. This situation was caused by the confusion over drafting and completing the Dexter speech, which had set back the entire schedule.

From Washington, Murphy struggled to get a draft ready for the second major address, on September 20 at the State Capitol in Denver. Since this was Secretary of Agriculture Brannan's hometown, it was easy to get suggested remarks from him. It was decided to emphasize the theme of conservation and use of natural resources, plus development of the West, at Denver. Murphy turned to the Department of the Interior for help, and gave them the Agriculture material to work into a draft. Richard Hipplehouser, a writer for the Interior Department, came to the White House and appeared to be on the right track, but days passed beyond the deadline, and still no draft. After repeated calls by Murphy and Bell, the draft came over one page at a time, and it proved to be rather poor in quality. Later, when I went to work at the White House, I used to hear Murphy or Bell use the expression, "Don't pull a Hipplehouser," and it was some time before I learned the meaning of that phrase.

As in the Dexter speech, there were echoes of William Jennings Bryan in the Denver address. Here the President charged that the Republican party was "controlled by silent and cunning men who have a dangerous lust for power and privilege. . . . I predict that they will turn back the clock to the day when the West was an economic colony of Wall Street."[20] He pointed to the positive Democratic record of conservation, hydroelectric and irrigation projects, and efforts to enact a good housing bill against the opposition of the Republican Congress and the real-estate lobby.

Elsey's knowledge of history spiced the whistle-stop speeches with references to the Pullman and Homestead strikes of the nineteenth century, and Frank Norris's muckraking book, *The Octopus.* In Colorado, Truman pointed to Pike's Peak and the other soaring mountains to compare them with high prices. Occasionally, he would cause pain among White House staff members, as when he repeatedly referred to his earnest hope that the voters would do right by him and relieve him of the worry of a personal housing shortage after January 20, 1949. Batt complained to Clifford on September 24 that "people are always more interested in what you can do for them than in what they can do for you." Elsey answered the next day: "We wince every time this is said, and every time that point approaches in a platform speech, we pray and cross ourselves and hope it won't come out."[21]

At Fresno, California, early on the morning of September 23, Truman did something he had never done before: He leveled a very personal attack against an incumbent Republican congressman. After damning the Eightieth Congress generally, Truman took off on the seven-term Republican veteran congressman, Bertram W. Gearhart:

> You have got a terrible congressman here in this district. He is one of the worst. He is one of the worst obstructionists in the Congress. He has done everything he possibly could to cut the throats of the farmer and the laboring man. If you send him back, that will be your fault if you get your own throat cut.[22]

Later that day, as *Washington Post* correspondent Edward T. Folliard was writing his story about the day's events, he recalls: "I felt somebody behind me and I looked around and it was the President. I said, 'Oh, Mr. President, I was just writing what you said about Congressman [Gearhart].' He said, 'Well, probably, I've re-elected the son-of-a-bitch.' "[23]

The results differed from the President's prediction. Gearhart was beaten by the Democratic nominee, Cecil F. White, whom Truman had praised at the Fresno meeting.

The President faced a somewhat smaller crowd than Dewey drew in Los Angeles the night after Truman spoke in Gilmore Stadium. Among the special guests who joined him on the platform were Humphrey Bogart, Lauren Bacall, George Jessel and an actor named Ronald Reagan, who supported Truman in 1948. Because of the strength of Wallace in California, Truman warned that communists were "guiding and using" the Progressive party, and that true liberals should stick with the Democrats. The disappointing crowd in Los Angeles spurred the President to instruct Connelly to get some assistance for Chapman to beef up the advance preparation for the Texas trip. Connelly got Dawson out of bed with a transcontinental telephone call, told him to get on the next plane for Texas, and impressed him with the critical need to contact local leaders.

Dawson did a brilliant job of advance work in Texas. Although the President did not campaign on the civil rights issue in the Lone Star State, Dawson, with Truman's encouragement, performed the daring feat of arranging a series of integrated rallies, a first for Texas. Despite some grumbling from local politicians, Truman made it a point to invite blacks aboard his campaign train, and Dawson was adept at rounding up all the important local leaders. Truman surprised the people of Alpine, Texas, by pointing out that he had been in Alpine before, when he was in his twenties, "with a bunch of people who were interested in irrigation problems on the Pincus River, and I had a great time going over the Davis Mountains."[24]

When he moved northward into Oklahoma on September 28, he found a hot Senate race going on between former governor and oil producer Robert S. Kerr and Senator Edward H. Moore. At his first whistle stop in Oklahoma, at Marietta, he delighted the crowd with a free-swinging attack on Moore.

> We need a man like Bob Kerr to take old man Moore's place. He never was any good in the first place. I know old man Moore. I served in the Senate with him for quite a while, and if he did anything for the people it was by accident and not intention.[25]

It was the kind of line that no ghost-writer could have dreamed up.

Meanwhile, Murphy was struggling to put together a major address on the loyalty of federal employees and on communism in general. The House Committee on Un-American Activities, headed by Representative J. Parnell Thomas of New Jersey, including as one of its members a young, first-term, ski-nosed Congressman named Richard M. Nixon, was staging a series of publicity shows featuring the sworn testimony of ex-communists like Elizabeth Bentley. At a news conference, the President agreed that the hearings were a "red herring" to divert attention from inflation. It was a remark that remained to plague him because the Republicans capitalized on it later.

David D. Lloyd of Batt's group, together with Stephen J. Spingarn of the Treasury Department (both of whom later worked at the White House), put together the first draft of an address slated for Oklahoma City on September 28. Murphy, Nash, Noyes and Carr also struggled with the Oklahoma City address, and after many telephone clearances with the campaign train it was finally put on a national radio hookup. This long and very serious address, delivered from the grandstand at the Oklahoma State Fairgrounds, was more an essay than a political rouser.

A crisis arose with the discovery that there was not enough campaign money to move the train out of the station in Oklahoma City. Oklahoma Governor Roy J. Turner staged a special shakedown of his wealthy friends aboard the presidential train and enabled the entourage to continue east to Washington.

True to his style of relating local interests to whistle-stop speeches, Elsey came up with a good one for Lexington, Kentucky. It was the year when the racehorse Citation won the Triple Crown. The President put it this way:

> You people know a great deal about horse races in Lexington, and you know that it doesn't matter which horse is ahead or behind at any given moment, it's the horse that comes out ahead at the finish that counts. I'm trying to do in politics what Citation has done in the horse races. I propose at the finish line on November the 2nd to come out ahead, because I think the people understand what the issues are in this campaign.[26]

After crossing the Ohio River, the President was greeted by ten thousand people in Huntington, West Virginia. The local newspaper printed one of those typically myopic editorials so characteristic of the press during the 1948 campaign:

The greatest service President Truman could render his country, before his retirement from the White House by the overwhelming decision of the American voters on November 2, would be to call off his political barnstorming trip across the country and get back on the job during one of the most critical periods in our Nation's history.[27]

When Truman had finished his Huntington speech, he turned to the Democratic candidate for the Senate, Representative Neely, and told the crowd: "If you people don't elect Matt Neely to the Senate, you don't know which side your bread is buttered on." Neely promptly slapped the President on the back and answered: "And if you folks don't vote for this man, you won't have any bread to put butter on." Then, on to Charleston for an evening radio address. The 140-speech trip, which had covered 8,300 miles, had its final whistle stop at 10:43 P.M. in Montgomery, West Virginia, before an overnight trip to Washington.

Mission to Moscow

During the early days of October, the White House staff was split by a strong argument that erupted over a proposal advanced by speechwriters Noyes and Carr. With the polls and press continuing to predict an almost certain Truman defeat, they argued that only a very dramatic development could turn the campaign around. They sold the President on the idea that he should send Chief Justice Vinson to Moscow to meet with Stalin, to stress that he was leaving no stone unturned in exploring the paths to peace.

Clifford, Murphy and Elsey were appalled by the transparent gimmickry in the proposal, but the President was persuaded to accept it. From Washington, Murphy voiced his opposition to no avail. When the subject came up on the presidential train, Clifford and Elsey put up the strongest possible arguments against the plan. According to Elsey,

> The Mission to Moscow matter caused enormous tensions within the staff. Clark and I argued vigorously—almost violently—against it. This was the only matter in which I ever tried to slug it out toe to toe with Matt Connelly, who defended the idea because it had come from Noyes and Carr.[28]

Perhaps against his better judgment, Vinson reluctantly agreed to the mission, following the importuning of his old friend. The President then asked Ross to arrange network time to explain this nonpolitical mission. Only then did he consult with Secretary of State Marshall, who was in Paris. The opposition of Marshall was so strong that it gave the President pause. He told Truman that such a unilateral move would cause widespread consternation among our allies. The President asked Marshall to return to Washington for consultations, and assured him that he would not go forward with the Vinson mission.

As luck would have it, the ill-fated project boomeranged despite its cancellation. Coming less than a month before a national election, it was not possible to keep the secret that the President had initially approved, then canceled, the mission to Moscow. On October 9, the news media broke the gory details of the sensational story. The leaks forced the President to issue a defensive statement the same day.[29]

When the brouhaha failed to stay off the front pages, and caustically critical editorials followed, the President again tried to explain the Vinson mission in an October 18 address to the American Legion. Fortunately for Truman, Dewey and his advisers felt they had the election already won without exploiting the issue. According to an October 12 report, Dewey's people felt the trip was "an error of judgment of such proportions that it could alone be sufficient to swing the election, if the contest were in doubt."[30]

"Lunatic Engineer"

Sometimes little incidents affect campaigns far more than the sweat, blood and tears that go into carefully prepared campaign addresses. Such an incident occurred on Columbus Day at Beaucoup, Illinois, where Dewey's campaign train abruptly backed up a few feet, almost plowing into the crowd. Ordinarily cool and collected, Dewey reacted with hysterical alarm and blurted out: "That's the first lunatic I've had for an engineer. He probably ought to be shot at sunrise but I guess we can let him off because no one was hurt." In the peculiar scale of political values, this blunder probably hurt Dewey more than the Vinson affair hurt Truman. Railroad workers and blue-collar laborers all over the country were properly aroused. Freight cars sprouted chalked slogans to drive the point home. Some newsmen, irked at Dewey's bland and soporific campaign, wrote sarcastic pieces about the incident. One joked that Dewey's train pulled out with a "jerk." Truman made the most of the glaring faux pas. He started out in a rather low-key way by praising all the train crews that his entourage had enjoyed. Then, he brought out the blunderbuss on October 21, reminding his listeners of the Dewey incident on a nationwide radio hookup, in the same breath that he reminded them of the Hoover depression:

> You remember that Mr. Hoover was an "efficiency expert," too. Also, as the Republicans presented him, he was the "Great Engineer." We have been hearing about engineers again recently from the Republican candidate. He objects to having engineers back up. He doesn't mention, however, that under the "Great Engineer" we backed up into the worst depression in our history.[31]

Truman's esteem for Herbert Hoover had been demonstrated as early as 1945, when he invited the former president to the White House to discuss the food situation in Europe and later appointed him as honorary chairman of the Famine Emergency Committee. Hoover's White House visit ended years of "exile" when Roosevelt had been President, an exile Truman later suffered under President Eisenhower. Hoover's appearance at the dedication of the Truman Library in 1957 was further indication of the warmth of feeling between the two men. Nevertheless, Truman had no compunctions about attacking Hoover sharply and repeatedly in the latter stages of the 1948 campaign and again when he campaigned for Stevenson in 1952. Murphy relates that Truman took out many of the references to Hoover that appeared in speech drafts, but on some occasions during October, the Hoover references escalated. One notable instance was an October 19 address at the Raleigh, North Carolina, State Fairgrounds. Murphy wrote a big part of the speech about "Hoovercarts," described by the President as "the remains of the old tin lizzie being pulled by a mule, because you couldn't afford to buy a new car, you couldn't afford to buy gas for the old one." Truman pointed out that the Republicans and big business favored having the people "ride out" the depression in these Hoovercarts. He closed his speech by stating: "I feel pretty sure that in 1948 the South is not hankering for another ride in a Hoovercart."[32]

Speech-Writing Assistance

A three-day foray into Delaware, Pennsylvania, New Jersey and upstate New York was followed in mid-October by a seven-day push through Ohio, Indiana, Illinois, Wisconsin, Minnesota and West Virginia. Clifford and Elsey, at times assisted by Ross, churned out an incredible series of speech outlines for the whistle stops, with the major burden falling on Elsey's broad shoulders. Jonathan Daniels came in at the President's request to help coordinate the process, after a hurry-up call to Judge Rosenman found him unable to drop prior commitments to devote full time to speech-writing. There were some unfortunate misunderstandings with Rosenman, which robbed the campaign of his speech-writing talent, with the exception of his work on the acceptance speech and a few specific speeches late in the campaign. Rosenman describes it this way:

> It had been agreed that I was to accompany the President on the campaign train, and I had made arrangements to do so by refusing to accept any legal work so that I could be free to do it. However, when a memorandum was passed around as to who was to go on the train, I found that my name was not included. I know it was not an oversight but a deliberate exclusion. I asked nobody to explain why, but I just didn't try to re-open the subject or get on the train, because apparently I wasn't supposed to. It has always been a mystery to me. I think the only two people who might know the reason would be Clifford or Matt Connelly, and I have asked neither of them, nor do I intend to. I make no secret of the fact that I resented it, was very angry about it—and still am.[33]

During the final month of the campaign, news columnist John Franklin Carter, whose pen name was "Jay Franklin," helped the speech-writers aboard the campaign train. In Murphy's eyes, Carter was one of the most dependable, high-speed, and effective writers, since his copy rarely had to be edited once it emerged from his smoking typewriter. In fact, there were times when Murphy even had to think up additional assignments for Carter, so speedy was his rate of production. Carter was greatly appreciated until just after the campaign when he made the mistake of writing two "kiss and tell" articles for *Life*. One of them, pretentiously entitled "Inside Strategy of the Campaign: One of the Advisory Board Tells How Truman Felt, Acted and Planned During His Winning Drive," was published on November 15, 1948. A second article, in the issue dated January 10, 1949, purported to describe a split between Truman and his cabinet over foreign policy. The articles, in addition to exaggerating Carter's personal role, infuriated the President. In his January 7, 1949, news conference, Truman went far out of his way to dissociate himself from Carter. He labeled Carter's speculation "absolutely without foundation in fact, in nearly every instance." He dismissed the author's knowledge of events by stating that "Mr. Franklin was one of the assistants in preparing speeches during the campaign, but I never had one private interview with him at all, on any subject."[34]

David D. Lloyd

Several weeks before the end of the campaign, David D. Lloyd was recruited to join the speech-writing team. Lloyd injected humor into the President's speeches. In general, Elsey noted that the President was not very good at reading a joke "in cold type in front of him," and also "a joke in a prepared text is not in good taste and falls rather flat."[35] However, Lloyd could weave humor into the substantive topic of the main body of the speech, rather than the "that reminds me of a story" type of joke. In preparing a speech for Pittsburgh on October 23, Lloyd concocted a hilarious imaginary dialogue between a patient (representing the American people) visiting a doctor's office (the doctor being Dewey). The doctor asks his patient whether he's been bothered much by issues lately, then warns him not to think about issues, but to take some of the doctor's brand of soothing syrup called "unity." The doctor refuses to tell the patient what is wrong with him, adding: "I never discuss issues with a patient. But what you need is a major operation. . . . It will just mean taking out the complete works and putting in a Republican administration."[36]

Murphy looked at the dialogue, expressed doubt that the President would use it, and was about to consign it to the cutting-room floor when Clifford telephoned. Clifford sharply stated that it was about time that more life be put into some of the speeches. When Murphy mentioned the visit to the doctor, Clifford crossed the street to take a look at it and was delighted with the dialogue. Truman had a lot of fun delivering the dialogue in his Pittsburgh speech, which was broadcast nationwide.

The Final Swing

Before leaving on his final campaign swing on the evening of October 24, Truman took care of a little piece of political business. Replying to a Dewey charge that he was vacillating on whether the Negev belonged to Israel or the Arabs, Truman issued an unequivocal statement on October 24, which reaffirmed the Democratic platform favoring the position that Israel's boundaries should include the Negev area. Clifford drafted the October 24 document, which strengthened the President's position among Jewish voters.

The most controversial campaign speech was delivered in Chicago on October 25. "When a few men get control of the economy of a nation, they find a 'front man' to run the country for them," Truman proclaimed, pointing out that in Germany "they put money and influence behind Adolf Hitler." He detailed "how Hitler used anti-Semitic propaganda as a way of stupefying the German people with false ideas while he reached out for power."[37] *The New York Times* ran a multi-column headline the next day: "PRESIDENT LIKENS DEWEY TO HITLER AS FASCISTS' TOOL."[38]

Once again, Dewey held his fire, although he was personally angered by Truman's Chicago remarks. The Dewey camp held to its view that since they had the election already won, it was better tactics not to be provoked into descending to that level of debate.

On the Truman whistle stops, Elsey once again shone with his pithy outlines. At Garrett, Indiana, Truman defined GOP as standing for "Grand Old Platitudes." At Hartford, Connecticut, he waved a copy of the *Wall Street Journal* quoting the nation's landlords as aiming to kill rent control with a double-barreled shotgun. At Springfield, Massachusetts, he talked about the first GI revolt in American history—Shays's Rebellion.

In Cleveland on October 26, the doctor who had first appeared in Pittsburgh showed up again. This time, like the Republican candidate, he was handing out "sleeping polls" to try to put the voters to sleep. Swinging back to New York the following night, Murphy and Carter tried to pep up a Rosenman draft. This time the doctor reappeared in a different form, as the White House physician whom Truman had to consult because he had a queer feeling that he was being followed. The punch lines brought the crowd at Madison Square Garden to its feet: "The White House physician told me not to worry. He said: 'You keep right on your way. There is one place where that fellow is not going to follow you—and that's in the White House.' "[39]

Clifford, Murphy and the speech-writing team decided to try something new for this speech. They had watched crowd reactions throughout the campaign, and were convinced that the contrasts between Truman and Dewey showed up most sharply in their differing personalities—the human being versus the efficiency machine. This became apparent in the strongly positive crowd reactions to items like the doctor stories. However, the press paid little attention to these items and concentrated instead on issue material. So Clifford and Murphy hatched a plan to include in the Madison Square Garden address all the amusing tidbits they could collect, thus forcing the press to write about some of them if they wrote anything at all.

After the speech was mimeographed on the train between Boston and New York and distributed to the press, several of the reporters came to Ross and Connelly, advising them as friends that the President should not deliver a speech as facetious as the text indicated. Murphy related: "We had a big pow-wow on the subject and serious consideration was given to pulling this speech back and not using it. But the President did decide not to pull it back and did decide to use it and I think it was a great success."[40]

But while Truman was having a grand time regaling audiences all over New York with his humor and his fighting predictions of victory, Clifford, Murphy, Elsey and Carter were struggling with a speech for the Brooklyn Academy of Music on the evening of October 29. They had worked in shifts the night before, one or two napping briefly as the others edited and revised. At 5:00 A.M., Murphy delivered a draft to the typist "with instructions to wake Clifford up when it was finished— having in my own mind at that time very little idea whether it was good, bad, or indifferent." The revisions during the day necessitated feeding the draft to the typists page by page, to have the stencil and reading copy cut at the last possible minute. "This was one of our closest shaves," indicated Murphy. By now, the worn-out speech-writing team was getting decidedly punch-drunk. But that night they reboarded the train for three final whistle stops at Bellefontaine, Ohio, Terre Haute, Indiana, and Mattoon, Illinois. Still ahead was the climactic address of the campaign, at 9:30 P.M. in the Kiel Auditorium in St. Louis.

The Best Campaign Speech

On Saturday night before the election, President Truman delivered an address that was far and away the best political speech of his entire career, bar none. How did he manage to do it? What were the ingredients that went into this superb performance?

Early in the week, Lloyd prepared a draft for St. Louis, which gathered dust as all hands were rushing around trying to keep up with the President's appearances in the East. Clifford and Murphy could not even think about the St. Louis speech until after the train left New York on Friday night. The President delivered three whistle-stop speeches on the way and it was late Saturday afternoon before Clifford and Murphy presented him with their best effort for the evening address. At that point, the President reiterated what he had already remarked several days before—that he wanted to speak off-the-cuff. Accordingly, Clifford and Murphy prepared an outline, trying to include those points which Ross had already told the press would be covered in the speech.

It was drizzling at 5:00 P.M. in Mattoon, Illinois, as the President stepped through the blue curtains at the rear of the *Ferdinand Magellan* and responded to a fulsome introduction by tall, tanned Senator Scott Lucas. He quickly reviewed the issues: the "do-nothing" Congress, which passed the Taft-Hartley Act "to tear up labor's bill of rights"; the lack of storage bins, which had driven the price of corn down forty-seven cents below the support price; and the positive progress of the Democrats to help the farmer, the worker and the small businessman. After this final whistle stop of the 1948 campaign, about three hours were left before the train rumbled across the Mississippi River into his home state.

What did the President do to prepare for his crucial speech? He just went to sleep. As always, he dropped off quickly and was refreshed when he awakened for dinner. Clifford and Murphy came back to join Mr. and Mrs. Truman and Margaret, Ross, Connelly and other aides for a family dinner. He did not seem to have a care in the world during the evening meal, but the minute he had finished his meal he quickly excused himself, went back to his compartment, and wrote out in longhand about two pages of notes.

Tumultuous applause reverberated throughout Kiel Auditorium as the President entered and took his place on the stage. The auditorium was jammed. The seats and balcony sloped steeply, giving the partisan audience an excellent view. The acoustics were ideal. The atmosphere tingled with excitement and the roars of the crowd echoed and re-echoed within the comparatively small auditorium. On the podium, the President placed his two pages of notes and one "prop"—the Republican document with the pointed suggestion that all good Republicans should donate their tax reduction to the Republican campaign coffers.

Leading off with several sure applause-rousers, Truman predicted a Democratic victory up and down the line. Then he launched into a thumbnail sketch of his three years, six months and eighteen days as President, from his decision to go forward with the United Nations Conference at San Francisco through his twenty-one-point program sent to the Congress on September 6, 1945, the election of the "do-nothing"

Eightieth Congress in 1946, and the thirty thousand miles he had covered since June. He ticked off the accurate statistics, from memory, of farm income and foreclosures under Republican and Democratic administrations. Unshackled by any manuscript, in top oratorical form, he fired a booming political salvo: "And I'll say to you that any farmer in these United States who votes against his own interests, that is, who votes the Republican ticket, ought to have his head examined!"[41]

Next he turned to the facts and figures about labor, how workers and others stayed away from the polls in 1946 and got what they deserved in the antilabor Congress. He pointed out how he had tried time and again to get Congress to raise the minimum wage from forty cents an hour to seventy-five cents. He added, "I would like to see those Republican congressional leaders try to live in Washington on $16 a week and support a family."[42]

Many of the cynical reporters who had written stories, frequently at the direction of their publishers, interpreting large whistle-stop crowds as merely curiosity-seekers, suddenly perked up and listened more closely. The crowd was responding with near-frenzied enthusiasm, which got the President's adrenaline flowing. Ordinarily a cool and phlegmatic observer, Murphy found himself "clapping and cheering as vigorously as anyone else—not just as a member of a claque, either, but because it was the kind of speech that generated a great deal of spontaneous applause."[43]

Next, the President turned to housing. He accused the Republican leadership of scuttling the Wagner-Ellender-Taft housing bill, by passing "a fake housing bill, a housing bill which was intended to build no housing." Then, to the utter delight of the crowd, the old artilleryman turned his biggest guns on Dewey. With dripping scorn and sarcasm, he thundered: "He has been following me up and down this country making speeches about home and mother and unity and efficiency, and things of that kind. He won't talk about the issues, but he did let his foot slip, when he endorsed the 80th Congress."[44]

Now he read the riot act on what had motivated the Congress— "they haven't done a thing that these good-for-nothing lobbies haven't asked them to do."

Using his prop to full effect, he demonstrated that the same Congress that didn't have time to help curb inflation passed a "rich man's tax bill," followed by Republican pressure to siphon the tax savings into political contributions. Schoolrooms, teachers' salaries, helping the average person pay his doctor's and hospital bills—Truman covered the waterfront without so much as a glance at his notes. Carleton Kent of the *Chicago Sun-Times* later reflected that "the response was just absolutely electric and thunderous."[45]

Turning to the one-party press, Truman ridiculed the press for claiming he couldn't win. He contended, "Ninety percent of the press is against us, but that didn't discourage me one little bit. You know, I had four campaigns here in the great State of Missouri, and I never had a metropolitan paper for me that whole time. And I licked them every time!"

In his peroration, the President confidently predicted that "People are waking up that the tide is beginning to roll." With perfect timing, he ended his masterful speech on a positive note:

> I am here to tell you that if you do your duty as citizens of the greatest Republic the sun has ever shone on, we will have a Government that will be for your interests, that will be for peace in the world, and for the welfare of all the people, and not just a few.[46]

The great St. Louis address went out over the radio, but very few newspapers caught the real spirit felt by the crowd. It just came too late in the evening. Perhaps its actual effect was minimal, because those present—and maybe some of those interested enough to tune in—were already committed. Nevertheless, there is some evidence that there was a swing to Truman among the uncommitted voters at the end of the campaign.

Election Eve

Even though the St. Louis speech was designed to climax the campaign, the President still had to deliver his traditional election eve remarks from his home in Independence.

Introduced by Barkley, he spoke on a coast-to-coast radio hookup. Instead of delivering the lofty generalizations customarily reserved for "get out the vote" election eve speeches, Truman ripped into the Republicans as "the party of privilege," and labeled the Democratic party "the party of the people." He affirmed that while the Constitution protects property, that document "is still more deeply pledged to protect human rights."[47]

Truman went right down to the wire with the same kind of fighting speech that had characterized his entire campaign.

Predictions

When Truman slipped out at 4:30 P.M. on Election Day, to motor thirty miles to the Elms Hotel in Excelsior Springs, Missouri, it looked as though he did not want to face the crushing defeat that had been predicted. What other politician would take a Turkish bath, have a sandwich and a glass of milk, turn on the radio briefly, then simply go to sleep before sundown when the election was hanging in the balance? The man who refused to admit defeat, who rallied his dispirited troops and almost singlehandedly achieved the impossible, was again demonstrating he was "the man of Independence." To the very end, he said he didn't need a George Gallup or some commentator to tell him what the American people were going to say.

Pollster Elmo Roper, whose prediction was only .3 percent off the mark in 1944, stopped polling after September 9, 1948, because he considered that Dewey "is almost as good as elected."[48] *Newsweek* made a well-ballyhooed announcement that its October 11 issue would carry the results of a poll of fifty of the nation's top political commentators, including Arthur Krock, Marquis Childs, Roscoe Drummond and the Alsop Brothers (whom Truman privately called the "Slop Sisters" or the "All Slops"). Clifford ducked off the campaign train to buy a copy of *Newsweek* as soon as the results were published. He was understandably embarrassed to discover the score read Truman nothing, Dewey fifty. He tried to hide the magazine under his coat, but the eagle-eyed President spotted him making the purchase, so Clifford sheepishly handed over the discouraging news.

"They just get more wrong all the time," Truman said.[49]

Elsey notes that in private Truman conceded early in the campaign that he was behind Dewey. Elsey recalls: "He knew he was behind and he said he was behind, but he was catching up and he was confident that by Election Day he would be out in front."[50]

By October 13, Truman gave Elsey his state-by-state prediction, which added up to a 340-electoral-vote victory (he actually received 303).

He candidly expressed his sentiments to his sister a few weeks before the election:

> It will be the greatest campaign any President ever made. Win, lose, or draw, people will know where I stand and a record will be made for future action by the Democratic Party.

We had tremendous crowds everywhere. From 6:30 in the morning until midnight the turnout was phenomenal. The news jerks didn't know what to make of it—so they just lied about it![51]

As the returns trickled in, Secret Servicemen James Rowley and Henry Nicholson awakened Truman about four o'clock the morning after Election Day, and they arrived back in Kansas City at six. In the early morning hours, despite Truman's two-million-vote lead in the popular vote, there appeared to be danger he would fail to get an electoral college majority, thereby throwing the election into the House of Representatives. But Ohio and California swung the balance, and by 10:30 A.M. Truman had a concession telegram from Dewey.

Showing 'Em Who Carries the Weight

Jon Kennedy, *Arkansas Democrat*

At a brief stop in St. Louis as the campaign train headed back toward Washington, someone handed the President a copy of the early edition of the *Chicago Daily Tribune,* headlined "DEWEY DEFEATS TRUMAN." The photograph of Truman holding the newspaper aloft is a classic.

The red-faced news media had more than their share of embarrassments. In its November 1 issue, *Life* magazine had the gall to caption a photo of Governor Dewey as "the next President." Some of the worst mistakes were made by overeager writers whose stories for postelection publication had obviously been written on the assumption Dewey would win. Subscribers to *Kiplinger* magazine were surprised to receive the day after the election an analysis of "What Dewey Will Do." Truman's old nemesis, Drew Pearson, had a column the morning after that started out: "I surveyed the close knit group around Tom Dewey, who will take over the White House 86 days from now." Some, like the Alsop Brothers and Harold Ickes, tried desperately to have their postelection columns killed when the startling election returns came in. The Alsops wrote that "events will not wait patiently until Thomas E. Dewey officially replaces Harry S. Truman." Ickes was more fortunate, and succeeded in having all his columns in the continental United States withdrawn. But Truman was amused when someone sent him a copy of the *Panama Star and Herald,* published in the Canal Zone, which treated readers to this Ickes account of the stupidity of the White House staff: "One may regret that he did not have about him, or at least within counseling distance, advisers who were able coolly to appraise the situation and frankly tell him that he could not win."

The President preserved his traditional neutrality at the confrontation between the Army and Navy football teams not long after the 1948 election. With Army an almost prohibitive twenty-one point favorite, there were rumors that Truman favored underdog Navy, which scrapped its way to a 21–21 tie. One of the high points of Truman's visit to the crowded stadium occurred as he approached the Navy side of the field. The President chortled when some midshipmen lofted a huge sign reading: "GALLUP PICKS ARMY."

7

A New Mandate: 1949

David H. Stowe, soon to become an administrative assistant to the President, noted a marked difference in the spirit of the White House staff at a certain stage. Stowe observed:

> One of the things that impressed me was the change after the '48 election.... The learning period had been accomplished; now Mr. Truman moved out into *his* program and *his* administration, and that infused a lot of vigor into the staff, through the staff meetings. We were watching things unfold as he would talk to us.[1]

The 1948 campaign also strengthened the forces of liberalism in Congress, with the election of senators like Hubert Humphrey and Paul Douglas. At the state level, new liberal governors came to office—Adlai Stevenson, G. Mennen Williams, Chester Bowles and others. The spirit of liberalism, battered and beaten in 1946 and split in the spring of 1948, had a strong resurgence after the Truman victory.[2] These forces strengthened the liberal group on the White House staff. ADA mogul Joseph L. Rauh, Jr., "noted with disgust that John Snyder, who had been conspicuously absent from the campaign, was back in the inner circle at the victory celebration,"[3] but those in the Clifford-Murphy-Elsey orbit were clearly in the ascendancy.

The aftermath of the election also marked the beginning of a brief honeymoon with the press for the President. Both Truman and Dewey addressed the Gridiron Dinner on December 11, 1948, and the President wrote to his sister: "You never saw such an ovation. Had to get up three times. Some of those old hard boiled Republican news men openly cried. So I guess it went over."[4] He also noted: "They ribbed Dewey unmerci-

fully. Had a lunatic engineer act that was a scream." The Gridiron sing-
ers rendered a hilarious parody starting "I'm a rambling wreck from
Georgia Tech, and a lunatic engineer."[5]

During the hectic campaign, many White House staff members were
away for weeks at a time. Even those who worked on the Washington
end of operations frequently had to spend long evening hours and week-
ends to keep current with the flow of business. It was not that these staff
members were "workaholics"; they simply had a sense of responsibility
about assignments from the President of the United States. When they
watched the thick file of papers that Truman brought home every night
and observed the thoroughness with which he read and absorbed everything he had to read, they couldn't help but be infused with that same
sense of responsibility about their own work. But staff members with
families suffered, since wives and youngsters frequently discovered that
Daddy came home only to sleep and tiptoed out of the house long before
breakfast. A strong family man who had a firm prejudice against divorce,
Truman also was sensitive and considerate about the work habits of his
staff. Frequently, the staff used circuitous ways to hide the amount of
overtime they were putting into their jobs. He usually found out, one
way or another, and would frequently caution his staff about personal
physical health and inquire about their general well-being. He made a
point of being sure that the families of staff members were invited to the
many ceremonies for foreign dignitaries, the presidential speeches delivered from the White House or in the Washington area, concerts and
other special events. Wives received invitations to certain state dinners,
receptions, concerts and other social events. The President loved base-
ball, and always took some of his staff along to Griffith Stadium to watch
the Washington Senators in action. Occasionally staff members and their
wives would go with him to the theater or for a performance at Constitution Hall. The President and his family rarely went to Shangri-la (later
renamed "Camp David") at Thurmont, Maryland, because they felt
the atmosphere of this mountain retreat was too cold and forbidding.
But White House staff members and their families at times used this
facility, even to the point of bringing their friends along for social
events.

Concern for the health of his staff led the President to open one staff
meeting by addressing some serious remarks to John Steelman. He told
Steelman he wanted him to take at least one hour off from work every
day. Then, turning to the rest of the staff, he said that he wanted every-

one to take it easier at times. He added that unless the staff kept in good
physical condition, it would affect the caliber of their work. The immediate cause of this serious talk was the sudden death of one of Truman's
close friends, Mayor Roger Sermon of Independence, Missouri, from a
heart attack.[6]

When he returned to Washington after the 1948 election, the President discovered that "the White House is in one terrible shape." He
wrote his sister that "there are scaffolds in the East Room, props in the
study, my bedroom, Bess' sitting room, and the Rose Room where you
and mamma stayed." Meanwhile, Mrs. Truman developed a bad cold
and sore throat, so serious that she couldn't talk. Her good and faithful
husband wrote to his sister, "I am up at an early hour (3:00 A.M.) because
I have to see that Bess takes her medicine at 3:30."[7] Although the President was restlessly eager to get on with planning for the new Congress,
to press forward his program, Dr. Graham prescribed a vacation at Key
West.

Key West

"I didn't know I was so tired until I sat down," the President wrote a
few days after he arrived in Key West.[8] If anything, the poker games got
more raucous as the staff celebrated. Before the arrival of Mrs. Truman
and Margaret, the President allowed a patch of gray stubble to sprout on
his chin.

"What's that, a Van Dyke?" quizzed a curious newsman.

"No, it's a Jeff Davis," explained the President, setting off speculation that he had indeed forgiven the errant Dixiecrats.

Clifford also grew a small beard, as did one or two others on the staff.
On November 11, with the appearance of Mrs. Truman and Margaret,
all faces were suddenly shaven clean. These were probably the most important developments during the entire two weeks of almost total inac-
tivity and complete relaxation.

The sun and surf provided magical recuperative tonics for tired
bodies and minds. But the vacation still meant two additional weeks
away from home and hearth for many White House staff members.
Aside from Mrs. Truman and Margaret, the only woman I ever saw at
Key West was Chief Justice Vinson's wife, and she didn't stay very long.
For the uninhibited language of the poker game, the President just felt
more comfortable with men around. In one of its annual skits the White

House Correspondents' Association put it accurately when they sang a
parody of "I'm Just Wild About Harry," which went like this:

> I go swimmin' with Harry
>   That's one thing Harry enjoys
> 'Cause there's no wimmin
>   To spoil his swimmin'
> He just invites the boys.

The period after Thanksgiving, especially between Christmas and
New Year's, is sometimes a "dead" period for federal agency and Capitol Hill employees, with Congress out of town and very little news generating. But for those responsible for preparing the annual budget, the
State of the Union address, and the President's economic report due
early in January, the atmosphere during this period is more like that of a
pressure-cooker. Once every four years, as in 1949, the inaugural address
imposes additional burdens. One of the White House staff members who
stayed behind while the presidential party went to Key West was
George Elsey. He felt it his first priority to think through the relationship between the State of the Union speech and the inaugural address.

The Inaugural Address and the Point Four Program

Earlier, the President had told Clifford that in view of the critical
international situation, he wanted to devote the 1949 State of the Union
speech to foreign affairs and then concentrate the inaugural on domestic
policy. Elsey disagreed, feeling strongly that foreign policy should be
the focus in the inaugural. He recalled that he had expressed his reservations to Clifford: "I finally wrote a long memorandum in which I argued
as persuasively, and as forcefully as I could, that the President had one
and only one inaugural opportunity and that he had other state of the
union messages and would have still future state of the union messages."[9]

Elsey won Clifford over to his argument. On another score, the President had originally planned to spell out his entire program in great detail, in a lengthy State of the Union message. He wanted to send a written message to Capitol Hill, since it would be too long to deliver in
person. Elsey, with Clifford's support, argued that a detailed exposition
of the President's plans was likely to stir more opposition from the Congress than a more general framework, which could set the stage for

working out the necessary compromises on specifics. Furthermore Elsey argued that a face-to-face presentation gave the added advantage of mobilizing greater popular support.

By this time, the Bureau of the Budget had requested that the various departments send in their recommendations for legislation. Clifford compared the State of the Union address to "having a skeleton and then you begin to pack the flesh onto the skeleton."[10] At Key West, Clifford gradually won the President over to the concept originally expressed by Elsey. On one occasion, Elsey flew down to confer further with Clifford about the State of the Union and inaugural addresses. Only after Truman's return from Key West was Clifford able to confirm that he would base his inaugural address on foreign policy.

As December wore on, it became apparent that the staff would have to start something soon if they wanted to develop a good theme before January 20. They were too occupied with current deadlines to do very much prior to mid-December. Elsey recalled:

> We had one or two self-appointed volunteers who were making suggestions, none of which seemed to me to be of the caliber we needed. I felt particularly heavily a sense of responsibility to see that we gave the President an outstanding speech because of the initiative I had taken in November in getting the contents switched from domestic to foreign.[11]

Within the musty corridors of the Department of State, there had been a few puffs of fresh air starting about the end of World War II. The so-called "striped pants boys" still ruled the roost, but at least some people had begun to realize that the department did not have a monopoly on wisdom. Inasmuch as popular support for foreign policy required public understanding, an Office of Public Affairs was set up in 1945. It was first headed by Dr. John Dickey, who later became president of Dartmouth College. Dr. Dickey was succeeded by Francis H. Russell, who had a deputy named Benjamin H. Hardy. A sensitive, soft-spoken man from Georgia, where his family owned a small-town newspaper, Hardy had a World War II naval career that exposed him to various developing countries of Latin America.[12] When he came to work as a speech-writer for the Office of Public Affairs, he had developed clear ideas on what was wrong with American foreign policy—which he felt concentrated too heavily on wealthy and powerful leaders without helping the average people of other nations gain better lives for themselves. Hardy believed that good will for the United States should not be cultivated with brass bands, parades, huge capital expenditures and high-level social receptions but by measures that would enable millions of people to grow better crops, get a better education, and improve their health.

When the call came for material to include in the inaugural address, Hardy sent up a memorandum through channels. It stressed technical assistance as an instrument of foreign policy, to provide low-cost help directly to people in underdeveloped countries, rather than the massive improvements funneled through governments. Hardy was distressed that his ideas were vetoed in the higher echelons of the State Department, with especially strong opposition being voiced by Undersecretary of State Robert A. Lovett, then serving under Secretary Marshall. Lovett sent a note to Russell, stating: "Francis, I'm not sure this is a good idea, but I'm quite sure that it's not appropriate for an inaugural address."[13]

At this point, Hardy was greatly disappointed. He wrote another speech draft, outlining in very general terms the superiority of a pluralistic society over a monolithic one. At the same time, he drafted a stronger memo, dated December 15, reiterating his deep conviction on the course that foreign policy should take. The material was in such a form that it could be included in the inaugural address if the President decided to commit himself to the concept of technical assistance. A strong idealist who bridled under the restrictions placed on him by the higher-ups at the State Department, Hardy had a long discussion with his wife as to whether he should risk going over Russell's and Lovett's heads to present the idea directly to the White House. The Hardys mulled over the dilemma until two or three o'clock in the morning. Without telling Russell or anyone else in the State Department, he decided the idea was too important for humanity's future to be buried in the bureaucratic bowels of an insensitive, old-line agency.

Hardy called on Elsey in his office in the east wing of the White House, and came quickly to the point. After eloquently outlining his views on technical assistance, he expanded on his conviction that this deserved to be a major point in American foreign policy. He told Elsey quite candidly of his frustration that the State Department was smothering a good idea with the excuse that it hadn't been through long cycles of "planning." He then left a copy of his original memorandum, along with speech material, with Elsey.

Elsey thanked Hardy for his memorandum and told Hardy he would carry the ball from that point. He then told Clifford that a State Department staff member had suggested an idea that could prove very useful for the inaugural address. Elsey later reported:

> Clifford was instantly intrigued, as was I, by the Hardy paper. There now ensued several days of typical bureaucratic maneuvering. A few discreet inquiries showed that a great deal of information to back up the Hardy suggestion was available in State and that it made sense.[14]

To pry some of this material loose, and at the same time to protect Hardy, who had stuck his neck way out by going outside of channels to present his idea to the White House, Clifford concocted a little dodge. He suggested that Elsey, on behalf of the President, send a memorandum to the State Department with the request that State propose to include in the President's inaugural address an expansion of American scientific and technical aid to underdeveloped countries. Clifford then telephoned Russell, telling him that he had the general memorandum on a pluralistic versus a monolithic society, but he needed something more specific.

Lovett continued to stonewall the Hardy idea, insisting to the bitter end that it contained "insufficient preparation and analysis." General Marshall, who had long wanted to be relieved of his onerous duties as secretary of state because of a series of kidney stone operations, was on his way out, and Lovett had been virtually running the department. On January 20, the President appointed Dean Acheson as his new secretary of state, with Budget Director James E. Webb as undersecretary, replacing Marshall and Lovett. But this changing of the guard had absolutely nothing to do with Lovett's attitude on the Hardy idea, which had not yet reached the President.

Ten days before Inauguration Day, Elsey and Lloyd came over to Clifford's office for a 10:30 A.M. meeting on the inaugural address. Intensive staff work proceeded from that point on. There was unanimous agreement that Hardy's idea would be included as one of the points in the President's program to protect "ourselves and other freedom-loving peoples."[15]

By early 1949, Bell had returned from a detail to the Budget Bureau. Along with Lloyd, whose liberal background made him an enthusiastic advocate of technical assistance, Bell immediately grasped the far-flung implications of this new idea. Lloyd helped push the concept, and Bell backed it up with hard economic data. Clifford and Elsey, with an understanding of the President's mind and their own long-standing interest in strengthening foreign policy, became the chief cheerleaders for the plan. Murphy also came aboard as an early advocate. With that kind of staff support, the Hardy idea was given a strongly sympathetic presentation to the President.

The President quickly endorsed the plan to include technical assistance in the inaugural address as a new pillar of his foreign policy. But he went far beyond the Hardy memorandum and the language offered by the White House staff in spelling out the down-to-earth meaning and application of this new idea. His knowledge of the success of the Tennessee Valley Authority in bringing new prosperity to the southeastern states, and his awareness, as an ex-farmer, of the way that scientific and educational programs of the Department of Agriculture had increased farm production spurred Truman's immediate interest in this program. He also elaborated on the potential of the Tigris-Euphrates Valley to become a modern Garden of Eden and granary for the Near East. He cited the Zambezi River Valley in Africa, and parts of southern Brazil that could be made to bloom with the help of technical assistance and American know-how.

As the inaugural address took shape, it included four points on which American foreign policy was based: support of the United Nations, the economic recovery program, the strengthening of freedom-loving nations against aggression, and, as a fourth point, "a bold new program for making the benefits of our scientific advances and industrial progress available for the improvement and growth of underdeveloped areas."[16] Because it was the fourth point in the inaugural address, the Hardy technical assistance program became known throughout the world as the "Point Four Program."

Once the objectives of Point Four were outlined, the President and his staff took a personal interest in seeing that they were implemented. Seven days after his inaugural, the President was asked at a news conference what steps would be taken to carry out the Point Four program. Without hesitation, he proclaimed:

> It's a policy of the administration over the next 4 years, and it's something that will have to be implemented gradually. I have asked the Secretary of State to get together with the heads of the departments of the Government, and try to work out preliminary plans for an approach to it. I can't tell you just what is going to take place, where it is going to take place, or how it is going to take place. I know what I want to do.[17]

In this initial comment, the President did not wish to undercut the new secretary of state. Thus, he did not indicate specifically how he intended that the program be managed. The President had the fullest confidence in Secretary Acheson. But as was so often the case, bureaucratic foot-dragging slowed the implementation of the Point Four program. The Policy Planning Staff, headed by Paul Nitze, had been against Point Four from the start and seemed determined to nickel-and-dime it to death through insistence on long delays for "planning" purposes before action got underway.

Much time and effort on the part of the White House staff was expended in trying to get the State Department to move, in an area that State felt it knew more about than the "politicians" at the White House. The dream of Point Four eventually did become a reality, because the President and his staff were able to extend its application, as he outlined in his inaugural address, through the United Nations and American business enterprises overseas. In a special message to Congress on June 24, 1949, Truman asked for $45 million to get Point Four off the ground. Congress balked, even though the President persuaded the Republican Eightieth Congress to appropriate billions of dollars for large-scale aid under the Marshall Plan. Not until June 5, 1950, did Congress authorize Point Four, with a $34.5-million appropriation approved on September 6, 1950. Working closely with the White House staff, the State Department set up the Point Four program under the Technical Cooperation Administration.

Truman named Dr. Henry G. Bennett, former president of Oklahoma A & M University, as first head of the TCA. On many occasions Dr. Bennett visited the White House, and he developed a deep and warm friendship with the man who had helped launch the program. Seeing his dream coming true, Hardy resigned his job with the Office of Public Affairs and joined Dr. Bennett to help carry out the program for which he had risked his job. The President took pride in these early accomplishments:

> By March of 1951 there were 236 Point Four trainees from thirty-four countries in the United States for advanced study, and plans were under way to bring in many more during the next six months.
>
> By the end of March the United States had concluded Point Four general agreements with twenty-two countries in the less developed areas of the world. Primary emphasis was put on food supply, since food is a key to all productivity. Other projects contributing to food supply, such as pre-

vention of disease, basic and vocational education, transportation, development of fibers and insecticides, were given an important place in the Point Four program.[18]

At Dr. Bennett's request, the President frequently met with Point Four trainees, talked with them in his office or in the Rose Garden, and helped infuse in them some of the spirit that motivated him to give such strong support to the program. There were attempts by later administrations to curb Point Four, but its success was proven in countless ways, from eliminating malaria to aiding irrigation, education, farm production, health and technical training. The highly successful Peace Corps established by President Kennedy was an outgrowth of this program.

On December 22, 1951, the program suffered a grievous loss when Dr. and Mrs. Bennett, Hardy and a number of other passengers were killed when their plane crashed in a blinding snowstorm a few miles northeast of Tehran, Iran. The bold new program went forward under new leadership and was one of the President's proudest accomplishments.

Admiral Leahy's Retirement

March 21, 1949, marked the retirement of Fleet Admiral William D. Leahy as Chief of Staff to the Commander in Chief, at the age of seventy-four. In a White House ceremony on March 25, the President awarded a Distinguished Service Medal to Leahy and reflected on his service during the four tumultuous years he had been on board.

It was difficult for the civilian staff at the White House to understand precisely how the relationship between Truman and Leahy operated. Most of their conversations took place either in the Oval Office or in the super-secret "map room" on the ground floor of the Mansion, with none of the White House staff present. Furthermore, Leahy never attended the President's regular morning staff meetings, which were always a useful conduit for the staff to find out what everybody was doing. He had an unapproachable air, with a stern and forbidding look as he peered out from behind his pince-nez. Of the other members of the White House staff, Elsey perhaps knew him best, from his apprenticeship in the map room, but even Elsey found it occasionally difficult to probe beneath the admiral's crusty exterior and know what he was really thinking.

Admiral Souers

Another White House "mystery man" was Rear Admiral Sidney W. Souers, a St. Louis business executive who attained the flag rank in the naval reserve. Souers worked closely with Leahy on the President's intelligence briefings, which followed the regular morning staff meetings. He was always so noncommittal about his activities that he would have shuddered at the thought of publishing any personal reminiscences of his work or conversations with the President. On December 21, 1949, the White House announced Souers's resignation as executive secretary of the National Security Council and his replacement by his assistant, James S. Lay, Jr. Souers thereafter served as a per diem consultant to the President on intelligence matters, frequently taking part with Lay in presidential briefings. Reflecting on his relationship with Truman, Souers wrote:

> President Truman was always determined to keep politics out of national security problems. All the time I served with him in the areas above mentioned, never once did he show any interest in partisan politics either in the selection of men or acting upon advice given to him. Really, for a man who was supposed to be partisan, he was the most un-partisan man I have seen in that area.[19]

Even after he formally joined the White House staff in 1949, Souers was so close-mouthed that he failed to develop an integrated relationship with policy makers on the staff. Neustadt recognized this when he wrote:

> The gap between the White House staff, as a politically oriented, totally presidential entity, and the neutral secretariat of NSC was never bridged in Truman's time on any systematic basis. Murphy, Bell, and others of this group were successful, on a relatively few occasions, but never intensively or for long.[20]

The Retirement of Clark Clifford

A startling change in the White House staff occurred as 1949 drew to a close. Clark Clifford announced his decision to leave his post as special counsel to enter the private practice of law. Clifford had performed brilliantly and effectively as the President's principal speech-and-message writer, with an articulate voice in formulation of policy along many fronts.

At his final news conference in 1949, the President announced matter-of-factly, "I am going to make Mr. Charles Murphy the successor to Clark Clifford."[21] Murphy was sworn in on February 1, 1950, and remained with the President until the end of his administration. At great personal sacrifice, during postpresidential years he accompanied Truman on many campaign swings on behalf of Democratic candidates. The change at the White House represented no alteration in policy, merely a difference in approach. The glamorous, highly visible Clifford was replaced by the low-key, methodical, more thorough Murphy.

Why did Clifford leave his prestigious post of special counsel? According to Connelly, who frequently clashed with him at the White House, Clifford wanted to become attorney general in 1949 at the time Attorney General Tom Clark was elevated to the Supreme Court, but Democratic National Chairman McGrath was picked for the post instead. Connelly felt that the reason for McGrath's selection was that since a Protestant was replacing a Catholic on the Supreme Court, it became advisable to appoint Catholic McGrath as attorney general.[22] Because of Connelly's poor relationship with Clifford, this account is suspect. Clifford himself indicates that he had reached the point in life when he felt, at age forty-three, that he should get started in establishing a new law practice in Washington. Raising a family on the special counsel's salary was not easy. Furthermore, some of the fresh bloom of working for the President in the early years had worn off. As Clifford notes, "I found that everything that I would write for the President would begin to sound like something else that I had written for him. It had a stale sound."[23]

Clifford attempted to keep his friendship with President Truman during the rest of his administration and also in the years after he left the White House. Even though he did not participate in policy-making after 1950, he was frequently on hand for White House social occasions and poker sessions on the *Williamsburg* and elsewhere. Clifford also kept in touch with the small stable of White House speech-writers and researchers who had moved in his orbit while he served as special counsel. On the second floor of the old Cosmos Club, across Lafayette Park from the White House, Clifford on a number of occasions regaled his old White House crew with graphic tales of days gone by in the legal profession and in working with Truman.

My Early Contacts with Truman's White House

As a hero-worshiper who was always trying to get some new inside information to enliven my political science classes, I was intrigued with Clark Clifford and Judge Rosenman. Here were two people who had the rare opportunity to be at the President's side, to share his inner thoughts, and to take part in the fascinating process of helping him to carry out his challenging responsibilities. I had a burning ambition to get to know these men better, and who knows, possibly to help them in their work.

Rosenman had a soft spot in his heart for his alma mater, Columbia University, where I was teaching in the late 1930s. Through one of my students I made his acquaintance, and before long he asked me to help with a massive research project he was doing for President Roosevelt. In compiling the thirteen-volume *Public Papers and Addresses of Franklin D. Roosevelt*, it was Rosenman's responsibility to write Roosevelt's personal explanations of the background and results of each of his speeches and public actions. In researching and writing these notes, and also helping Rosenman with a later book of his own entitled *Working with Roosevelt*, I tasted the heady wine of being close to a great person. At times he would invite me to visit for brief periods while he was at the White House, or ask me to draft a letter that President Roosevelt had asked him to send to some organization.

Clifford and Elsey were symbols of the effective staff that helped Truman during his dramatic upset victory in 1948. I first met Clifford when he talked with some of my students from Princeton University, where I taught after World War II. At this session he clued us in with graphic details on Truman's uphill whistle-stop fight. Elsey, a Princeton graduate, spent some time telling how the whistle-stop outlines had been prepared on the train. He also came up to Princeton on January 10, 1949, for a complete presentation of the 1948 campaign to my two-hundred-member class.

It was a lucky break that enabled me to work at the White House. Rosenman wrote to Clifford recommending me in the fall of 1949. While most of the staff was preoccupied with preparing the State of the Union message, Truman suddenly asked for a research study of subsidies to business. The administration was being attacked for "handouts," and he was interested in showing that these so-called "welfare state" benefits had persisted since the days of Alexander Hamilton, but were only opposed when the federal government tried to help people get a better education, better housing, better health care and a minimum wage.

Elsey contacted me to do the subsidy study as a temporary, one-shot effort. Clifford liked it, sent it on to the President with a covering note on December 22, 1949, and said he wanted to circulate it among several cabinet members "as background information for speeches by them."

My status was still uncertain when, two days later, I wrote the following letter to a friend, a copy of which I recently discovered:

Dear Mary:

So I was minding my own business day before yesterday, when a call came through from George Elsey saying that my presence was requested at the White House, after the President's press conference, in order to shake hands at the annual Christmas party. After I hung up, I thought it might be interesting to see the press conference—the first since President Truman's return from Key West. The last press conference I attended was with Judge Rosenman on August 16, 1941, and that took a lot of wire-pulling. Steve Early grumbled that the correspondents did not like to have outsiders muscle in; I watched from the back, and could scarcely see President Roosevelt. He bantered a lot with the news people in the front rows; there were lots of laughs and "inside jokes."

This was a little different. It was just a case of Elsey saying "Sure," without hesitation, and I doubt if Press Secretary Charlie Ross even knew I was there.

Just before the news conference, there was a lot of friendly small-talk as the reporters waited in the big outer lobby just as you enter the West Wing. The stay-at-homes were greeting those with Key West tans, and everybody was asking about Christmas plans. There is a big, tall Secret Service man named Bill Simmons, who used to be stationed out in Huntington, West Virginia, until President Roosevelt recruited him. I reminded him I had last seen him in 1941, and he had some nice things to say about Judge Rosenman. "I still think he ought to be appointed to the U.S. Supreme Court," Simmons said.

Some people were talking shop. There was a tall colonel from the Corps of Engineers who was talking loudly about the cornerstone of the White House they are reconstructing: "So we tried the mine detector to locate the original cornerstone, but it was no use. Every little nail and piece of iron caused the detector to hum. Who wants that old cornerstone anyhow except some newspaperman?"

Somebody asked: "Did the bell ring? I guess we can go in." The crowd poured into the Oval Office. The first thing I saw was a bronze bust of Roosevelt, and also a magnificent portrait of FDR. This time, unlike 1941, I got down to the front row, about ten feet from the President. Clark Clifford, his face very deeply tanned, was sitting to the President's left. Ross, Matt Connelly and the aides were distributed around the back.

President Truman exchanged a rapid fire of greetings with the correspondents as they poured in. He really looked fit, in a double-breasted suit, with a carefully placed handkerchief. And such vigorous activity. The last time I was in that office, Roosevelt was sitting immobile in his chair, a long cigarette holder angled upward from his upraised chin. He gave an appearance of majesty; you wouldn't dare to reach out to pat him on the shoulder. This President bobs around and seizes the initiative. He looks like your Uncle Dudley.

"I wonder if they take down all these joking remarks people are making to the President," I asked the reporter standing next to me. "Sure," he said, "Truman wants them for his memoirs. Look at that steno who is taking down every word, even when somebody swears."

"Biggest conference I've ever seen," said another reporter behind me, as the office jammed up. "All in," somebody boomed from the back, and it's amazing how the babble of conversation stopped on a dime.

The President started out on a benign note, wishing the press corps a Merry Christmas and a Prosperous and Happy New Year. Then all of a sudden his eyes began to twinkle, as he added: "I think the vast majority of you have been as kind to me as I deserve." The way he said it made you feel, here is a guy who takes no guff and gives none, and just doesn't go through the motions to be polite.

He said he had persuaded David E. Lilienthal to stay on until February 15 on the Atomic Energy Commission. Then he announced that Charlie Murphy would succeed Clark Clifford. There was a low whistle from one newsman. I heard Elsey's secretary mumble something about Murphy not being the glamor boy Clifford was. I like Murphy. But, gee, what a big pair of shoes he has to fill! It may take time before he can build up the tremendous prestige which Clifford generates. Clifford looks like a Greek god, and Murphy looks like your next-door neighbor. But then, isn't that the difference between Roosevelt and Truman? I know Murphy stands for the right things. Clifford said he couldn't afford to keep the job. I heard the Judge say once that he had to quit in 1946, because he had to go up to New York and reach into his safe deposit box to get a security to sell every now and then, and the last time he reached into the box all he could find was cold steel. So he said he couldn't live on $12,500 a year. Personally, I'd pay them to get a permanent job here, and would be willing to mop the floors after hours to earn enough to eat.

These reporters are really persistent. One guy wanted to know why there was so much trouble in selecting someone to succeed Gray on the Labor Relations Board. The President stretched his arms out, palms upward, to show he had nothing to conceal. With an air of complete innocence, he zeroed in on the word "trouble," and shot back: "There isn't any trouble that I know of." Then his jaw stuck out, and he said with authority: "I am just not ready to make the appointment." Somebody mumbled: "What Gray was that," and President Truman pointed a finger like a schoolteacher putting down a student who hadn't done his homework: "Copeland Gray."

Now a reporter with a bass-voiced Southern drawl allowed as there had been "a sort of drought down South" on Presidential appointments. The President interrupted his question and challenged his premise: "Are you right sure about that? I would like to call the roll for you. I think you will find that the South is still running the Government." There was a lot of laughter at this exchange, and the reporter yielded with a mild, "I will say no more then."

Roosevelt had been more inclined to philosophize in his answers, to give an expansive sketch of historical background where necessary, and to tie in his answers with other developments in related fields. Roosevelt often filibustered at length when he really didn't want to come to a direct point, or when he may not have known the specific answer to the question actually asked. Truman was very short and snappy; at times he sounded like he knew the answer long before the reporter had asked even half the question, which is why there were lots of interruptions. Roosevelt would sometimes pause after a question for effect, and everybody would hang on his answer. Truman was like an impatient dynamo.

I liked the way Truman wheeled around and faced every questioner directly. Roosevelt was more inclined to gaze off into space as he was answering. On the other hand, you had the feeling that Roosevelt was always the complete master of what he wanted to convey, nothing more and nothing less, whereas Truman seemed more interested in answering every question quickly. When he wanted to dodge, he either said no comment or if he was asked about an appointment or resignation he didn't want to reveal, he'd simply say: "There isn't a word of truth in it," when sometimes you had the feeling that something might be brewing.

Truman scolded the press on occasion. When they started asking about whether General Eisenhower was a candidate, he reminded the press that when rumors were flying in 1948, that he had told them Eisenhower wouldn't be a candidate "and none of you believed me."

Then came the Christmas introduction line. I remember that it was one of the proudest moments of my life when the Judge took me in to see Roosevelt in 1941. The Judge gave a nice little pep talk saying I had read every word of FDR's speeches, executive orders and press conferences. The Judge saw to it that I was with Roosevelt alone. The circumstances were not quite as good when there is a long line pressing to get through. Elsey told President Truman what I was doing, and the greeting I got was warm and genuine, but I'm going to have to wait for another occasion to try and get to know this President better. He is really decisive and incisive.

Over New Year's I'm going to try and get down to Memphis and New Orleans. In case I leave this job, I want to make a personal inspection of Beale Street and Basin Street, to qualify for another type of work.

Yours,

Ken

Like the man who came to dinner, I came to the White House on a temporary assignment at the end of 1949, and stayed until after Truman left office in 1953.

8

Whistle-Stopping in 1950

"About Christmas of 1949, the president gave me a paper to read which, as I understood it, had been prepared by the Departments of State and Defense," recalls Charles S. Murphy.[1] "I took it home with me that night. What I read scared me so much that the next day I didn't go to the office at all. I sat at home and read this memorandum over and over, wondering what in the world to do about it."[2] The memorandum warned about the weakness of the American defense posture in the light of worsening international developments. Murphy added: "So I recommended to the President that he put this into the machinery of the National Security Council where it had not been before. That is how it became the paper that got so well known as NSC-68."[3] In addition, Murphy made sure that the views of Leon H. Keyserling, chairman of the Council of Economic Advisers, were considered in assessing how much the American economy could stand for the necessary strengthening of defense. According to Murphy: "From time to time we would turn to Leon and ask, 'How much can the country afford to spend on defense?' And Leon would say, 'I don't know exactly, but you have not reached the limit yet.' "[4]

This is only one illustration of the difference between the speech-writer's and special counsel's functions in the Truman administration, as contrasted with subsequent White House operations. In Truman's time, the special counsel's office and speech-writers were heavily involved in the implementation of policy, foreign and domestic. Consequently, Murphy and his staff spent a great deal of time on current operations, a field that those who draw boxes on charts usually liked to assign to Steelman. As Neustadt points out,

In the first place, messages, speeches, Executive Orders, and the like are not merely vehicles for *expressing* policy, they are devices for getting policy *decided.* They have deadlines attached. And there is nothing like a deadline on the statement of a policy for getting a decision on what that policy shall be.

Thus Murphy had not only the power that goes with choosing the words but also the power that goes with presenting the issues for decision. And as a corollary, he had the responsibility for determining what the issues were, clarifying them, counteracting the premature commitment, counterbalancing the one-sided presentation, flushing out the hidden controversies, and surveying the alternatives.[5]

Richard E. Neustadt

In the spring of 1950, Richard E. Neustadt was recruited by Murphy to join the White House staff. He was one of the crop of bright young public administration graduates who joined the Bureau of the Budget in the post–World War II period, during the expansion of the Executive Office of the President. Neustadt was Budget Director Webb's special assistant, and also frequently dealt with the White House through his work with Roger W. Jones, assistant budget director in charge of legislative reference. He helped assemble recommendations by the federal departments on whether legislation was in accord with the President's program. This "legislative clearance" work was superb training for a prospective White House staff member. Murphy confesses that one of the reasons Neustadt was hired at the White House was his frequently expressed eagerness to work there.[6] When he came aboard in May 1950 he captured the title of youngest member of the staff from Bell, who in turn had taken it from Elsey. Neustadt more than compensated for his shortness by his resonant, basso profundo voice and his addiction to bow ties. He had a booming and infectious laugh and, as Murphy recalls, "You could hear Dick Neustadt laughing across the hall, and then the rest of us laughed too."[7]

He started out as an assistant to Stephen J. Spingarn during the summer of 1950, and with Spingarn's elevation to the Federal Trade Commission, he became an all-around assistant to Murphy. He handled issues relating to the President's legislative program, worked with Bell on economic problems, and was a part of the speech-writing team working on the President's addresses, messages, public policy letters, and other documents. During 1952, he helped on campaign speeches and wrote the first draft of the 1952 Democratic platform, and he wrote the President's farewell address in 1953.

Scare Words and the Jefferson-Jackson Day Speech

The President made reference to some of my material on subsidies to business in his news conference on the budget.[8] But by early 1950 the attacks on his program had veered away from criticisms of the "welfare state," and I had a new project to work on. Although I had been warned not to keep a diary, I recently discovered some notes that describe this new study.

Friday, January 20, 1950: 3 P.M. Elsey and Lloyd said that preliminary talks had been started about the Jefferson-Jackson Day speech, to be given February 16. Lloyd has been commissioned to draw up the first draft. They asked me to check back for the past twenty years in official statements of the Republican National Committee and Republican platforms to get some "calamity-howlers" or "scare words," i.e., predictions of despair which sounded silly in light of the facts of today. . . .

Both Lloyd and Elsey said the President was more interested in general predictions covering the economic scene, since the Jefferson-Jackson Day speech would probably cover a review of the prosperous economic condition of the country and the fortunate economic position of every group in society. When this was contrasted with Republican predictions of doom, it would not only knock the stuffing out of the predictions but would also make the current predictions of the Republican National Committee look very stupid.

Saturday, January 21, 1950: I spent the morning at the Democratic National Committee, pawing through their files on the Republican Party and Republican campaigns. I am shocked at the skimpy and poorly organized material they have on the Republican party. Seems to me this is a first priority for political intelligence: know your enemy. They had plenty of dope on the issues of the day, good background material for Democratic speeches, and a well-organized file on speeches and releases of the Democratic National Committee. I talked with a number of officials, pointing out how important these items were for any winning campaign. They just didn't seem to be interested in the Republicans at all. I am amazed. They ought to have some research people who are pulling all these boners together, so they can be pulled out quickly. Are we going to have to do all this at the White House, in addition to other duties? (Batt's research group was dismantled after the 1948 campaign.)

Friday, February 3, 1950: Received phone call at 11 A.M. that Elsey wanted to see me at 3:30. We discussed a draft for the Jefferson-Jackson Day dinner. Elsey and Lloyd said: "Since this will be a political dinner and a political crowd, we can pull out all the stops. The Democrats and Republicans should be singled out by naming the parties, and why one is constructive and the other stupid. We must play down the old historical stuff about Jefferson and Jackson and what they stood for, and the differences between the two parties down to the present. The President tried that in the 1948 Jackson Day speech, and it really laid an egg. It was the quietest speech he ever made. We've had enough of quiet speeches. We want to hear some noise at this one. It should be an emotional speech rather than a rational one. Praise the Democratic record, and kick the Republicans.

"Then point out that we have a two-party system. The Republicans are against everything, and the Democrats are *for* everything. Then use some of your quotes to show that the Republicans have used the same pessimistic predictions for years and years, which they are using now. Show the real difference between the Democrats and the Republicans."

I grabbed a quick dinner, and worked until about midnight on a draft.

Saturday, February 4, 1950: I came in about 8:00 A.M., checked a few references on tax and world peace issues with Elsey at 10 A.M., and completed typing a 13-page, triple-spaced, legal-size-paged draft. I brought it in to Elsey about 11:30 A.M. It had lots of pretty pointed applause lines on it.

Elsey's first comment was that the style was "like the Boss speaks." He then told the story about the time someone suggested that Arthur Schlesinger, Jr., be enlisted to help the President with speeches, and David Lloyd had replied that "Schlesinger does not write on the same conceptual level as the President." Elsey said that was a wonderful comment on Schlesinger, Lloyd and the President all in one brief sentence. He added that anything which Schlesinger wrote for the President would stick out all over as a ghost-written job. He said that our job was simply to mirror the manner, style, and thought of the President, and not to try and play God. He pointed out several soft spots where I had not put enough political whiplash at the end of certain paragraphs.

Monday, February 6, 1950: Elsey and Lloyd called me in shortly before noon, and said it was OK; Elsey was more enthusiastic than Lloyd, who called it "just a stump speech."

Tuesday, February 7, 1950: "Where do we go from here?" I asked Elsey. "We'll have a huddle on this draft, and everybody will comment," he said simply. "What happens at a speech session?" I asked. I soon found out. Everybody came in and fingered a copy of my draft. There was very little said. Murphy looked at the ceiling. Lloyd got up and looked out the window. For five minutes nobody said anything. I really don't remember exactly how the meeting broke up, but when it was finished I knew I had flunked my first effort at speech-writing.

Thursday, February 16, 1950: I got a free ticket to the Democratic dinner, which drew a huge crowd in the National Guard Armory. There were six quotations which I had found which the President used in his address. The general tone of the speech was far more statesmanlike than I had suggested, although a number of my original ideas were preserved. Yet I guess in editorial content, I flunked the test.

Elsey came over a couple of days ago, and said that the White House was very much concerned about the issues I had been raising with respect to a Research Division at the Democratic National Committee. He said he agreed 100 percent with the suggestions I had made about the void which had to be filled at the National Committee. Then he shocked me with the suggestion that since I knew the White House personnel and needs, and recognized the shortcomings at the National Committee, that I was obviously the prime candidate to head up the Research Division. I shot back pretty sharply, I guess, telling him that he and I had academic training, that we were both interested in applying that training in broader and more constructive fields than in the cauldron of straight partisan politics. We had an interesting discussion of the distinction between helping the President in his role as head of the Democratic party, and working on strictly partisan slants such as the National Committee does. He said that the National Committee needed more academic people. I told him: "Count me out, thank you." I then told him of my fascination with the work I had been doing at the White House, and asked him to be patient and the White House wouldn't regret the investment in the future.

After the Jefferson-Jackson Day dinner, I completed the collection of "scare words" with index and cross-references so it was easy to find predictions of gloom. We forwarded choice quotations to friends on Capitol Hill, although the material was originally stockpiled for the exclusive use of the President. Before long, the National Committee had mimeographed the collection, boiled down to about 120 pages, and started running excerpts in "Capital Comment" and other publications.

Local Color: Collecting Material for Whistle Stops

A development early in March 1950 assured my future at the White House. Elsey came over from a presidential staff meeting, lugging a collection of timetables and brochures, and threw them all on the black leather couch in my office. "You are now our local color man," he said simply. "The President is taking a trip out to the West Coast early in May, and you are nominated to pull together an analysis of every city and town he will visit. Here's the tentative schedule," he said, indicating a list of some thirty or thirty-five stops.

The major purpose of the trip was the dedication of the massive Grand Coulee Dam in Washington on May 11. Bell successfully urged that the President make several speeches in southern Idaho, although he failed in his attempt to route the train through Williston, North Dakota, on a Sunday so there could be an excuse for not speaking. He noted that Williston "has had a long and bitter feud with the Corps of Engineers over the height of the Garrison Dam."[9] An early attempt was made to route the trip through Denver, a key population center and political battleground. Wyoming Senator Joseph C. O'Mahoney raised violent objections, because a Denver stop would have meant cutting out the President's swing through Wyoming. So political and personal pressure won out over population. The entire process was an intriguing example of how a potpourri of conflicting claims produced a schedule that for the most part was built around where the railroad runs. Two conclusions were certain: There would be no unplanned, off-the-train motorcade such as produced the disaster at Carey, Idaho, in 1948; and the schedule was frequently expanded. What started out as about thirty stops eventually ballooned into fifty-seven.

In a memorandum to Murphy, Bell urged:

> In connection with any speech on resource development and the Columbia
> Valley Authority, it would seem to me desirable to use the quotation tech-
> nique, and, if you approve, I would suggest that we ask Ken to find us some
> quotations along two lines: (1) the conservative yelps in the late '30's and
> early '40s that Grand Coulee and other power projects would be "white
> elephants," that after the projects were built, we would have "power run-
> ning out of our ears," etc.; (2) the opposition of the conservatives to TVA,
> with particular emphasis on their claim that it was socialism and that it
> could destroy local control of local affairs.[10]

That night, I found a beautiful quotation in an old *Congressional Record* for January 26, 1936. A Republican Congressman from New York, Francis D. Culkin, told his colleagues: "But I say to you, Mr. Chairman, that up in the Grand Coulee country there is no one to sell power to except the coyotes and jack rabbits, and there never will be." The President got a great kick out of the phrase, and decided right off the bat to use it at Grand Coulee.

The White House staff pondered how to develop a theme for the trip. They were concerned that a "nonpolitical" trip that put too much heat on Congress would be branded as too political. Recalling that a Congressman in the 1930s had put out a "stockholder's report" in a letter to his constituents, I suggested that perhaps this theme could be used. "It should be sort of a profit and loss report of the President's stewardship," I said. This was initially dismissed as being "pretty tame," but eventually it was decided to kick off the trip as a "report to the people."

Assembling the background material was an eye-opening experience. It involved contacts with every federal department and agency affecting the area through which the President traveled. It required original research on the interests of the cities and towns. When the tentative itinerary became available early in March, I went up to Deck 10 of the Library of Congress annex every evening to leaf through all the published information in the local history collection. At the newspaper room, I made notes on recent articles covering the areas the President was to visit. Washington, D.C., is a great melting pot, and somewhere in the nation's capital are knowledgeable residents who grew up in these towns. Getting them to talk was easy—in fact, at times too easy, because they wanted to relate long stories about their ancestors and other tidbits having little relevance to the basic data needed. Newspaper correspondents were excellent sources both for local color and for advice on whom I could contact. But I had to be extremely careful to warn that there was a strict embargo on any published reports that the President might visit a town; premature publication would upset local officials if the schedule changed. The anticipated wrath of Connelly, who was authorized to release the President's schedule through press secretary Ross, was a good deterrent against leaks.

I usually started with the Works Progress Administration state guidebooks, which contained useful historical material. These were supplemented with material at the Library of Congress, locally published Chamber of Commerce or Farm Bureau publications, commercial and marketing data, plus personal conversations. House and Senate offices were helpful, as well as mayors, librarians, and local elder statesmen. Some political information was also available at the Democratic National Committee, and all local and state leaders had their own ideas about which issues should be stressed or avoided.

For the President's personal use, as well as to help the speech-writers and others, I prepared for each whistle stop a two-page analysis of local economic and political conditions, plus background history, personalities and current issues. Up-to-date employment information and federal projects were also included. At a glance, the President could tell something about the local Congressman and his stand on Truman legislation, recent election returns, how the county had voted since 1896, and just what the meeting would be like.

The White House carpenter shop built a small box and bookcase, which fit snugly into a train compartment. In it, the staff placed basic reference materials, including six volumes of the *Dictionary of American History,* all of the President's messages to Congress and economic reports, party platforms, and folders on every conceivable subject that related to federal projects and local interests—even down to the grasshopper situation in Wyoming.

An unwritten rule at the White House is that new staff members (and most old ones too) are supposed to stay out of the newspapers. This much-touted "passion for anonymity" was observed quite strictly, even though the White House press corps was always looking for some new angle about the staff. After I had been running all over Washington asking questions about places the President was going to visit, I guess somebody finally put two and two together and told a Scripps-Howard reporter that there was a former Princeton professor collecting data to help the President on his next political tour. I was horrified to receive a telephone call one day from a reporter who had been talking to people I had interviewed, and he seemed to know what I was doing. I tried to discourage him from writing a news story about me, which is the last thing a person should do if he wants to minimize a story. I was so nonplussed that I said: "Well, I'm really not here. You see, this is very—how shall I put it?—sub rosa." The reporter felt that was such a good quote he decided to use it verbatim in his syndicated story, which appeared April 4.

"EX-PRINCETON PROF NAMED TRUMAN AIDE," the headline blared. I was shocked to see the account, which read:

> President Truman has hired a new political handler for his planned stumping tour for Democratic Congressional candidates.
>
> The White House adviser is Ken Hechler, a former Princeton University professor, who once worked in the executive offices of President Roosevelt. He coordinated the war history efforts of executive departments.
>
> Mr. Hechler's first assignment is to make the President's western trip in May bigger and better than any of the junkets Mr. Truman took as presidential candidate in 1948.
>
> Mr. Hechler refused to discuss the details of the President's May trip. When it will start and Mr. Truman's itinerary will be announced soon from Key West, Fla.
>
> The Princetonian has an office in the White House. He has been there a very short time and doesn't like it known. Asked how long he expected to stay, Mr. Hechler replied:
>
> "Well, I'm really not here. You see, this is very—how shall I put it?—sub rosa."

Down at Key West, where he was vacationing with the President, press secretary Ross was naturally puzzled when a reporter asked a question about somebody whom he had barely met at that point. Had it not been for my amusingly stupid quotation, and my evident efforts to avoid rather than generate publicity, the story would have caused more embarrassment.

Meanwhile, an out-of-town girl friend sent me a telegram that read "CONGRATULATIONS ON BEING QUOTE NOT THERE END QUOTE ACCORDING TO WORLD TELEGRAM."

Speech Drafts

The staff had begun to sketch out topics for the major speeches, with final decisions being made by Murphy in consultation with Bell, Lloyd and Elsey, as follows:

Lincoln, Nebraska	— Domestic farm program, especially in Great Plains
Casper, Wyoming	— Conservation and reclamation
Cheyenne, Wyoming	— Small business
Laramie, Wyoming	— Foreign policy
Pendleton, Oregon	— An expanding national economy
Grand Coulee Dam, Washington	— Reclamation, Columbia Valley Authority
Gonzaga University, Spokane, Washington	— Freedom and civil rights
Butte, Montana	— Labor and social legislation
Fargo, North Dakota	— World trade; International Wheat Agreement
Madison, Wisconsin	— Peace
Chicago, Illinois	— A political "State of the Union" address

In general, the first drafts we received for these speeches were not very scintillating, with the exception of a foreign policy speech written by James L. Sundquist of the Bureau of the Budget. The Sundquist draft was delivered by the President almost intact. Keyserling put together a meaty draft for the Pendleton speech containing some good ideas, but unfortunately it was heavily loaded with statistics and economic theory and had to be pepped up. The Agriculture drafts included some good material and sparkling phrases, but lacked a central theme. The State Department drafts wandered around in a quasi-maze. At a crucial time during April, Lloyd became ill and could not come to the office. Fortunately, the White House was able to get Sundquist's help for the speeches at Cheyenne and elsewhere. He also contributed substantially to the whistle stops at Cumberland, Maryland, and several other points.

As with the selection of topics for the major speeches, the topics for the whistle stops were picked in order to cover all domestic and international programs, as well as relate to the local interest of the town. Beginning about three or four weeks before the start of the trip on May 7, rough drafts of the whistle-stop outlines were under way. The outlines were three to four triple-spaced, legal-size pages for five-minute stops, and a couple of pages longer for ten-minute stops. As in 1948, the outlines were loosely arranged, somewhat as follows: (1) an initial greeting to the people of the community and state, always with an indication of how glad the President was to be there; (2) the main theme of the speech; (3) concluding sentences, which summarized many aspects of the Fair Deal program, as well as indicating the President's commitment to work for world peace. Truman indicated that he wanted to devote at least one speech per day to the theme of world peace; this speech was usually reserved for the final evening whistle-stop.[11]

On May 6, the day before the President's departure, two of the major speeches, at Lincoln and Casper, were frozen. The status of the whistle-stop materials was explained in the following memorandum from Elsey to the President:

> There are being prepared for your use materials for every daylight stop on your trip to the Pacific Northwest.
>
> Each town will have a two-page description, containing historical and political information.
>
> There will also be a speech outline for each town which the President may use in one of several ways. The outline is written in such a fashion that it may be read as a speech text; or it may be used as an outline, with the President interpolating freely and at any point he chooses. If the President chooses to speak completely "off the cuff," it is suggested that he talk on the theme set forth in the outline as that theme was chosen after careful consideration of current local conditions and after discussions with persons familiar with the local picture.[12]

In addition to the political and economic summaries, I gave the President a general political profile of the areas. In a memorandum entitled "Political Batting Averages of the Northwest," I showed that although there were Republican Congressmen in ninety percent of the communities, the President had carried two-thirds of these areas in the 1948 election. Furthermore, William Jennings Bryan, Theodore Roosevelt and Bob LaFollette (1924) had all run strongly in this territory.

Speeches and Whistle Stops in Illinois, Iowa and Nebraska

United States Senator Paul H. Douglas, who attended the first whistle stop of the trip, at 8:50 A.M. on May 8 in Galesburg, Illinois, was agreeably surprised by what he saw and heard. He had expected some rather crass "politicking" at this conservative Republican college town. Instead, he heard a reasoned analysis of the dangers of isolationism, strong support for the United Nations, and an eloquent exposition of paths to world peace.

Truman also captivated the audience completely by ad-libbing that Mrs. Truman had a great-uncle who was a graduate of Knox College "and one of our great circuit judges in Jackson County, Missouri." The crowd of eight thousand knew he wasn't just reciting a rehearsed, ghost-written speech when he folksily referred to "my first 'sashay' into politics" in 1892 when he wore a white cap labeled "Cleveland and Stevenson." He got a big laugh by recalling that "some big Republican boys took my cap away from me and tore it up, and the Republican boys have been trying to do that to me ever since!"[13] He noted that it was his sixty-sixth birthday and the fifth anniversary of V-E Day. The crowd sang and shouted "Happy Birthday."

Transportation agent Dewey Long, glasses perched on the end of his nose, worried aloud on that first day of the Western trip: "He got seven cakes, each of 'em so big it took three or four men to carry. There must have been a ton of cake on that train."[14]

Damp, chilly weather greeted Truman as he entered Iowa at Burlington, but fifteen thousand people jammed around the rear platform and warmed the reception. He edged into his favorite subject this way:

> A lot of people are expecting me to talk about what the 81st Congress has done on these matters, just as I told the country 2 years ago the truth about the 80th Congress.
>
> I will say one thing, and say it emphatically, the 81st Congress has done a lot better than the 80th ever did, and it is going to do a lot more than it has done up to date.[15]

Sleek cattle, fat hogs, and rich farmland stood as visible evidence of the Truman prosperity he bragged on all the way across Iowa. At Ottumwa, thirty-five thousand people crowded around a special platform near the railroad stop. The size of this crowd astounded Victor Johnston and Philip Willkie, sent by the Republican National Committee to follow the President. Johnston called the thirteen-car campaign train a "traveling medicine show," but had to admit to reporters that "nobody hates him." Johnston was startled when the President spotted him in the audience and invited him to ride the train if he would buy a ticket. During his remarks, the President said this about Johnston: "I sincerely hope that he has been as highly pleased with the reception I have had this morning and with the crowds as I have been, and I hope he will make that report to the opposition so that they can govern themselves accordingly."[16]

Columnist George Dixon, after interviewing Johnston, reported:

> He merely wants to find out how this bespectacled little fellow from Independence, who used to be considered a complete washout as a public speaker, talks these people into stringing along with him.
>
> I think student Johnston will find out it's no magic. Truman just talks to people about the things they are personally interested in, in terms they can understand. He did that in 1948; and Tom Dewey didn't.[17]

At Ottumwa, the President used the first of a long series of "scare words" that I had compiled—this one from a Missouri Congressman who railed against an 1887 measure to finance agricultural experiment stations. Congressman William Henry Hatch had denounced a modest fifteen-thousand-dollar annual appropriation as "absolutely destroying the independence and freedom of individual conduct, and subverting the theory on which the government is based."[18] The President noted that Hatch's speech sounded just like the modern-day attacks being made against any progressive measure. He gently reminded his audience that nobody's freedom was being limited by the State Agricultural College and its experimental station a few miles north at Ames.

There was a driving thunderstorm when the President spoke from a canvas-covered stand in Lincoln, Nebraska, with a major farm address on his first day of the whistle-stop tour. There he thundered against Republicans who had branded New Deal soil conservation measures "communistic," making farmers "dominated and regimented for all time."

Acorn Minds and Oak Trees

Writing about the Northwest trip, Margaret noted that at Missoula, Montana, her father "came up with one of his best metaphors."[19]

Prior to the trip, I had called on Montana Representative Mike Mansfield to inform him that the President planned to sign the recently passed National Science Foundation bill in Missoula. He lit his pipe slowly, and commented:

> No—categorically no. I got one letter on that subject, from a zoology professor who probably had been told to write it. We need cheaper power in

the Missoula area. People are really excited about the Hungry Horse Dam, which is being built. That's what President Truman ought to talk about at Missoula. It will also mean flood control, cheaper phosphates for the farmers, and will make the whole region bloom.

Mansfield then talked about each of the Montana cities and towns the President planned to visit, gave me brilliant thumbnail sketches for the "local color" summaries, and also went into depth on the issues. We talked about many things—his job as a Congressman, recent literature he had been reading, how the White House was organized, his future ambitions—and I came away with a high impression of this scholarly legislator.

My reaction was expressed in a letter that I wrote at the time to Judge Rosenman:

> I was so impressed with the clarity of Mansfield's thinking that I went home to bang out a tribute to him to start the Missoula speech. Then I got to thinking about what kind of a guy he was, got to looking at George Norris's picture on my desk, and decided there was something similar in their breadth of outlook. Why is it, I asked myself, that Mike Mansfield can look at some things and see the broad future while others see only the narrow past? It seemed to me like an *acorn;* some people could look at an acorn and all they would see would be the acorn; others like Mansfield would see the oak.[20]

I wrote a rough draft for the Missoula speech, which went through several revisions, both by myself and by other members of the speech-writing team. The President took the draft and used his best whistle-stop style to improve on it when he delivered it.

Even though it was fairly early—just past 7:00 A.M.—when the President's train pulled into Missoula, the crowd was cheering loudly. Mike Mansfield boarded the train in his hometown to introduce the President, and Truman responded: "After that introduction, I will have to deliver the goods, won't I?"[21] Commenting on the early hour, the President joked: "Of course, we farmers think this is pretty late in the day." He went on to say:

> One reason I like this city is because it has given me one of the finest men I know in public service, and that is my good friend Mike Mansfield. . . . There are few men in this country, in the Congress or out, who can equal him in the farseeing grasp he has of the country's international and domestic problems.
>
> You know, some people will take a look at an acorn and all they can see

is just an acorn. But people of Mike Mansfield's type are something different. They can see into the future. They can see a giant oak tree, with its great limbs spreading upward and outward coming from that acorn.

In Washington there are some men, no matter how hard they try, who can only see little acorns. I don't have to call any names, you know who they are. Even give them a magnifying glass, or even a pair of spyglasses, or even a telescope, they just shake their heads and all they can say is, "I'm sorry, I can't see anything but an acorn there."

Then he launched into a story about opposition to the Hoover Dam. The President noted that "one Congressman from the same political party as the gentleman after whom the dam is named, had this to say about it in Congress: he said it would damage industry, it would waste the taxpayers' money, and it would lead us into communism. That's real acorn thinking, I think."[22]

The press had a field day with Truman's Missoula speech. Writing in the *Baltimore Sun*, the President's future press secretary, Joseph H. Short, wrote:

Speeding eastward across rugged Montana, President Truman declared today that the way to avoid the danger of domestic communism was to keep from power "little men with acorn minds."

An "acorn mind" was defined by the Chief Executive at Missoula as one who saw only little acorns and not the giant oaks which grow therefrom.[23]

The *Baltimore Sun* carried a front-page headline: "TRUMAN RAPS 'ACORN MINDS' OF LITTLE MEN." *The Washington Post* headlined a front-page story: "FAIR DEAL OPPONENTS CALLED 'ACORN THINKERS' BY TRUMAN."[24] In the *New York Daily News*, another front-page headline read: "TRUMAN BLASTS POLICY CRITICS AS 'ACORN-MINDED.'"[25] The inside page headline in the *Baltimore Sun* repeated: "TRUMAN SCORES 'ACORN MINDS,' SCOFFS AT CRIES OF SOCIALISM." The press car buzzed with renewed interest at the slogan. Later, the *New York Daily News* ran a special little box with the impish headline, "TRUMAN COINS ACORNY TAG."

The favorable reactions to the Missoula speech may have been affected by the two hindquarters of a freshly butchered elk and 175 newly caught trout that were placed aboard the train at Missoula. The President shared his generous gifts with the press and other train travelers.

North Dakota, Chicago and Maryland

Moving to North Dakota on May 13, the President assured the residents of Williston that the Garrison Dam would not flood the city. He praised the flood protection work of the Corps of Engineers. His biggest and most enthusiastic crowd turned out at Fargo, North Dakota, where the Secret Service estimated that up to thirty-five thousand people jammed around a platform near the depot. Murphy remembered the weather was cool, and he was afraid the crowd would get restless while Truman talked about the International Wheat Agreement. Murphy recalls: "I thought that was sort of a high-water mark when you get a crowd to cheer for the International Wheat Agreement, that's doing very well."[26]

In Chicago on May 15, the President gave a rousing speech at the climax of a three-day Democratic conference. He reviewed the aims and accomplishments of the Fair Deal. In the backyard of the *Chicago Tribune,* he threw out the challenge: "To achieve peace, we must cooperate with other countries in strengthening and improving the United Nations." Reading the facts on doubled corporate profits, doubled new investment in plant and equipment, and a sixty-percent increase in industrial production over the past decade, Truman charged: "All this talk about weakening private enterprise is sheer political bunk."[27] He taunted and twitted Victor Johnston, the Republican "spy" who had followed his trip in a private plane.

Batt, Sundquist, and I had worked up the material for the final whistle stop of the trip at Cumberland, in western Maryland. When we had finished and mailed the speech to the train, I suggested to Sundquist and Batt that we ought to pile into the car and drive to Cumberland for the noon address. Unfortunately, when Truman spoke, the wind kicked over one of his pages, and I'm sure some of our pearls of wisdom were lost to history.[28] But we all felt it personally as, in the final words of his seven-thousand-mile, sixteen-state tour, he looked out over the audience and said: "You have welcomed me at the end of what I think has been a most successful tour to make a report to the people of the United States as President of the United States."[29]

There was much back-slapping and renewal of old acquaintances at Cumberland. Murphy took me aside and asked if I wanted to ride the presidential train back to Washington. Although I hated to desert the friends with whom I had driven to Cumberland, it didn't take much arm-twisting to get me aboard for the leisurely trip in to the nation's capital. Tired and worn though they were, Murphy's crew were optimistic and enthusiastic. The President was overjoyed with the results he had achieved and made no secret of it. Wandering forward to the press car, I found the bedraggled newsmen full of admiration for the performance of Truman and his staff. They were still swapping stories about some of the funny incidents that had occurred:

Bill Bray, a Steelman assistant and former Farley aide who helped Connelly with the reception of local politicians, drew laughs one day as he emerged with a huge Dewey button attached to his coattails by Associated Press correspondent Tony Vaccaro.

At the Spokane stockyards, when the head of the livestock show pinned a huge purple livestock champion's ribbon on the President's lapel, Truman cracked: "Am I the grand champion pig or cow?"

A reluctant lamb noisily protested having a blue ribbon pinned on him by the President, until the President called him a "Republican sheep," after which the animal miraculously subsided.

In Casper, Wyoming, the President interrupted a major address to tell an audience in the high school auditorium that he remembered his mother telling him about the time the grasshoppers were so bad they ate the handles off the pitchforks.

George Dixon said, "He doesn't miss a local trick. I'm glad we're not going to Alaska on this trip, as he would undoubtedly come up with a batch of tasty recipes for cooking whale blubber."

They remembered the sturdy farmer who, when the President made his last speech of the day, after 10:00 P.M. in Broken Bow, Nebraska, yelled with great fervor, "Thank you, Harry."

In Baker, Oregon, he enchanted the crowd by saying he had come out "so that you could see me and find out if I have gone 'high hat' since you elected me in 1948." There was unanimous agreement he had not.

A Well-Planned Trip

Two days after his return, the President was asked at a news conference whether he thought the Republicans had gotten their money's worth in chartering a private plane for Victor Johnston to tail him. "Read Tony Leviero's letter to Johnston to take back to his people, I think that answers it," the President responded.[30] He was referring to an "imaginary" letter that Leviero suggested in a Sunday column in *The New York Times*. It was remarkably accurate. It described the

> pretty fat loose leaf binder Mr. Truman has in front of him, even for the simplest speech. . . . In this fact book he has a lot of interesting and homey facts about every single place where he made a speech. He reads this stuff over at least twenty-four hours before he reaches a place and works it into those aforementioned off-the-cuff speeches. . . . The one thing this man Truman has been hitting harder than anything else, however, is the charge of "socialism" we keep throwing at him. He gets to a place where the Rural Electrification Administration brought in electricity, or to another where the Reclamation Bureau made farming possible. He gets sarcastic about the "mossbacks" who opposed those things and claims they were crying "socialism" against them as far back as 1887.
>
> And he asked the crowd do they think it's socialism when they can have these things? Somehow, when he puts it that way these socialistic projects don't sound as bad out here at the grass roots as they do in Washington.[31]

There were quite a few analyses written of the President's Western trip, all of them very complimentary. Even Johnston admitted publicly:

> It was a good show; a hoopla medicine show, maybe, but good.
>
> The President epitomizes the common man. Also, he is a very masterful politician. He has an exceptionally good staff, and fine research work behind him.[32]

Murphy's favorite press story involved the young lady who wrote about the effectiveness of the White House staff work, and "said that if that train stopped at a little town out there somewhere for five minutes, and if they had crooked cue sticks in the pool hall, that we would know about it and the President would say something about it."[33]

The President returned from his Western trip with renewed confidence that his programs for strengthening the economy and moving toward world peace were attainable goals. Privately and publicly, he expressed appreciation to the White House staff for the smooth operation of the whistle-stop trip. On May 20, he told a Democratic women's dinner:

> There has been a great deal of conversation about a successful jaunt which the President took just a few days ago. If that trip was a success, it was due to the fact that the President had the most efficient staff that has ever been gotten together for the purpose.[34]

The roseate glow of success encouraged Truman to feel that in 1950 he might reverse the historical pattern of voting against the party in power at the mid-term elections.

The whole picture changed suddenly at the end of June 1950, as North Korean troops stormed across the Thirty-eighth Parallel. The crisis produced an early semblance of national unity, which later crumbled in the face of Republican attacks on "Mr. Truman's war." The blunderbuss attacks by Wisconsin Senator McCarthy stirred up the issue of "communists in the federal establishment." As attention was diverted to the conflict in Korea, President Truman's domestic program suffered declining support in Congress. The events in Korea also resulted in significant changes in both the organization and emphasis of the White House staff.

9
The Politics of
Congressional Relations

I saw an immediate change in the President's personal mood in the closing days of June 1950. As I watched the visitors to the Oval Office, more and more military and diplomatic officials trooped in and out. Those who had political and domestic concerns suddenly found it was difficult to see the President. He put on his commander in chief's hat, and his political hat gathered dust. From Capitol Hill came a steady stream of grim-faced House and Senate members to discuss military and diplomatic issues. The President was personally concerned about the effect of the war on the domestic economy, and how the economy would adjust to a quick expansion of our military strength.

Crisis in Korea

Truman doggedly insisted that the war in Korea should be played down and labeled a "police action." But in his own scheduling, emphasis, and personal mode of operation, there was a radical shift. Getting a domestic program through the Eighty-first Congress and the congressional election campaign of 1950 were suddenly placed on the back burner.

On Saturday morning, June 24, the President dedicated Friendship International Airport outside of Baltimore—"why I don't know," he wrote. He added: "I guess because the Governor of Maryland, the two Senators from that great state, all the Congressmen and the Mayor of Baltimore high pressured me into doing it."[1] From that point on, he was less receptive to congressional pressure. But those were the days of innocence, when the President could easily write (the day before the invasion), "I'm going home from Baltimore to see Bess, Margie and my

brother and sister, oversee some fence building—not political—order a
new roof on the farmhouse and tell some politicians to go to hell!"[2]

That night he received a telephone call in Independence from Secretary of State Acheson, informing him of the sketchy news about the first
North Korean troops invading South Korea. After midnight in Kansas
City, assistant press secretary Eben A. Ayers was awakened with a detailed follow-up message from Washington on the seriousness of the invasion. The American ambassador in Korea, John Muccio, labeled it an
"all-out offensive." Unfortunately, Ayers decided to go back to sleep,
concluding that little could be done until the next day. It was an error of
judgment.[3] When the President learned of the seriousness of the developments in Korea by another phone call from Acheson on Sunday, June
25, he made immediate arrangements to fly back to Washington and
convene a Sunday evening meeting of diplomatic and military leaders at
Blair House.

Averell Harriman's Return

Since Leahy's retirement in 1949, the President had felt the need for
additional high-level assistance at the White House on foreign policy
and geopolitical issues involving the military. In the early days of the
Korean crisis, he decided to ask Harriman to return from assignment in
Paris, where he was helping to administer the Marshall Plan. After talking with the President by telephone on the morning of June 27, Harriman took the afternoon plane to Washington and arrived in time to join
the meetings that followed during the rest of the week at Blair House.
He set up a small staff located in the Executive Office Building. This
group worked on military, political and financial issues, largely through
interdepartmental committees.[4] In 1951, the President named Harriman
director for mutual security and also senior adviser to the President on
foreign and military policy.

Harriman's return was no sudden decision prompted entirely by the
Korean conflict, but it was speeded by the crisis. As early as the spring of
1950, Harriman had informed the President of his desire to return from
Europe, since the aid program had become fairly well established by
that time. The President was concerned about growing personal friction
between Secretary of State Acheson and Secretary of Defense Johnson,
and had asked Harriman to return to Washington by the end of July or
early August to work in the White House on coordinating foreign policy
and defense matters.[5]

The rift between Acheson and Johnson became deeper after the out-break of hostilities in Korea. The President was irked at Johnson's behav-ior on the Sunday evening when he flew back from Independence to confer with his advisers at Blair House. As the group was waiting on the patio prior to dinner, Johnson suddenly asked General Bradley to read a memorandum from General MacArthur on the importance of Formosa. The President cut him short, saying he wanted no policy matters dis-cussed before dinner and prior to the withdrawal of the Blair House staff. There was a clear feeling that Johnson was trying to upstage Ache-son.[6]

A stark example of Johnson's conduct came to light early in July. Harriman told the President he had been in the Secretary of Defense's office when the latter was congratulating Senator Taft on a speech criti-cizing the President for not consulting Congress. Johnson then shocked Harriman by telling him that if they could only get Acheson out, he would see that Harriman became secretary of state.[7] Harriman was the wrong person to approach with such a comment. He was completely loyal to the President; he also happened to have been a contemporary of Acheson's at Yale University and respected his ability and integrity. Fur-thermore, Harriman rarely engaged in "palace politics," or intrigues aimed at some higher office. Despite Truman's obligation to Johnson for his yeoman work in raising funds for the uphill campaign of 1948, it was now evident that sooner or later Johnson would have to go. In Septem-ber, he was replaced by General Marshall, recalled once again from re-tirement. The President privately jotted down the inside story:

> Today I had a most unpleasant duty to do. For some time I've known that Louis Johnson could not continue as Secretary of Defense. I've known him for thirty years personally—helped make him National Commander of the American Legion, appointed him treasurer of the National Democratic Committee in 1948, in which position he did a bang-up job. Then I ap-pointed him Secretary of Defense when I saw Jim Forrestal was going to crack up. Mr. Johnson did a good job with Forrestal and the unification of the armed forces. Then he came forth with a complex. I don't understand what happened to him. He talked out of turn to the press, the Senate and the House—and kept it up. He talked to the lying, crazy columnists—Pearson, the Sop sisters (Alsops), Doris Fleeson, and others. He succeeded in making himself an issue both publicly and in Congress.
>
> He is inordinately ambitious and an egotist. When I told him that for the good of the country he'd have to quit, he said "You are ruining me." That answers the question of what comes first—my sentimental attachment to Johnson or the country.

I had to tell him he'd have to quit. I felt as if I'd whipped my daughter which I've never done. Johnson's done. Too bad. He had a grand opportunity.[8]

Consultation with Congress on Korea

Following up on Secretary Acheson's telephone contacts with a bipartisan group of congressional leaders on June 26, the President decided to call a full-scale meeting on the morning of June 27 to brief House and Senate members of both parties. Included in the bipartisan group were three Republican Senators, Alexander Wiley, H. Alexander Smith and H. Styles Bridges, and two Republican House members, Charles Eaton and Dewey Short.

After these discussions in the Cabinet Room, the President issued a new statement to congressional leaders, again denouncing the invasion and indicating that United States air and naval forces would give Korean troops "cover and support."[9] The same day, he exchanged telegrams with his 1948 campaign opponent, Governor Dewey, and thanked Dewey for stating that the President's action "should be supported by a united America."[10]

A good deal of my work during this period involved documentation of the extent of bipartisan support for the decision to commit American forces to Korea. By the end of the week, it became apparent that American ground troops would have to be committed. What was also evident was that some Republicans were already starting an attack of major proportions on the President's decisions. One of my major tasks was to document the background of Republican and Democratic statements on Korea in light of subsequent efforts to make a partisan issue out of "Truman's war."

Senator Taft was the spearhead of attacks on the President's actions in the Korean conflict. Taft contended that the attack had been invited by an address by Acheson at the National Press Club in January 1950, placing Korea outside the defense perimeter that the United States would defend. Every time Taft or some other opponent brought up this point, we had to respond that in the same January speech Acheson had clearly stated that the United Nations would be called on in the event of an attack outside this American defense perimeter—which is exactly what happened.

When the fighting broke out, Taft's initial comments were somewhat muted, in contrast to his later strident attacks. In fact, his first speech expressed approval of the "general policies outlined in the President's statement." This caused great joy at the White House, and Ross proclaimed, "By God! Bob Taft has joined the U.N. and the U.S."[11] Although denouncing the President for exceeding his authority in sending American forces to Korea, in a June 28 Senate speech Taft acknowledged that "if a joint resolution were introduced asking for approval of the use of our Armed Forces already sent to Korea and full support of them in their present venture, I would vote in favor of it."[12] Taft later became the leading critic of the President's Korean policy.

At the White House, Harriman urged the President to obtain a joint resolution of support from the Congress. At the time, sentiment was running strongly in favor of such action. A long-time foreign policy critic of Truman, Senator William F. Knowland, Republican of California, praised the President's action in a June 27 Senate speech and urged that "he should have the overwhelming support of all Americans regardless of their partisan affiliation."[13] Had the President followed Harriman's advice, it would certainly have blunted some of the subsequent Republican criticism of his actions. Harriman explained the reason for the President's decision not to seek a joint resolution:

> He said that he would not do so because it would make it more difficult for future presidents to deal with emergencies. . . . Later when Robert Taft and others began criticizing the president, I was convinced that the president had made a mistake. This decision, however, was characteristic of President Truman. He always kept in mind how his actions would affect future presidential authority.[14]

A far larger bipartisan meeting was convened by the President on June 30, with the Vice-President, members of the cabinet, Joint Chiefs of Staff, and fifteen Democratic and Republican Senate and House members attending. For the first time, Republicans like Nebraska Senator Kenneth Wherry (the Republican floor leader) openly challenged the President's constitutional authority to proceed without congressional consent. The President was firm on the point, indicating he would seek congressional support, but not advance approval. At many more bipartisan meetings, the President spent considerable time and effort briefing congressional leaders on his actions in Korea.

Supplying Information to Congress

As Republican attacks mounted, a better-organized effort was necessary to supply ammunition to answer these attacks. The State Department, burdened with the day-to-day conduct of our foreign policy and concerned about preserving bipartisanship, acted as though there was something unclean about two-fisted political arguments. The Office of Public Affairs sent out many speakers, arranged forums on foreign policy and answered correspondence, but could not seem to produce hard-hitting speeches with the "sex appeal" needed for the rough-and-tumble of debate. Many of us at the White House continued agitating for the re-establishment of the research division at the Democratic National Committee, abolished after the 1948 election. Truman's Missouri friend William M. Boyle, Jr., Democratic National Chairman, was more of an organization man than an issue man. We had great difficulty getting Boyle to move. This put an increasing burden on the White House to produce research materials. During the summer of 1950, the National Committee named Charles Van Devander of the *New York Post* public relations director. After some pressure from the White House he hired Philip Dreyer, an Oregon veteran of the 1948 research division, to head research. Unfortunately, as in 1948, research was always a stepchild at the National Committee. Beyond that, personality differences erupted between Van Devander and Dreyer. By September, Dreyer was forced out, and we faced a difficult mid-term campaign without the research division we had so long sought.

Vice-President Barkley

President Truman's regular weekly meetings with the "Big Four"—the Vice-President, House speaker and Senate and House majority leaders—were an essential feature of his relations with Congress. Prior to 1949, when he did not have a Vice-President, Senate President Pro Tempore Kenneth D. McKellar of Tennessee came instead. Senator McKellar and President Truman did not see eye to eye on many issues; thus the President was pleased when Vice-President Barkley took office in 1949.

Barkley cannot be classified as a powerful Vice-President. He was seven years older than Truman, and although he had served as Senate majority leader he had never exerted a strong influence with Congress.

Truman was sensitive that the constitutional powers of the President should not be delegated. Although he invited the Vice-President to attend cabinet meetings and always called on him first at these meetings, the President rarely used him for special legislative assignments. Perhaps here, too, Truman was still smarting from the difficult assignment given him in 1945 by President Roosevelt, who directed Truman to twist the necessary Senate arms to obtain the confirmation of Henry A. Wallace as secretary of commerce.

The presidential bug bit Barkley every four years, and his rousing keynote speech at the 1948 convention prompted some forces to try to use his candidacy to upset Truman. Again in 1952 he made a bid for the presidential nomination, and found himself vetoed by a group of labor leaders. In between times, Vice-President Barkley seemed more interested in his new home life with an attractive second wife, the former Mrs. Carleton Hadley, introduced to him by Clifford on a boat cruise. The Vice-President's role in helping Truman legislation get through Congress, in summary, was not very large.

Legislative Liaison

As a former senator, President Truman had clearly pronounced views on what should be appropriate relations with the Congress. He had been on the receiving end of "must" legislation from President Roosevelt. He had also seen the counterproductive results of strong-arm lobbying by some White House emissaries like Tommy Corcoran, whom Truman came to dislike intensely.

Because he was well acquainted with the leaders and most of the Senate and House committee chairmen, the President considered it undignified to allow staff subordinates to call on prestigious legislators. Also, as a consummate politician he knew the background of the issues involved, and felt that if anybody should contact these leaders, he should do it himself. In the Truman period there was also a great deal more centralization of legislative authority in the speaker and committee chairmen, whose power has since been dispersed. Truman was never reluctant to pick up the telephone and call congressional leaders. Murphy reports:

> He would make phone calls to key people in Congress in support of a piece of legislation if I made a recommendation that he do so and if he thought

the recommendation was right. A good deal of this went on; these phone calls were usually very short, but they were usually quite effective.[15]

When Murphy became special counsel in 1950, it was his central responsibility to brief the President prior to "Big Four" meetings. The President preferred to conduct these meetings with no White House staff present, so Murphy would be available in the anteroom, and occasionally Truman would call him into the meeting to clarify a technical point or a matter of fact or judgment of strategy. For the most part, the President felt the "Big Four" would be more amenable to his suggestions if he made them face-to-face without staff present.

Another factor militating against a powerful White House congressional relations staff was the feeling that the best way to handle legislative matters was to allow the executive departments and agencies, with their own information and expertise, to work with Congress. Of course, this practice frequently led to a spotty record, depending on which agency had the best liaison staff or the most attractive program, and frequently the Truman program suffered.

Not until 1949 did the President allow the addition of two legislative assistants, attached to Connelly's office. Joseph Feeney in the Senate and Charles Maylon in the House could scarcely be labeled effective lobbyists for the President's legislative program. He probably cautioned them to keep their operations at a low-key level. Their time was devoted primarily to listening to complaints or performing the minor chores for constituents that are the bread and butter of every Congressman's work. Occasionally, they came up with a "head count" or prediction on pending legislation, although we suspected these predictions came from central sources like Leslie Biffle, secretary of the Senate, or Speaker Rayburn in the House.

I began to sense the weaknesses of the congressional liaison operation a few weeks after starting work at the White House. One day I received a telephone call from Kenneth Harding of the House Democratic Congressional Campaign Committee. Ken told me that the dean of the California House delegation, Harry Sheppard, wanted me to have lunch with him at the Capitol. Naturally, I asked what was the reason for the meeting, and he answered that Congressman Sheppard just wanted to talk with someone from the White House. Being new and naive about the rigid rules requiring clearance with Connelly before arranging such meetings, I blithely went ahead and met the two gentlemen in the

House restaurant. After the luncheon, I sat for over an hour as Sheppard went through many of the problems he was facing in California. I did nothing more than ask leading questions and listen quietly. As the luncheon and its aftermath drew to a conclusion, I was surprised when Sheppard arose with a grin, grasped my hand warmly and said with sincerity: "I've met lots of people down there at the White House, but you are one of the smartest." Only then did I realize that there are quite a few of the 435 Congressmen who aren't members of the Big Four, and who aren't on the President's list to receive occasional telephone calls. They became frustrated when they didn't have someone from the White House to whom they could pour out their troubles.

Connelly did what he could to act as a channel of communication for congressmen who wanted White House help. As he put it: "Of course, every Congressman and every Senator wants to talk to the President, and if that happened there wouldn't be room for anybody else, so it had to be done on a lower level (myself)."[16]

The President's reluctance to set up effective congressional liaison made him easy prey to the type of problem about which he protested to his cousin Nellie Noland:

> One old Congressman who rides in a wheeled chair and who is a chairman of a key committee talked to me for forty long, nerve wracking minutes about his favorite candidate for postmaster in a town of a million people where there are two other Congressmen with a favorite. Seven people stood on first one foot and then another outside my door. That's one example. A Mayor of a city with a million people and lots of smoke and soot, and a Senator almost talked me into nervous prostration over the appointment of a Federal Judge—whom I had no intention of appointing. There are two examples of dozens and I have to grin and bear it and make them like it.[17]

Changing circumstances and shifting congressional majorities prompted President Truman to change his tactics. In the face of a crushing defeat in the mid-term elections of 1946, at his next news conference the President made a public statement that was firm but conciliatory, rather than belligerent. "I shall cooperate in every proper manner with members of the Congress, and my hope and prayer is that this spirit of cooperation will be reciprocated," he said.[18]

From 1947 to 1949, facing a Republican-controlled Congress, the President cultivated a warm personal relationship with Senate Foreign Relations Committee Chairman Arthur H. Vandenberg, which paid rich dividends. He achieved remarkable success in getting congressional approval for a sweeping program to contain communism.

Congressional Republicans were convinced that Truman was destined to be a one-term, "caretaker" President, but the fact remains that the President persuaded the Republican-controlled Congress that it was in the national interest, and in their own interest, to support these programs.

Despite his strident attacks on the Eightieth Congress, Truman consistently preserved a policy of bipartisanship in foreign affairs. During 1950 alone he made seventeen different public statements expressing his determination to carry forward a bipartisan foreign policy.

Research on Bipartisan Foreign Policy

On February 13, 1951, I was handed a memorandum concerning an address that Vice-President Barkley was scheduled to make in Topeka, Kansas, on February 24. The memorandum stated:

> In this connection, the President has asked that we get up a memorandum for the Vice-President's use, setting out facts to show the extent of bipartisan cooperation and congressional consultation in foreign policy matters.
>
> The President mentioned particularly that we should point out the bipartisan character of the United States delegations to such international meetings as Bretton Woods, the San Francisco conference that established the United Nations, and our United Nations Delegations. He mentioned specifically Senator Austin and John Sherman Cooper.
>
> He also mentioned the bipartisan consultations that took place in connection with the Marshall Plan. He spoke about how he consulted the bipartisan group on the Korean situation as soon as it was practicably possible after the communist attack. He also made quite a point of the way the Congress, with members of both parties concurring, has from time to time in legislative action given its approval to the course being followed. Particularly, he mentioned the Defense Production Act as a ratification of the course taken last summer.[19]

In compiling this material, I went through Rose Conway's files to get a full, accurate picture of all the meetings the President had held involving Republican leaders. I also consulted the notes that the President frequently wrote on five-by-eight pads following these meetings. Jack McFall's office at the State Department supplied additional data on bipartisan consultations, both those involving State and those involving the White House. My initial report, done under some pressure to meet the Vice-President's deadline, was about twenty pages long. But the subject was so interesting that I kept working on it after the Topeka speech and expanded the document to about three times its original size.

We had a struggle deciding how to get this material published. Obviously, it couldn't be done by the Democratic National Committee, since it involved a study of bipartisanship praising Republican cooperation. I tried to persuade the staff of Texas Senator Tom Connally, Chairman of the Foreign Relations Committee, to issue it as a committee publication. They shuddered, claiming that anything connected with the White House was far too "political" to touch with a ten-foot pole. They argued there was a possibility Connally might run for re-election in 1952, and there were lots of people in Texas who probably disliked President Truman. I doubt if his aides had read the document, which the State Department had checked for accuracy and objectivity.

Finally, I found a kindred spirit in John Horne, administrative assistant to Alabama Senator John Sparkman, a prominent member of the Foreign Relations Committee. Horne read the document, and wrote out an introduction for Sparkman, who obtained Senate permission to have it printed as a Senate document. It was entitled "Review of Bipartisan Foreign Policy Consultations Since World War II."[20]

In addition to the information asked for by the President, the document listed the leaders in formulating the policy; explained how it developed and what it had accomplished; and contained many illustrations of the great triumphs achieved—in the UN, in the Rio Treaty, in the Marshall Plan, in NATO, and in other areas.

The document sketched in the basic reason for the policy: Farsighted people in both political parties "were determined that the bitter history of partisan opposition to the League of Nations must not be repeated in the post–World War II efforts to maintain peace." It also analyzed six manifestations of the development of the policy, as specifically encouraged by the President:

1. Frequent White House conferences with congressional leaders of both parties. . . .
2. Bipartisan congressional representation on U.S. delegations to many international conferences.
3. The inclusion of leading members of both political parties on United States delegations to the United Nations.
4. Frequent consultation on major policies between the Department

of State and the bipartisan membership of various congressional committees. . . .

5. The bipartisan planning and development of major policies with
the assistance of congressional leaders of both parties, as well as private individuals and outside groups representing both political parties (for example, the development of the Marshall Plan, the international information
program, and the technical assistance program).

6. The appointment of leading members of the Republican Party to
high policy positions in the Department of State, and in other agencies
dealing with foreign policy matters (for example, the appointment of John
Foster Dulles as a special representative of the Secretary of State to negotiate the peace treaty with Japan and the 50 other nations at war with Japan,
Paul G. Hoffman as the administrator of the European recovery program,
former Vermont Republican Senator Warren R. Austin to head the U.S.
mission to the United Nations, and former Nebraska Republican Governor
Dwight P. Griswold to be chief of the American mission for aid to
Greece).[21]

The President was pleased with the study and called attention to it
in his news conference of August 14, 1952. During a discussion of presidential plans for having the Central Intelligence Agency brief both presidential candidates in 1952, Truman added:

I would like very much, though, to have each one of you familiarize yourselves with a Senate document. It is Senate Document 87. It was issued on
October the 20th, 1951, by the Foreign Relations Committee of the United
States Senate. It is a unanimous report on the bipartisan foreign policy, and
the history of the operations of that policy almost from its beginning. You
can get some very good information out of that document.[22]

Central Clearance at the Budget Bureau

Truman was an expert on relations with Congress. He knew what he
wanted to accomplish, had a personal stake in setting up effective machinery, and knew how he wanted it done. One aspect of executive-
legislative relations, however, emerged quietly as institutionalized machinery, rather than through Truman's initiative. In the Bureau of the
Budget, a process was developed to provide central clearance of legislative proposals, along with coordinated advice to the President on
whether to sign or veto bills passed by the Congress.

Advice on pending legislation and whether departmental or congressional legislative proposals were "in accord with the program of the

President" started when Roosevelt was President. Under the leadership of Budget Director Harold D. Smith, the process developed and expanded. While Truman was President, the Budget Bureau's Legislative Reference Division addressed reports to the White House executive clerk on bills that had cleared Congress. These reports included a complete file of the bill, the House and Senate reports, the executive department recommendations on approval or disapproval, and a covering letter from the Budget Bureau with its own recommendation for action.

During the war years, when Judge Rosenman was Roosevelt's special counsel, he usually received these reports from the Budget Bureau. Since Rosenman remained as special counsel to President Truman until February 1, 1946, the same process continued with the same close working relationship with the Budget Bureau. Rosenman was the architect of the President's legislative program, and with his departure, the scepter of leadership in that area passed to Clifford. Yet whether the special counsel was named Rosenman, Clifford or Murphy, there was never any question who made the final decision and who was in charge: the President of the United States.

Even on some reports on relatively minor legislation, Truman read the complete file thoroughly before signing or vetoing bills. For example, H.R. 9087 called for the payment of seventy-five dollars for relief of one H. Dale Madison, who had rented a black horse to the Forest Service for use by forest rangers to help the Army in aircraft warning duties. The rented horse chewed through his tie rope one night and broke away, only to meet an unfortunate end when he caught his right hind shoe in the rope. The Budget Bureau slipped in this sentence in its report to the President: "While this is a case of a horse and not a Missouri mule, we are betting that the President will give Mr. Madison the $75, so he can buy another horse to rent to the Forest Rangers and start all over again."

Truman indicated that he really read these obscure reports by penning this note at the bottom of the Budget Bureau report: "The President is in agreement. No Missouri mule would ever so entangle himself. H.S.T."

A legislative issue close to President Truman's heart was the Atomic Energy Act of 1946. In direct opposition to Pentagon forces favoring military control of atomic energy development, Truman successfully fought for civilian control. His leading ally on Capitol Hill was Connecticut Senator Brien McMahon. The President's main concern was the ultimate objective; hence he probably did not pay much attention to the power struggle going on within the Executive Office legislative clearance machinery. On Capitol Hill, Charles S. Murphy, in the Senate legislative counsel's office, noticed that the Atomic Energy Act was handled for the White House through the Office of War Mobilization and Reconversion.[23] OWMR's director, John W. Snyder, apparently remarked to an aide: "I simply do not see why [legislative] *policy* is any business of the *Budget* Bureau."[24] Budget Director Smith, who initially impressed President Truman by his objectivity, orderly approach to administration, and professional competence, lost favor because he unwittingly clashed with Snyder, who was an old friend of the President. Desperately, Smith argued that fewer individuals should have access to the President. Truman not only favored his old friend Snyder in the controversy, but in July 1946 replaced Smith with James E. Webb as budget director. As Neustadt accurately put it: "By mid-summer, 1946, the Budget Bureau's status in the presidential orbit had reached its lowest point. OWMR seemed superficially to be assured a strong, perhaps a permanent position."[25] Coincidentally, the head of the Budget Bureau's Legislative Reference Division, aging F. J. Bailey, was near retirement and in no mood to fight for the prerogatives that were slipping away to the OWMR.

Several shifts in the cast of characters had a dramatic effect on the Bureau of the Budget's work of legislative clearance and helped with the President's legislative program. In 1946, the President appointed Secretary of the Treasury Vinson as Chief Justice, then moved Snyder from OWMR over to head the Treasury Department. Early in 1947, Murphy came to the White House with a strong interest in keeping tabs on the President's legislative program. Shortly afterward, Bailey retired and was replaced by the energetic and imaginative head of the Bureau's Legislative Reference Division, Elmer B. Staats. His deputy, Roger W. Jones, later moved up to direct the division as Staats was promoted to executive assistant director. Meanwhile, Webb, who appreciated that one of the best ways to gain support was to furnish able assistance, solidified his relationship with the White House by offering to detach any of his staff to help the White House whenever needed. A whole string of Budget Bureau personnel suddenly found themselves either on detail or permanently transferred to the White House rolls. Bell, Stowe, Kayle, Andrews, Enarson, Neustadt and I were Bureau alumni.

In addition, the White House expanded the process of formulating the President's legislative program. Every year, the Budget Bureau

The President congratulates his retiring special counsel, Judge Samuel I. Rosenman, as he awards him the Medal for Merit on January 24, 1946. (*International News Service—UPI*)

President Truman applauds Britain's wartime prime minister, Winston Churchill, at his March 5, 1946, address at Westminster College, Fulton, Missouri. Others on the platform are Fleet Admiral William D. Leahy, Captain Clark M. Clifford, and Major General Harry H. Vaughan. (*Terry Savage, Courtesy Harry S. Truman Library*)

A lifelong friend and school classmate, Press Secretary Charles G. Ross was probably the only person who dared to sit on the President's desk. (*Associated Press Photograph*)

Dr. John R. Steelman, Charles S. Murphy, President Truman and Rear Admiral Robert L. Dennison aboard the U.S.S. *Williamsburg*. (*U. S. Navy, Courtesy Harry S. Truman Library*)

Using his characteristic chopping gestures, President Truman electrifies the Democratic National Convention with his rousing acceptance speech on July 15, 1948. (*Photoworld*)

A galaxy of screen stars, including Ronald Reagan, actively supported Truman in 1948. On the stage for Truman's address at Gilmore Stadium, Los Angeles, are, from left, Ronald Reagan, Humphrey Bogart, Lauren Bacall and George Jessel. (*Photograph by Rene Laursen*)

The President gleefully displays the early edition of the *Chicago Tribune*, headlined DEWEY DEFEATS TRUMAN. This classic photo was snapped in St. Louis, November 4, 1948, as Truman's train made its triumphant way back to Washington. (*Courtesy Harry S. Truman Library*)

The President meets with some of his staff in the Oval Office. From left, Donald S. Dawson, Charles S. Murphy, Matthew J. Connelly, William J. Hopkins, David E. Bell, Major General Harry H. Vaughan, Major General Robert B. Landry, David D. Lloyd, William D. Hassett, Dr. John R. Steelman, James S. Lay, Jr., Joseph H. Short, Roger W. Tubby, Joseph G. Feeney and Irving Perlmeter. (*Alfred Wagg, Photoworld*)

President Truman throwing out the first ball at a 1951 game celebrating the 50th anniversary of the American League. From left, Chief Justice Fred Vinson, Charles S. Murphy (partially hidden behind Vinson), David H. Stowe, Martin L. Friedman, President Truman, Clark Griffith (president of the Washington Senators), unidentified man, Henry J. Nicholson (Secret Service). (*Department of Defense, Courtesy Harry S. Truman Library*)

Picnic lunch at the Little White House at Key West. From left, Milton P. Kayle, a steward, Ken Hechler, Dr. John R. Steelman, Margaret Truman, Mrs. Truman and the President helping themselves to hamburgers and hot dogs. (*U. S. Navy, Courtesy Harry S. Truman Library*)

Staff members enjoying a hamburger lunch on the lawn of the Little White House at Key West: George M. Elsey, Roger W. Tubby and David E. Bell. (*U. S. Navy, Courtesy Harry S. Truman Library*)

Press Secretary Joseph H. Short briefs the White House press corps on the dismissal of General Douglas MacArthur, 1 A.M., April 11, 1951. (*Acme Newspictures—UPI*)

Truman staff relaxing at Key West. Standing, from left: Dr. John R. Steelman, Richard E. Neustadt, Donald S. Dawson, Milton P. Kayle, Russell P. Andrews. Seated, from left: Ken Hechler, Dallas C. Halverstadt, Major General Harry H. Vaughan, the President, David M. Noyes. (*Paul Begley, Courtesy Harry S. Truman Library*)

Part of the crowd of 5,000 that greeted the President at Crestline, Ohio, on September 1, 1952. Mingling with the crowd during a presidential whistle-stop speech was one of the author's favorite chores (see tall, bespectacled figure in center of photo). (*Courtesy of D. K. Woodman, Editor Emeritus, Mansfield News-Journal*)

Aboard 1952 campaign train. A speech strategy session with the President, Charles S. Murphy, David D. Lloyd and Matthew J. Connelly. (*Wide World Photos*)

began to solicit from the departments their own recommendations for legislation. Occasionally, as with the Point Four program, the initiative came exclusively from the White House over the objections of the department involved. Only high-priority items would be included in the President's legislative program. Other departmental recommendations, not significant enough to be packaged with the "President's program," still had to be cleared with the White House for their budgetary implications. Jones observed:

> The key to what I consider to be the outstanding success of the whole operation was the availability of the White House staff. Almost any issue could be taken there, some of them calling for the development of legislation. . . . Through Mr. Murphy's intervention, and with the president's full support, we were able to move anywhere in the White House in the developmental process.[26]

Staats added:

> Given the close adjunct relationship which this function had with the special counsel's office (first Mr. Clifford and then Mr. Murphy), we were never quite sure who we were working for, the budget director or the counsel, but that didn't really make too much difference. The only time that the budget director said we had to come and check with him was if a very large amount of money was involved; otherwise we went ahead and worked with Clark Clifford and Charlie Murphy.[27]

Starting in 1948, the Budget Bureau took the initiative in helping to draft administration bills. This frequently involved assembling teams of experts around the conference table to coordinate the development of important legislation involving differing interests or agencies. Under this procedure a working team from the Executive Office, usually including the Budget Bureau's Legislative Reference Division, hammered out the details of legislation. The Housing Act of 1949 and the Social Security Act Amendments of 1950 were drafted in this fashion.[28] As new Executive Office agencies like the National Security Resources Board and the Office of Defense Mobilization were established, they too took the lead on occasion.

My Contacts with Capitol Hill

President Truman's successful 1948 campaign had brought a number of young, liberal Democrats along to victory on his coattails. There was a new spirit in the Eighty-first Congress, which seemed destined to enact many of the measures on which the President had been rebuffed by the Eightieth Congress. Among new House members with whom I worked closely were Richard Bolling of Missouri and Sidney R. Yates of Illinois. John A. Carroll of Colorado had been one of the three Democrats in the nation to replace a Republican in 1946, and I got to know him even better. These three Congressmen and others frequently commented on how poorly they felt the President's liaison with Congress was operating. They were critical of Colonel Maylon, the President's liaison with the House, who did little to push the President's program.

As time went on, I began to expand my contacts with House and Senate members and their staffs. I got the same comments from the Senate about the low quality of White House congressional liaison. There was a thirst for new ideas, a desire to check developments with knowledgeable people in the White House, and a reluctance to disturb the President to test emerging strategy. Legislators frequently expressed a low opinion of the Democratic National Committee's failure to supply more than a few slogans and wisecracks to clarify issues. Some of Truman's restless supporters on Capitol Hill felt that he and the Democratic party were somehow letting them down, because they needed facts and figures to back up his program. Often all they could obtain from federal departments was gobbledegook or dense circumlocutions. I spent a lot of time after 1950 meeting with House and Senate contacts at luncheons or in small groups, at both the White House and the Capitol. I also started a small mailing list to send them background research materials.

Missouri Congressional Relations

Like most party leaders, one of the President's cardinal rules was to stay out of party primaries. But he frequently made an exception in his home state of Missouri. He made no secret of his disappointment with two-term Democratic Representative Roger C. Slaughter, an opponent of President Truman's policies, representing Truman's home district. At his July 18, 1946, news conference, the President stated, "As a member of the Rules Committee, Mr. Slaughter has been opposed to everything that I have asked the Congress to do" in 1945 and 1946.[29] He acknowledged that he had conferred with Kansas City leader James M. Pendergast, and "I don't think Mr. Pendergast is going to be for Mr. Slaughter." The organization succeeded in replacing Slaughter in the August 1946 Democratic primary with Enos Axtell, but Axtell was defeated in the

Republican landslide in November. Although the President was chagrined that the seat went Republican, he was glad to be rid of Slaughter, who had cast the deciding vote in the House Rules Committee against Truman's efforts to establish the Fair Employment Practices Committee, a key point in his civil rights program. He explained privately to Pendergast his bitterness because Slaughter had gone back on his word, the violation of a sacred obligation in Truman's eyes:

> He has become insufferable to the Administration, because of his actions as a member of the powerful Rules Committee of the House. He owes his position on that Committee to me. After giving Speaker Rayburn and myself unqualified assurance that he would go along without question on Administration measures Rayburn appointed him to the Committee. That happened while I was in the Senate.
>
> After I came to the White House, Slaughter again assured me that he would cooperate. The meanest partisan Republican has been no more anti-Truman than has Slaughter.[30]

But the unseating of Slaughter had its repercussions. The *Kansas City Star* discovered some suspiciously lopsided precincts where the totals seemed to point to corrupt practices by the Pendergast machine. Although there were only a few minor violations uncovered, the reaction probably helped elect a Republican Representative in 1946.

Another home-state thorn in Truman's side was Missouri Republican Senator Forrest C. Donnell, elected in 1944 after Truman ran for Vice-President. A bookish, precise lawyer, Donnell irked the President by his self-righteous speeches. When Truman nominated his friend Robert Hannegan as postmaster general, Donnell talked for two hours, denouncing Hannegan as a crooked politician. Although the Senate confirmed Hannegan by a 60–2 vote, Truman took Donnell's remarks personally.

When Donnell came up for reelection in 1950, Truman tried to unite the Democrats behind the ranking member of Missouri's State Senate, Emery W. Allison. "I know Emery Allison very well," he told a 1950 news conference. "I like him, and I think he would make a wonderful United States Senator from Missouri."[31]

Several months before the Missouri Democratic primary in August 1950, the President tried to give a further boost to his candidate Allison. He wrote a note asking for a compilation of Senator Donnell's "more asinine" speeches and statements. I got the assignment. Donnell was a good friend of mine. Prior to entering politics, he had dined at our home on several occasions. My father, who graduated from and then taught animal husbandry at the University of Missouri, was a contemporary of Donnell at the university. On a number of occasions, he had interrupted his duties as a senator to receive groups of students I brought to Washington while teaching at Princeton.

It took me about two seconds to decide where my loyalties were in this conflict. I spent many evening hours examining Missouri newspapers at the Library of Congress, researching every reported speech and statement he had made, combing the *Congressional Record* and the files at the *Congressional Quarterly* building for examples of his obstructionist tendencies. This was not too difficult, for Donnell was something of a backward isolationist who fought against such measures as the establishment of the North Atlantic Treaty Organization. When the research was completed in mid-June 1950, I pulled it all together in a punchy speech draft. In August, Allison was nosed out by Thomas C. Hennings, Jr., for the Democratic senatorial nomination, at which point I immediately sent the same material to Hennings, who unseated Donnell in the November general election.

Research Ammunition for Democrats

After the Korean outbreak, we began to prod the State and Defense departments to turn out affirmative fact sheets on foreign policy and defense. At the White House, I compiled voting records, excerpts from speeches, debating points on specific issues, and challenging questions to ask Republicans, to forward to Democratic candidates. I became sort of a clearinghouse for this material, especially after the closing weeks of September 1950. The National Committee argued that the Republicans had won the 1946 elections primarily with their slogan "Had Enough? Vote Republican!" And the Committee argued that the Democrats had won in 1948 through President Truman's effective attacks on the Eightieth Congress rather than "dry, factual material." Therefore, they reasoned that the way to win in 1950 was to keep it simple. We agreed that congressional candidates should not just spout dry statistics, yet we argued that Truman had more than slogans at his disposal in 1948, that the National Committee was a logical source for such ammunition and thus that the Research Division should be revived. But the National Committee continued to drag its feet.

I produced, mimeographed, and distributed a number of special spot studies to meet congressional inquiries. Two of these were "The Facts

on Demobilization" and "Lest We Forget"—the former a compilation
of President Truman's efforts to extend selective service and establish
universal military training, with a collection of quotations from leading
Republicans like Taft, Dewey and MacArthur, pressing for quicker demobilization of our armed forces after World War II, and the latter a
collection of friendly and supportive statements about the Soviet Union
made by prominent Republicans during World War II. Although these
documents may not have swung any elections, a number of congressional candidates indicated that they used the ammunition effectively
when charged with weakening our defenses or being "soft" on communism.

An Analysis of the 1950 Election

Certainly events in Korea dictated the results of the 1950 elections more than did research materials. The high tide of popularity that
President Truman enjoyed immediately after his successful May cross-
country trip to the Northwest was quickly dissipated as the reality of
war was brought home to more Americans. The President did not make
any more extended campaign trips in 1950, although he made a windup
address in St. Louis, where once again he stated that any farmer who
voted for the Republican party ought to have his head examined.[32]
He explained that the international situation precluded his going on a
whistle-stop tour. The Democrats suffered a net loss of twenty-eight
seats in the House and five in the Senate, including that of Majority
Leader Lucas of Illinois.

Right after the 1950 election, the President asked me for an analysis,
by congressional districts and economic groups, of what had happened
and what issues had predominated. After collecting a vast amount of
material, and through letters and telephone calls to congressional candidates and political leaders, I concluded that while the defeat was serious, it was not as bad as portrayed. In his news conference on November
16, 1950, the President commented: "You want to bear in mind that this
is an off-year election and it is the smallest loss for the party in power
since 1916, with the exception of 1934, so I don't think there is anything
to be very blue about. At least, I'm not blue."[33]

The same day Lloyd wrote a memorandum to Murphy stating:

Ken Hechler has made a very good start, it seems to me, on analyzing the
1950 election returns. His first analysis confirms the general impression that

we lost in the cities and urban areas. I think intensive research ought to be continued on this angle until we find out what actually did happen in the cities.

While a good deal could be done through phone calls, talks with candidates, and studies of the figures that are available in Washington, I don't believe that a complete answer could be produced unless an investigation is made on the spot. I think that Ken Hechler ought to make a field trip, going to a selected number of the big city areas, talking there with the Party leaders and the leaders of the labor political organizations, going over their figures, interviewing precinct workers, etc. . . . He could take about three days apiece in Chicago, Pittsburgh, Baltimore, Los Angeles and Denver.[34]

Although this sounded like an interesting trip, I was not convinced it would change any conclusions. The urban losses occurred in heavily Catholic areas, disturbed by McCarthy's charges and by reaction to local corruption issues stirred by Senator Kefauver's investigations. There was a low turnout in labor-dominated urban areas, where jealousies developed between local labor and Democratic organizations. The mid-term election was a preview of the 1952 defeat for the Democratic party, when the Republicans successfully capitalized on the issues of "Korea, corruption and communism." I pointed out that through frequent public appearances the President had attempted to explain our presence in Korea, but "there is no great, unified, patriotic emotion which would accompany an all-out war against our main enemy. The people do not fully understand how much better off they are than if this should develop into an all-out war. The administration has not succeeded as well as it should in convincing the people, in simple terms, of the rightness of the course we are pursuing." I also noted that city casualty lists seemed to have a cumulative, adverse effect, that reserve units taken from certain cities made a dent, that residents of some cities even felt more vulnerable to atomic attack, and that McCarthyism's virus spread more rapidly in urban Democratic areas. The AMA proved a potent political force in attacking "socialized medicine," as did the organized attacks in the Middle West against the "Brannan Plan" for agriculture.

I put in a further plug for a favorite idea when I stated that "the 1950 campaign underlines the need for an aggressive research division at the National Committee. The story of our foreign policy was not sufficiently understood by the voters."

I guess there was a selfish reason why I discouraged Lloyd's efforts to have me make major political probes in a field report. Working for President Truman was a political scientist's dream. I loved the people I was working for and with and savored the thrill of taking part in a great program whose ramifications were worldwide. The last thing I wanted was to get typed as a "political analyst" who worked exclusively with politicians instead of with the entire breadth of government activity. Fortunately, I heard no more of the proposed trip.

Prospects for 1951 and the New Congress

Despite his brave performance at his November 16 news conference, Truman was privately discouraged over the prospects for the new Congress. He complained that he had a majority,

> made up of Republicans and recalcitrant Southern "Democrats"—who are not Democrats. So I get the responsibility and the blame. There are liars, trimmers and pussyfooters on both sides of the aisle in the Senate and the House. I'm sorry. I wish I had straight out opposition and loyal support. I guess it is too much to ask for![35]

On the same day he was penning these pessimistic comments, the President held a disastrous news conference. Reporters' questions led him to make dangerous comments that he was considering use of the atomic bomb in Korea, and made it appear that this might even be a tactical decision by military commanders in the field rather than by the President. The press interpretation clearly indicated that the President had been caught off guard by the questions, and the headlines reverberated across the Atlantic as a shocked Prime Minister Attlee flew to Washington for clarification. To add to the difficulty there were serious setbacks in Korea. The President had told his November 28 staff meeting: "We've got a terrific situation on our hands. General Bradley told me that a terrible message had come from General MacArthur. MacArthur said there were 260,000 Chinese troops against him out there."[36]

Relations with the New Congress

With the convening of the Eighty-second Congress, Capitol Hill buzzed with controversy over the President's clear-cut statement in his January 4 news conference that he had the constitutional authority to send additional American troops to Europe without congressional approval. The President elaborated on his constitutional powers in subsequent statements, also indicating that he would continue to consult Congress. These statements set off a "Great Debate" in Congress over the President's powers as commander in chief. Interestingly enough, the troops were being sent to strengthen General Eisenhower's command in Europe. One wing of the Republican party was already looking forward to drafting Eisenhower as the 1952 GOP standard-bearer. Eisenhower's chief rival for the nomination, Taft, attacked the President's interpretation of the Constitution on the grounds he lacked authority to send troops without congressional approval. On the White House staff, Lloyd took the lead in mustering constitutional arguments to support the President's authority.

The Eighty-second Congress convened in an atmosphere of Republican elation over election victories. A new senator from California named Richard M. Nixon was sworn in, fresh from a triumph over Representative Helen Gahagan Douglas in a dirty campaign during which Nixon charged his opponent with being soft on communism and linked her votes on such issues as public housing with those of communist sympathizer Vito Marcantonio. Equally unscrupulous tactics were used to defeat Maryland Senator Millard Tydings, including the doctoring of a photograph to make it appear that Tydings was friendly with communist leader Earl Browder.

Increasingly preoccupied with international developments, the President continued to use his limited time for congressional relations by meetings of the Big Four (with Arizona Senator Ernest McFarland, after 1951 the majority leader, replacing defeated Senator Lucas), personal conferences and telephone calls.

Following the President's order relieving General MacArthur of his command on April 11, 1951, I received a telephone call from Denver, from John A. Carroll, who had served two terms in the House of Representatives before making an unsuccessful race for the Senate in 1950. Carroll told me that people in the mountain states, while encouraged by the dramatic reaffirmation of the President's exercise of civilian control over the military, nevertheless felt the need for more action in areas relating to the economy. He said he would like to come to Washington to help the President, particularly in alerting members of Congress concerning both the MacArthur issue and inflation problems. A "Memorandum for the President" included the following:

John Carroll telephoned from Denver and asked that you be informed that the people of the entire mountain region are stirred by your courageous move. Above and beyond any personal issue, it has awakened the people there to an excited discussion of world problems, and the necessity of rallying to the support of every effort toward world peace. The Denver *Post* is doing a magnificent job in helping follow up on the issue which the President has crystallized.

Carroll added that he would like to return to Washington to assist the President, Bill Boyle or Speaker Rayburn to mobilize sentiment in this vital situation. Carroll feels that a great deal can be done by (1) talking with members of Congress and keeping them fully informed and alerted on which issues to stress; (2) helping the National Committee to have a more active relationship with Congress.[37]

Carroll's call could not have come at a more timely moment. The President felt keenly that his program was in trouble on Capitol Hill, and that a storm of public opposition would arise from his action in firing a popular general. He knew that it would require a major effort to get the facts to Truman supporters in Congress and throughout the nation. Murphy argued convincingly that the weak congressional liaison operation was insufficient to handle the impending firestorm over MacArthur's dismissal. Elsey and other members of the staff, particularly press secretary Short and his assistant Tubby, echoed Murphy's argument. Although Carroll was the kind of ideological liberal who in prior years might have roused presidential opposition, the President recognized that Carroll had a record of strong Truman support. Furthermore, he checked out very well with Secretary of the Interior Chapman, also from Denver. The President made an immediate decision to ask Carroll to come in to help.

When staff members or other federal employees are considered for positions, it usually takes weeks before the necessary civil service and other clearances can be accomplished and they can start work. Carroll's employment probably set a speed record in cutting red tape. As soon as I got the President's favorable reaction, two days after MacArthur's dismissal, I telephoned Carroll and told him to pack his bags and take the next plane to Washington. Then, on April 16, Murphy sent this note to the President: "John Carroll is coming in today for a 'trial run' of about two weeks. It is proposed that he be assigned to the job of coordinating the efforts of the Executive Branch in getting the facts concerning General MacArthur before the Congress."[38]

Carroll was a self-starter. From the minute he was installed in the spacious Executive Office Building office once occupied by World War I commander General John J. Pershing, he began a series of conferences and phone calls with State and Defense officials and members of Congress. He fitted in quickly with the White House staff, and his experience proved helpful in clarifying many legislative problems facing the President.

Truman liked Carroll, invited him to attend some staff and cabinet meetings, and encouraged him to broaden his work beyond the Mac-Arthur issue to cover inflation and stabilization of the economy, as well as other special issues confronting Congress. Carroll and others encouraged the President to hold a series of evening meetings with House and Senate members at Blair House, for free-wheeling discussions of the President's legislative program. He proved especially helpful in these meetings, because he had the knack of pulling a rambling discussion by legislators sharply into focus.

About a month after Carroll's arrival, Murphy was so pleased with his success that he felt it was time to make Carroll a permanent member of the White House staff. Murphy advised the President that Carroll might be designated as an "administrative assistant." He suggested:

> I would think that it might be well for him to have some kind of charter to see that the National Committee does an effective job of helping and supporting our friends in Congress. I think that this is going to require a major addition to the National Committee's staff before it is ever done on a proper basis.[39]

During this period, I had been helping Carroll in his contacts with Congress and the National Committee, as well as continuing with the production of special political research studies. Of course, it was personally gratifying to know that since 1950 I had been doing a lot of the work accomplished by six professional staffers in the National Committee's research division in 1948. Nevertheless, I felt that exclusively political work should not be done on the federal payroll, neither in the departments nor in the White House, and should more properly be undertaken on a full-time basis at the National Committee. Carroll too had other interests. He was looking forward to another try for the Senate in 1954 (he failed in 1954, but succeeded in 1956), and was anxious to get away and mend his fences in Colorado. Therefore, an arrangement was worked out to retain Carroll as a "consultant."

An illustration of the kind of back-up work I was doing appeared in a memorandum I wrote to Murphy:

I had dinner last evening with Emil Rieve (Textile Workers) at Max Kampelman's house and I needled him repeatedly about labor's apathy in connection with the Defense Production Act. As usual, Rieve ranted and roared about the way the 1950 act had been administered, and showed little disposition to get his troops over-excited about strengthening the present act. We engaged in a first-class yelling match and over and over I posed these questions: When is the labor movement going to get out and fight? What better issue than stabilization can they fight for? When is everybody going to look to the future and stop raising recriminations about the past?

Beneath his roars, Rieve showed that labor is still deeply disturbed and resentful about Wilson [Charles E. Wilson of General Electric, Director of Defense Mobilization], about excess profits tax loopholes and the developments of the past 6 months. The fighting spirit just isn't there.

I believe it is important to get labor thinking about the future. The President's time and energy is limited, but labor is such a vital force when it fights enthusiastically that an early Blair House session with leading labor men might pay dividends.[40]

The President did arrange the labor meeting at Blair House for July 10, including Rieve among those invited. The session stimulated labor to a clearer understanding of its stake in the President's program, as well as helping labor to arouse its friends on Capitol Hill.

During the balance of 1951, and in the early months of 1952, Carroll effectively beefed up White House congressional relations. He gave that operation a more realistic and more effective issue-oriented direction, rather than the haphazard head-counting and hand-holding that had characterized the Feeney-Maylon operation. Carroll's work with the National Committee only spotlighted the glaring deficiencies that the White House staff had already spotted and tried repeatedly to correct.

National Committee Research Division

Lloyd summarized his own conclusions about Chairman Boyle and the National Committee, after working in the 1948 research division:

1. Bill Boyle has taken affront on this whole research division question, and made it a matter of his personal tenure as Chairman.
2. Boyle is the Chairman, and has the President's confidence.
3. We should avoid further aggravation of the situation. Therefore, I believe:
    1. We should not pester the Committee any more about research.
    2. We should have as little to do with them as politely possible.

3. We should lay the foundations for getting our own research done for us through some other means—so we are ready for '52.
4. We should peddle stuff direct to the Hill where necessary.[41]

Later in 1951, Boyle's reputation was tarnished by Senate hearings revealing that his law firm had received fees in connection with an RFC loan to the American Lithofold Corporation. He resigned as National Committee chairman in the fall of 1951, and on October 31, 1951, he was replaced by Frank McKinney, an Indianapolis banker.

Not until the campaign of 1952 loomed ominously over the horizon did the National Committee finally move to set up a full-time and well-staffed research division, under Bertram M. Gross, who had been executive director of the President's Council of Economic Advisers. From that point on, my own work shifted to the more appropriate task of helping to coordinate departmental input into issues material being prepared by the National Committee. I also acted as White House liaison with Capitol Hill and other Washington personnel developing campaign materials or formulating strategy for the campaign. This activity involved organizing or participating in a series of dinner meetings, usually attended by about twenty to thirty people, to discuss strategy and issues.

As an illustration of the contacts I built up with a large number of House and Senate members, excerpts follow from letters and memos to and concerning Missouri Representative Bolling, who had a lively Town Hall debate on communism with Republican Representative Charles J. Kersten of Wisconsin on October 2, 1951:

September 27, 1951

Dear Dick:

Attached are copies of the Civil Service Commission's annual reports, which give brief official descriptions of the nature and the progress of the Loyalty Program. Attached also is a copy of a speech by the Honorable Hiram Bingham, Chairman of the Loyalty Review Board, which contains some useful material despite its endorsement by people with whom you and I may not agree. Attached also is a copy of a speech by Robert Ramspeck which contains some useful suggestions. I think you will be interested in the President's American Legion speech, which deals with the subject and I am attaching a copy.

September 28, 1951

Dear Dick:

In connection with your Town Meeting, you may be interested in the attached advance copy of a speech by Burton L. French of the Loyalty Review Board. Mr. French will not deliver this address until October 11th, and it was with great difficulty that I obtained an advance copy.

I am sure that you will respect the confidential nature of this document in advance of its delivery, but there is no reason in the world why you should not use the figures or the substance of the material, without reference to Mr. French or the occasion of the speech.

October 3, 1951

Dear Dick:

I listened to your Town Meeting performance last night, and I want to congratulate you on a magnificent job. You are probably the first person on this or any program who received a round of applause after the very first sentence of your remarks. I think you were on top from the opening gun and, as can be expected, Kersten dodged most of the direct issues.

June 26, 1952

MEMORANDUM FOR MR. MURPHY:

Dick Bolling called to say that he had heard some talk among northern liberals about opposing the Defense Production Bill on final passage, because of the fact the stabilization sections had been shot full of holes. Bolling feels very strongly that this would be a tragic mistake, on account of having the production titles of the bill enacted. He hopes that no Administration encouragement will be given to opposing the entire bill, and that the President will support the bill because there is no better alternative.[42]

The President did sign the Defense Production Act Amendments on June 30, 1952, along with a statement condemning the many shortcomings of the bill. When Murphy joined the White House staff, he encouraged the President to include analytical statements when he signed legislation, clarifying the specific intent of certain sections to aid the courts in future interpretation, and indicating those sections to which he was opposed.

September 6, 1952

Dear Dick:

Since Congress left town, I have been neglecting to send out copies of the President's speeches, and I am glad that you jogged me on it. Attached is a set of the President's speeches on his recent trip to Milwaukee. I was lucky enough to tag along on this trip, and the results were terrific.

I am not developing very many independent materials here, because I am routing everything I have to Bert Gross, and I assume that you are latching on to the good things the Research Division is producing. Their campaign handbook will be out next week. I think that you should also get a copy of the excellent CIO publication called "A Speaker's Book of Facts," which has just been put out.

As you know, the President hopes to make a speech in your area on the swing back from his trip through Montana and the Northwest early in October.[43]

Measured by the standards of other administrations, President Truman's machinery for congressional relations left much to be desired. His major political successes were scored by attacking the Republican Eightieth Congress on domestic issues and winning the bipartisan support necessary to achieve major foreign policy goals. On the home front, his advanced positions on medical care, education, housing, civil rights and civil liberties remained a beacon of inspiration for the future. Yet it is unfortunate that the Truman White House staff was not better equipped to help the President lead Congress on many of the key issues that concerned the President and the nation.

10

Korea, Communism and Corruption: MacArthur, McCarthy and McGrath

The constitutional issue of civilian control over the military, MacArthur's repeated refusal to obey orders not to release foreign policy statements, his public insistence on the superior wisdom of using Nationalist Chinese troops on Formosa to join in attacking the Chinese mainland, his belligerent March 24, 1951, message that torpedoed the President's delicate effort to negotiate a cease-fire in Korea—all these factors contributed to MacArthur's recall.

In his *Memoirs*, the President indicates that the key factor in his decision to dismiss MacArthur was the latter's March 24 message, threatening the Communist Chinese with military annihilation, at a time when Washington was trying to get a cease-fire. "It was in open defiance of my orders as President and as Commander in Chief. This was a challenge to the authority of the President under the Constitution," wrote Truman.[1]

General MacArthur's Defiance of the Commander in Chief

It seems more probable that the final decision was not made until House Republican Leader Joseph W. Martin, Jr., read a message from MacArthur to the House of Representatives on April 5. MacArthur was responding to and commenting on a blatantly political message from Martin, which included the statement, "If we are not in Korea to win, then the Truman administration should be indicted for the murder of thousands of American boys." In his answer, MacArthur congratulated Martin on his statement and added "you have certainly lost none of your old-time punch." He renewed his argument for using Chinese Nationalist troops, and pooh-poohed those who felt it important to be concerned with the communist threat in Europe: "Here we fight Europe's war with arms while the diplomats there still fight it with words."

Assistant press secretary Tubby rushed into the President's office shortly after 3:00 P.M. on April 5, with the United Press news ticker outlining Martin's speech quoting MacArthur. The President was reading General Omar Bradley's book, *A Soldier's Story*. The President seemed unconcerned at first, passing it off as "more politics," and indicating that "the newspaper boys are putting him up to this." As he returned to his book, Tubby blurted: "Mr. President, this man is not only insubordinate, but he's insolent, and I think he ought to be fired." The President picked up the ticker sheet again and read it, as though for the first time, and said firmly: "By God, Roger, I think you're right."[2]

Next day, the President wrote in his diary that the Martin speech "looks like the last straw."[3] He reviewed another example of "rank insubordination" by MacArthur—his message of the preceding summer to the Veterans of Foreign Wars (pressing for use of Nationalist Chinese troops on Formosa), a message that the President had ordered withdrawn.

At this point, the President called in his principal advisers, including Harriman, Marshall, Bradley and Acheson. He revealed on April 6: "I've come to the conclusion that our Big General in the Far East must be recalled. I don't express any opinion or make known my decision."[4]

The same team met with the President again at the week's end, and the President reported, "It is the unanimous opinion of all that MacArthur be relieved. All four so advise." Marshall was particularly outspoken. After having read the entire Defense Department file on MacArthur, he commented: "The S.O.B. should have been fired two years ago."[5] Harriman had already reached that conclusion.[6]

On Monday, April 9, the President went over his recall orders to MacArthur with the same four advisers, reviewed a suggested public statement, and decided to ask Secretary of the Army Frank Pace, who was on an inspection tour in Korea, to take the recall orders to Tokyo and deliver them personally to MacArthur before he heard about the action through the news media or other sources.[7] Unfortunately, this courtesy backfired because Pace was at the front when the orders arrived, and did not get the message in time.

Staff Meeting

On Tuesday, April 10, the President told his staff what had occurred. He expressed his feeling that MacArthur wanted to be fired. Certainly his repeated violations of clear directives indicated either that the President was right, or that MacArthur had concluded the President would not dare remove him. The press picked up this theme. On April 10 *The Washington Post* screamed: "MACARTHUR RECALL RULED OUT BY PRESIDENT, 'HILL' HEARS." Cartoonist Herblock, frequently in President Truman's corner, ran a cruel cartoon depicting "Captain Harry Truman" shaking with fright as he slept on his World War I army cot, too scared of a five-star general to exercise his responsibilities as Commander in Chief. The President's remarks indicated that he planned to act, regardless of the consequences.

The night of April 10 was hectic at the White House. It had been planned to prepare the presidential statements, with supporting documents, in an orderly fashion for release on April 11 after Pace had informed MacArthur of the action. Harriman and his counsel Theodore Tannenwald, Jr., Connelly, Murphy and his staff, press secretary Short and his assistant Tubby, Acheson and his assistant secretary of state Dean Rusk, Bradley and several others worked on the statement. About 6:00 P.M., the President went across the street to Blair House for dinner, as the others continued their work while sandwiches were sent in. Tannenwald, mindful of the public outcry that would follow the action, urged that "the statement should contain a reference to the fact that the President was doing this on the unanimous consent of his principal military and civilian advisers."[8] Murphy and others rejected this reference, on the ground that it would confuse the central point, which was that the President was making the decision on constitutional grounds.

The Chicago Tribune *"Leak"*

Now a strange twist upset the orderly scenario. Just before 7:00 P.M., Walter Trohan of the *Chicago Tribune* received a telephone call from his managing editor that there was a rumor circulating in Japan that there would be an "important resignation." Trohan went to the White House, where Short responded, "There's nothing to it." Tubby got a call from the *Tribune*'s Pentagon correspondent, then a call from the Mutual Broadcasting System in New York with the identical information. He answered that he "didn't know what it could be," but he was convinced there was a big leak.[9] Over at the Pentagon, excited aides alerted Bradley when they received the same information. Acheson was in Georgetown persuading John Foster Dulles to go to Tokyo and reassure the Japanese there would be no change in our Far Eastern policy. This made Rusk the senior State Department official at the White House. A heated debate ensued whether, if the rumor were true, it would mean MacArthur would resign with an impassioned blast at the President. Always cool under fire, Murphy argued against making a precipitous move to change the timetable.

Despite Short's denial, Trohan decided to write his story anyhow. Then he received another phone call from his managing editor, stating: "Forget that MacArthur tip. We've checked this source in Tokyo, and it turns out the fellow doesn't know what he's talking about."[10] Trohan tore his story out of his typewriter. He didn't think it important enough to tell Short of the second call, but by this time the rumor had ricocheted back and forth in the White House as everybody heard it repeated. About 9:00 P.M., the President recalled, "General Bradley came rushing over to Blair House. He had heard, he said, that the story had leaked out and that a Chicago newspaper was going to print it the next morning."[11] Harriman, Rusk, and Murphy came to Blair House to see the President. Bradley urged that MacArthur not be allowed to outmaneuver the President by resigning. "He's going to be fired," the President replied grimly. The staff reassembled in the Cabinet Room, now facing a frantic deadline as pressure mounted to get the statement with supporting documents frozen, mimeographed, and out to reporters who had not yet been notified there would be an announcement that night. Endless minutiae had to be telescoped into a short period. Extra telephone operators had to be summoned late at night in anticipation of the flood of telephone calls that would certainly jam the White House switchboard.

The President returned to the Cabinet Room for the customary "freezing session." Tannenwald tried again to persuade him to indicate the approval of the military and civilian advisers. "I am taking this decision on my own responsibility as president of the United States, and I want nobody to think I am sharing it with anybody else," Truman answered.[12]

Why the Announcement Came at 1:00 A.M.

In order to release the President's statement prior to MacArthur's supposed resignation, the White House correspondents were summoned for a 1:00 A.M. news conference. When the news was flashed around the world, the circumstances were initially very shocking. No official word came to MacArthur until an aide heard it in a radio newscast. He had no opportunity to break the news to his troops with a farewell message. The opposition in Congress was emotional. Why did it have to be done in the middle of the night? Senator McCarthy charged that "treason in the White House" resulted from the President's being plied with "bourbon and benedictine."

Lincoln and McClellan

The President had asked that I prepare an analysis of the relations between President Lincoln and General George B. McClellan. When I started this, I wasn't sure what it was designed to prove. I missed the excitement at the White House, because I was hiding in the Library of Congress stacks long after closing time, researching Carl Sandburg and other biographers of Lincoln and McClellan. The memorandum was in the President's hands early the next morning.[13] I discovered that the President had put his finger on a striking historical analogy, which he was adept at doing. I documented that McClellan was a brilliant, egotistical field commander who felt his Commander in Chief was a crude, ignorant and uncouth Middle Westerner with no appreciation for military strategy, at which McClellan was a self-acknowledged expert. Repeatedly McClellan ignored President Lincoln's orders, the only difference from 1951 being that Lincoln felt McClellan was going too slowly, while Truman feared MacArthur might start a land war with both China and the Soviet Union by attacking Manchuria. Like MacArthur, McClellan had political ambitions, and actually ran against Lincoln in the 1864 presidential election. When McClellan disobeyed a direct order from Lincoln to advance, pleading his horses were fatigued, Lincoln telegraphed: "Will you pardon me for asking what the horses of your army have done since the battle of Antietam that fatigues anything?"[14]

Finally, on November 5, 1862, the President relieved McClellan of command of the Army of the Potomac. *The New York Times* on November 10 editorialized that "at the hotels, crowds have been discussing the subject, and occasionally the feelings of some have found expression in language disrespectful to the President and disloyal [to] the Government. It is certain that Mr. Lincoln never performed a duty which gave him so much pain as did the removal of McClellan just at this time."

On the front cover of my study, I placed this quotation from Sandburg's biography of Lincoln:

> Gen. McClellan occasionally made political statements on non-military matters. President Lincoln was once asked what he would reply to Gen. McClellan's advice on how to carry on the affairs of the Nation. President Lincoln answered: "Nothing—but it made me think of the man whose horse kicked up and stuck his foot through the stirrup. He said to the horse, 'If you are going to get on I will get off.' "

In numerous informal conversations and speeches to small groups, President Truman cited the analogies between MacArthur and McClellan. In his *Memoirs*, the President wrote that during this trying period, "I reflected on the similarities in the situation that had faced Abraham Lincoln in his efforts to deal with General McClellan." Then he repeated the story about the horse sticking his foot through the stirrup.[15]

Once again, Truman showed that his knowledge of history was not confined to a series of dates and events. He grasped the essence of broad trends, knew how to separate wheat from the chaff, and had an instinct for the heart of any subject.

"Belt Him a Couple for Me, Roger"

On the night the President relieved MacArthur, he slept soundly, as always. Others on the White House staff weren't as lucky. Tubby stayed on duty until the last reporter left, about 3:00 A.M., and then collapsed on a couch in the Secret Service office in the west wing. He was awakened only three hours later when James Rowley, Chief of the White House Secret Service detail, was moving around, getting ready for the President's early morning walk and other activities.[16] Tubby walked along the portico between the west wing and the Mansion, pausing at the small "gymnasium," where he got a surprise: "I went into the gym to try to clear the cobwebs out of my brain; and as I was punching a heavy bag I heard a familiar chuckle behind me, and Mr. Truman said, 'Belt him a couple for me, Roger.' "[17]

At the morning staff meeting, the President commented: "I discovered my press man over here punching the bag this morning after sleeping on a couch in the secret service room. Roger, you should have come across the street. I've got some colorful pyjamas, and there are at least fourteen beds over there!"[18]

Another assistant in the press office, Irving Perlmeter, recalled, "He was so sincere about it and it was such an unlikely thing for anybody to do that everybody thought it was quite a joke."[19]

Press secretary Short summarized the press reaction to the momentous events. It was hostile to the President. At breakfast at a restaurant on Pennsylvania Avenue, Tubby heard angry comments. One man referred to the attempt on Truman's life the preceding November and said, "It's too bad those Puerto Ricans didn't get him!" Another said, "At least he ought to be impeached!"[20] Short told the morning staff meeting that most of the telegrams that had come in during the night were condemnatory. The President replied: "When I was a Senator, I once received several thousand such telegrams. I burned them all up. I'm not surprised by this reaction."[21] Tubby recalls:

> There were bushel baskets of telegrams, overwhelmingly against the President. I remember picking up a bunch of those telegrams and just holding them up, not saying what was in them, and the President said, "See that fireplace over there, Roger? Go put them in there and set a match to them. The American people will come to understand that what I did had to be done. Now, what's next on the agenda?"[22]

April 11 Address to the Nation

There was little rest on April 11 for the speech-writing staff, as the President prepared to address the nation that evening. It was a broad speech, which explained once again why we were in Korea and the importance of standing firm against the spread of aggressive communism in both Europe and the Far East, while at the same time trying to prevent a third world war. Not until the end of the radio report did he mention MacArthur, explaining simply and clearly that MacArthur did not agree with a consistent policy aimed against broadening the conflict in the Far East. One small incident illustrates the President's mood during this period. Having finished work on the speech he was about to deliver at 10:30 P.M., the President found he had a little over half an hour before he was to go on the air. Under these circumstances, the average individual would probably have nervously fingered his speech draft and practiced his delivery and points of emphasis. Instead, the President went into correspondence secretary Hassett's office, purposefully moved some books from a sofa, curled up and within a minute or two was sound asleep.[23] He awoke, refreshed, and went into the Oval Office to address the nation.

It is difficult to overestimate the emotional wave of bitter opposition that first greeted President Truman's decision. Of the first thirteen thousand letters and telegrams reaching the White House, executive clerk Hopkins noted the ratio was running about two to one against the President.[24] The wires ranged from the mild epithet "little ward politician" to such terms as "red herring," "imbecile" and "Judas." A Hearst newspaper, the *New York Journal-American*, suggested the President had been drugged by the State Department. "The happiest group in the country will be the communists and their stooges," cried Senator Nixon.

In one of the many analyses I prepared for Carroll to brief him on the MacArthur issue, I was slightly chagrined to discover some years later that I unwittingly used the phrase "dirty tricks," which came to prominence during the Nixon Watergate fiasco. In relaying to Carroll what the National Committee was planning to do, I mentioned, among many other items,

> some miscellaneous work on MacArthur materials which may be useful if the debate ever reaches the "dirty tricks" stage. For example, Van Devander, in cooperation with Representative Pat Sutton, is having the Signal Corps dig out the photographs of the wading ashore at Leyte. These photographs, when pieced together, show the wading ashore was done in the face of a barrage of newsreel cameras, while on the edge of the photographs are a number of engineers and other service troops landing dry on a solidly-constructed pier. I have my doubts about the usefulness of such materials, but have no objection to assembling them.[25]

General MacArthur's Address to Congress

When MacArthur flew back to the United States, he was greeted as a conquering hero during the early weeks of his return. Congressional leaders invited him to address a joint meeting of the Congress on April 19, and the nation's capital prepared for one of its biggest celebrations. The President graciously canceled a speech that had been scheduled the same date, and also issued this statement on April 13: "I am happy to learn from Speaker Rayburn that Congress is planning to invite General

MacArthur to address the Members of both Houses. I regard it as fitting that Congress bestow this honor on one of our great military men."[26]

On the day that MacArthur addressed Congress, Harriman invited a number of the members of the White House staff to his spacious house in Northwest Washington for a buffet luncheon. I was especially interested to hear the reaction of the group as they watched the dramatic address while clustered around the television set. It was unquestionably a superb oratorical performance. When it had concluded, to the overwhelming applause of the assembled legislators, Samuel Berger of Harriman's staff began to pick it apart on legalistic grounds, contending that Mac-Arthur's knowledge and interpretation of the United States Constitution were obviously faulty. Elsey spoke up, suggesting that MacArthur had stirred up a real hornet's nest, since his emotional address had contained convincing arguments that inspired support not only in Congress but also in the nation. He stressed that the arguments needed to be answered.

Senate Hearings

The answers came in joint hearings of the Senate Armed Services and Foreign Relations committees, starting May 3. When the Joint Chiefs of Staff, Marshall, Acheson and other civilian and military leaders had finished testifying, MacArthur's insubordination became glaring and somewhat embarrassing even to Republicans. Stripped of its rhetoric, it seemed peculiarly out of tune with American constitutional principles. The aging general tried to extend the triumphal welcome he had received in New York, Washington and several other cities, but soon found his crowds dwindling. By June 21, the President could record in his diary: "MacArthur is now a 'drug on the market' with the Senate Republicans. His Texas trip was a dud. And the witnesses by telling the truth have left the joint committee with[out] a real headline for weeks."[27]

A month following MacArthur's recall, the volume of telegrams, cards and letters to the White House was down to a trickle. Furthermore, the percentage of adverse mail was down to fifty-five percent pro-MacArthur and steadily falling.

At the Republican national convention of 1952, MacArthur delivered the keynote address. Like most convention audiences, the delegates and visitors seemed preoccupied with talking among themselves, rather than listening to what was going on at the podium. The seventy-two-year-old general did not command the respect he had received when he addressed the joint session of Congress in April 1951. He tried in vain to recapture his audience by command. The convention, and indeed the nation, was far more interested in another general, named Eisenhower, from a different theater of war. By 1952, MacArthur had indeed faded away.

Communism and McCarthy

"Any move to abridge the rights of the individual under the Constitution—no matter in what form—is a danger to the freedom of all," the President wrote in his *Memoirs*. The Bill of Rights was the most sacred part of the Constitution in Truman's eyes, and he fought against every attempt to encroach on those rights. Even before Senator McCarthy began to find communists under every bed, Truman was deeply disturbed by the wholesale smear tactics of the House Un-American Activities Committee.

For some of the same reasons that he had disliked the televised ballyhoo of the Kefauver crime hearings, the President compared the Un-American Activities hearings unfavorably with his own thorough and objective senatorial investigation of war contracting, construction and procurement procedures. Truman, as a committee chairman, had insured that witnesses were not badgered, that reports were carefully prepared and not sensationalized, and that constructive achievement was the hallmark. As President, he reacted against publicity-seeking committees that gained notoriety by ruining the personal reputations of individuals at the expense of the Bill of Rights.

In 1950, the perjury conviction of Alger Hiss, the triumph of the Chinese communists, and Acheson's vow that "I do not intend to turn my back on Alger Hiss" stirred a wave of hysterical criticism of Truman for allegedly harboring communists in the federal government. Some Republicans, like McCarthy, Jenner, Mundt, Nixon and Taft, saw pay dirt in the communist issue.

Long before McCarthy made his first stab at "discovering" hundreds of communists in the government in February 1950, the President was expressing concern about the type of hysteria that had produced demagogues like McCarthy down through history. On April 29, 1949, Clifford indicated to Elsey, "Some weeks ago the President handed to me a memorandum by Max Lowenthal entitled 'The Sedition Bills of 1949.' " He turned the memorandum over to Elsey. The document sounded an alarm bell concerning the punishment of nonconformists and witch-hunts threatening freedom of expression, manifested in recent state statutes and a disturbing mood in the nation.

At this point an unlikely character moved onto the stage. The President's Air Force aide, Brigadier General Robert B. Landry, was neither an old friend, like military aide Vaughan, nor an officer to whom the President gave many varied assignments, as he did naval aide Dennison. But as Landry recalled in 1954, here is what happened one spring day in 1949:

> The President called me one morning. I was sitting in my office. It was about eleven o'clock in the morning, and the President said, "Bob, I want you to do a little job for me. I want you to make a study on hysteria and witch hunting. . . . I want you to go back to the days of 1692, the old Salem days when witch hunting was at its peak in this country, and I want you to go on through the days of the 'Know-Nothings' and the Sedition trials. . . . You needn't be in a hurry; you take as much time as you want. . . . I think you'll find it quite interesting; it will be a good education for you."
>
> I said, "Yes, sir." I was completely bewildered. . . . The first thing I did was call the Air Force and ask, "Have you got a good man who is a good historian and who knows American history?" Well, they had a man named [Murray] Green. He had a master's degree in American history at Harvard. A lot of his language was too flowery, and I had to put it in my own. . . . I guess [the President] gave it to me because he thought I had some time to devote to it. It took six months to make it.[28]

On October 31, 1949, Landry presented to the President an elaborately bound, impressive-looking document entitled "A Study of Mass Hysteria and Witch-Hunting in America." The President wanted to have it edited, adding material on other demagogues like Huey Long and Father Coughlin.

The document suddenly assumed greater importance after McCarthy made his Lincoln Day speech in Wheeling, West Virginia, on February 9, 1950, charging, "I have here in my hand a list of 205" communists in the State Department. I was asked to edit and revise the document on witch-hunting in accordance with the President's instructions. I found the study rather spotty, not particularly well organized, and containing a great deal of rambling and irrelevant material, as well as lacking a strong, positive conclusion regarding the most constructive

ways to fight communism. I did a lot of original research, expanded the
section on the Alien and Sedition Acts, which were quite relevant to the
hysteria and thought control that characterized McCarthyism, edited
out a lot of the surplus language and irrelevancies, and wound up with a
section on strengthening the economy within the Bill of Rights as a
means of combating communism. "In order to prevent the internal success of communism, democracies have discovered that the most powerful antidote to communism is a virile government which can fulfill the
needs of all classes of people," the conclusion read, adding that "the exercise of the freedoms guaranteed in the Bill of Rights serves to counter-
act the effects of hysteria."[29]

The only portion of the President's instructions I rejected was the
advice to include a section on Huey Long and Father Coughlin. I knew
about the President's contempt for Long while they served together in
the Senate, and I certainly held no brief for the Sunday radio rantings of
Coughlin during the early New Deal days. Yet I felt that somehow those
two gentlemen, although certainly demagogues, did not fall into the
same category as the far more dangerous witch-hunters who had black-
ened personal reputations. When he read the revised document, the
President did not comment on this "dodging" of his instructions, but
told a number of people how much he liked it. He frequently used it as
the text for informal speeches, both as President and after he left the
White House.

Campaign of Truth

The study I perfected was a companion piece to a ringing address
the President delivered to the American Society of Newspaper Editors,
calling for a "campaign of truth."[30] At the end of 1949, Edward Barrett,
formerly of *Newsweek* magazine, was named to head the State Department's Office of Public Affairs. At the White House Elsey worked
closely with Barrett and was the principal draftsman for the President's
"campaign of truth" address. We began to see glimmerings of improvement in the stodgy approach traditionally taken by the State Department
toward communicating with the average American in everyday English.

About this time I had dinner at the home of Marshall Shulman, an
excellent speech-writer and an aide to Acheson. Another guest was pollster Rensis Likert, who told us the disturbing fact that support for the
President's foreign policy was slipping among lower-income groups.

Apparently, McCarthy's appeal among these groups was gaining. The President fought back, not by direct attacks on McCarthy, but through emphasis on truth and justice, the hallmarks of the American system. He followed his address to the newspaper editors with a dinner address to the Federal Bar Association, calling attention to the federal loyalty program he had established in 1947 and its objectives:

> I was determined, as far as it was humanly possible, to see that no disloyal person should be employed by our Government, whether he was a Communist or a native American Fascist of the Silver Shirt or Ku Klux Klan variety. I was equally determined that loyal Government employees should be protected against accusations which were false, malicious, and ill-founded.[31]

He said that his administration would fight communism "without headlines or hysteria," with full protection of the Bill of Rights. He bluntly stated that he was not going to turn the FBI "into a Gestapo secret police," and "we are not going to turn the United States into a rightwing totalitarian country in order to deal with a leftwing totalitarian threat."

The President kept his "witch-hunting and hysteria" research study handy, and made frequent references to it. He told his news conference on July 27, 1950, that "We want to be very careful in times like these that we don't get in the alien and sedition mood of 1798. The Bill of Rights is still a part of the Constitution of the United States, and a most important part. That doesn't mean that we are going to overlook any operation to see that traitors and saboteurs are properly taken care of."[32] He followed up these remarks with a special message to Congress on the internal security of the United States. In his August 8 message, he again reviewed some of the historic threats to freedom posed by the hysteria of the moment. He branded the Alien and Sedition Acts "repugnant to the free spirit of our people." He added that since the time of the Alien and Sedition Acts, in periods of danger there are "those who, in good faith or bad, would severely limit the freedom of our people in a misguided attempt to gain greater security."[33] The immediate stimulus for the President's August 8 special message was the pellmell rush in Congress to enact the restrictive McCarran Act, which the President subsequently vetoed with an eloquent message on September 22.[34] Congress promptly voted to override the veto.

At a late August Big Four conference, the President discussed with Vice-President Barkley, Senate Majority Leader Lucas, Speaker Rayburn and Majority Leader McCormack the research study on witch-hunting and hysteria. He then wrote each of them a note on August 28, stating, "Here is the 'Study of "Witch Hunting" and Hysteria in the United States' which has just been prepared. It is as interesting as can be, and I think you should have a copy."[35]

On August 31, he met with the members of the United States Advisory Commission on Information, which had made an intensive study of such overseas information programs as the Voice of America. The chairman of the commission was Mark Ethridge, publisher of the Louisville *Courier Journal* and *Times.* Following their meeting with the President, Ethridge dropped a note to Connelly, including the following:

> When we talked with the President this morning he told us about a pamphlet he had written on the "Cycles of Hysteria in the Country." He was going to give it to us, but he forgot. I would appreciate it very much if you could mail a copy to us.[36]

In sending the research study to the members of the Commission, Elsey noted: "It was prepared at [the President's] direction, as useful background information in considering some of the demands which are being made for unwise and extremist internal security measures."[37]

We made a number of copies of the study available to people on Capitol Hill, the Democratic National Committee, and various labor, farm and liberal organizations, as well as sending them out with the President's correspondence on that subject. More frequently, as McCarthy's attacks became sharper during the 1950 congressional campaigns, the President used the text as background for informal remarks. Unfortunately, not all of these remarks were recorded, and some were therefore lost to history. Drew Pearson, who frequently incited Truman's anger by his attacks on some White House staff members, wrote what was probably an accurate account of one of these off-the-record talks in September 1950:

> Sometimes the President's off-the-record remarks that never reach the papers are his best. Those present thought this was the case when Truman addressed the joint session of the AFL-CIO last week.
> Speaking without notes and obviously straight from the heart, the President made a plea for tolerance in wartime.
> To a considerable extent it was a historical speech. The President reviewed the different periods of hysteria which have gripped the country—the Alien and Sedition Act in the early days of the republic, the Know-Nothing Party, and Ku Klux Klanism.

He pointed out that the Know-Nothing Party had been anti-Mason and referred to the fact that he, himself, was a Mason. The Klan, he recalled, was first against the Negro; then when revived in the 1920's, against the Jew and the Catholic.

These were evidences of intolerance which did not truly represent the American people, he said, and he was absolutely confident that the good judgment of the American people would always win out.

The President did not mention the Mundt-Nixon bill or the McCarran bill, but it was obvious he had them in mind. For he referred to congressional witch-hunters who wave the American flag while persecuting alien immigrants and trampling on the rights of loyal Americans.

"This is the raw material of totalitarianism," he said.

While fighting the intolerance of totalitarianism, he emphasized, we must not take on the methods of totalitarianism. Recalling that totalitarian regimes had persecuted labor unions, religious groups and fraternal organizations, he pointed out that under the Alien and Sedition Act, naturalized citizens hardly dared to say anything in public about the Government for fear of being thrown in jail, and this, he inferred, might also happen under the Mundt-Nixon and McCarran bills.[38]

It cannot be claimed that any of Truman's counter-measures had much immediate effect in curbing McCarthy's excesses, despite the considerable time and effort that he spent trying to figure out the most effective means of fighting the evils of McCarthyism. The White House staff joined in this effort. The loyalty and security procedures were constantly under review to insure that subversives would indeed be weeded out and that those appointed and employed by the federal government would be carefully screened for security. Maine Senator Margaret Chase Smith, in a noteworthy "Declaration of Conscience" at the end of May 1950, joined six other Republican senators to declare on the Senate floor that they did not want to see the Republican party win the congressional elections on "the four horsemen of fear, ignorance, bigotry and smear." Asked to comment at his June 1, 1950, news conference, the President diplomatically answered: "I wouldn't like to make a comment as strong as that about the Republican Party."[39] Despite Senator Smith's efforts, McCarthy continued to ride high. When Senator Tydings's committee issued a devastating report that exposed and denounced the bankruptcy of McCarthy's tactics, the Wisconsin senator marked Tydings for defeat in the 1950 elections. After McCarthy made good his threat in one of the dirtiest campaigns in history, more and more congressmen turned tail and sent out the word that they weren't going to say anything that was critical of McCarthy.

The Nimitz Commission

On January 23, 1951, the President appointed a nonpartisan Commission on Internal Security and Individual Rights, chaired by Fleet Admiral Chester W. Nimitz. The Nimitz Commission was charged with considering "how this Nation can best deal with the problem of protecting its internal security and at the same time maintaining the freedoms of its citizens."[40] The leering figure of McCarthy was one of the main reasons for the establishment of the commission. Its membership was carefully chosen for their standing with the public. Included were former Connecticut Republican Senator John A. Danaher, Harvey Firestone, Charles H. Silver (vice-president of the American Woolen Company), Russell C. Leffingwell (a former partner in Morgan & Company), and several distinguished bishops and others. The business members of the commission and prospective staff soon discovered that conflict-of-interest statutes precluded their service on the commission without considerable personal loss. Nimitz asked the President for a congressional waiver for his part-time commission, as had been done in other instances. The House of Representatives readily passed such legislation, but one of the President's inveterate Senate foes, Nevada Senator McCarran, blocked the legislation in his capacity as chairman of the Judiciary Committee. In his memoirs, Truman noted that McCarran's "record for obstruction and bad legislation is matched by that of only a very few reactionaries." He described the results of McCarran's act:

> By this obstruction McCarran succeeded in killing this legislation and kept the Nimitz Commission from making a nonpartisan and honest study of the government's loyalty-security program.
>
> This was another move by McCarran calculated to check the administration's program and to encourage the demagogues in the Congress. It left the Nimitz Commission with no choice but to resign as a body.[41]

Blair House Meeting

Behind the scenes, the President was trying to get the best advice on what could be done to check McCarthyism. One such secret meeting was held at Blair House on the evening of February 28, 1951. News of the meeting did not emerge until the publication of a book by John Hersey in 1980.[42] Despite the passage of almost three decades before he wrote his recollection of the meeting, Hersey gives a revealing portrait of President Truman. A Pulitzer-prize–winning novelist and journalist, he had persuaded the President to allow him to sit in on a number of meetings. Hersey received permission to spend a "social evening" at Blair House.

When he arrived at 8:00 P.M., Murphy cautioned him that the meeting was to be off the record and he was to take no notes. Also present at the discussion were Clifford, Senators Clinton Anderson, Mike Monroney, Thomas C. Hennings, Jr., and John J. Sparkman, Congressman Brent Spence, Attorney General McGrath, Solicitor General Philip B. Perlman, and Democratic National Chairman Boyle.

As the President entered and sat down at a large oval table, he immediately asked what antidote he should use against the poison of McCarthy. Hersey summarized one line of suggestions, which amounted to proposing "that McCarthyism might be done in, once and for all, by a stroke of McCarthyism." The suggestion was this:

> A thick and devastating dossier had been assembled over a number of years, detailing, complete with dates, the hotel rooms in which Joseph McCarthy had stayed and the names of the Senator's bedmates in all those rooms. The list was practically guaranteed to blow Senator McCarthy's show sky high.[43]

Hersey recalls this phase of the discussion clearly because it "so moved me that I have never been able to forget it." Here is Hersey's account of the President's reaction:

> Truman listened to this presentation and to some supporting statements.
> Then the flat of his hand came sharply down on the table. His third-person self spoke in outrage; the President wanted no more such talk.
> Three pungent comments of Harry Truman's on the proposal that had just been made have stuck in my mind ever since. This was their gist:
> You must not ask the President of the United States to get down in the gutter with a guttersnipe.
> Nobody, not even the President of the United States, can approach too close to a skunk, in skunk territory, and expect to get anything out of it except a bad smell.
> If you think somebody is telling a big lie about you, the only way to answer is with the whole truth.[44]

It was difficult to get much of a laugh out of the efforts by the White House staff to combat the insidious forces unleashed by McCarthy and McCarran, but we did our best to keep our spirits up during those grim days. One of my choice tidbits was a telegram purloined from the White House mail room, which I hope to return to its rightful repository in the Truman Library. From his home in New York, one Abner Green wired the President to ask him to veto the McCarran internal security bill. Western Union made a minor typographical error, and the telegram implored the President to veto the McCarran bill "or any similar legislation" because "it threatens basic American free loving."

Senator McCarthy and the 1952 Campaign

McCarthy figured personally as well as symbolically in the 1952 presidential campaign, in which the Republican party made its central issues Korea, communism and corruption. It was one of my tasks to follow Eisenhower's public statements and to document them by subject for analysis. One of the subjects I researched was Eisenhower's reaction to McCarthy.

The first hint came in the general's Abilene news conference over a month before the Republican convention. In response to the direct question, "Do you favor the re-election of Senator Joseph McCarthy of Wisconsin?" the answer was revealing: "I should say again I am not going to indulge in any kind of personalities under any pretext whatsoever."[45]

It was generally concluded that the nomination of Taft would lend far greater support to the forces of McCarthyism, especially since Taft had publicly called on McCarthy to keep bringing up communist charges until he could find one that would stick. Truman felt that Taft's control over organization delegates gave him the best chance of winning the Republican nomination.[46] He candidly expressed his reaction to Taft's convention performance in this fashion, in a private letter to his cousin Ethel:

> It looks very much like my candidate for the Republican nomination has beaten himself. Of all the dumb bunnies—he is the worst. Son of a President and a Chief Justice, in the Ohio Legislature, U.S. Senator, three times candidate for President—and look what he's done to himself. When a fellow is not honest intellectually, what can we expect.[47]

A year before the Republican convention, in a Senate speech, McCarthy had accused General George C. Marshall of treason. Indiana Senator William Jenner branded Marshall's life a "living lie." This challenge to the integrity of a man whom the President considered the greatest living American touched a raw nerve in Truman. I recall the occasion when the President accepted the first volume of Jefferson's papers at a Library of Congress ceremony on May 17, 1950. The audience applauded politely as the distinguished guests on the platform were introduced in turn. When Marshall was introduced, the President suddenly stood up and began applauding vigorously; of course, this immediately stimulated the entire audience to rise and do likewise, with feeling.[48]

After Eisenhower defeated Taft for the Republican nomination, the McCarthy issue came up again on August 22 in an Eisenhower news conference in Denver. In a lengthy circumlocution, during which the reporters were furnished with several examples of the candidate's muddy syntax, he said he supported the "uprooting of subversion." The closest he would come to criticizing McCarthyism was this sentence: "I think that conditions were serious enough so that serious measures were necessary, but un-American methods, as far as I am concerned, are never justified." He immediately went into a qualification of this statement and concluded that the "Legislature should be of the same party" as the President. "For that reason, I have to accept the decision of the voters of a State, as much as I can," he finally said.[49]

To pin it down, a reporter asked: "Will you oppose Senator McCarthy if you go to Washington?" Eisenhower had an easy answer for that: "I don't know. I haven't gone yet." Then someone wanted to know if he would appear on the same platform as McCarthy, to which he hedged again, but noted that "appearing on the same platform with somebody does not seem to me in itself to be such a heinous crime."[50]

As the campaign warmed up, Eisenhower moved closer to McCarthy. In Appleton, Wisconsin, on September 3, he called for the election of a great Republican "team" in Wisconsin, "from the Governor himself through the Senate and the House."[51] Then on October 3, Eisenhower took the irrevocable step that incited Truman to go after him with one of his toughest criticisms of a presidential candidate. At Green Bay, Wisconsin, Eisenhower said:

The differences between me and Senator McCarthy are well known to others. But what is more important, they are well known to him and to me and we have discussed them. I want to make one thing very clear. The purposes that he and I have of ridding this government of the incompetents, the dishonest and above all the subversive and the disloyal are one and the same. Our differences, therefore, have nothing to do with the end result that we are seeking. The differences apply to method.[52]

In another address on the same day, planned for Milwaukee, Eisenhower's advance text included a passage of praise for Marshall, as if to answer those who were charging he was stabbing his old chief in the back. But when he delivered the address, Eisenhower deftly deleted the praise contained in his advance copy. Some sources contended that the section had been stricken at McCarthy's insistence, as his price for riding the Eisenhower campaign train. Eisenhower himself states that Governor Walter Kohler of Wisconsin made the request, and that he deleted the passage in the interests of party unity.[53]

At Colorado Springs on October 7, Truman let Eisenhower have it with both barrels:

> If there is any one man to whom the Republican candidate owes a great debt of loyalty and gratitude, that man is General George Catlett Marshall. It was General Marshall who promoted him to a position of responsibility in the War Department General Staff. It was General Marshall who made him our commander in the European Theater. It was General Marshall, according to the candidate's own book, who made the decision to give him command of the invasion of Europe—a command that Marshall could himself have had, if he wanted to take it. . . .
>
> This great man has been the subject of an infamous attack by two Republican isolationist Senators. Acting from purely partisan motives, these two moral pigmies have called this great American a "living lie," a "front for traitors" and the center of an infamous conspiracy. . . .
>
> Now what has the Republican candidate done about this outrage? Has he condemned these two slanderers? Has he denounced their lies about his great friend and benefactor?
>
> I'll tell you what he has done. He has endorsed them both for reelection to the Senate. . . .
>
> Now what do you think of a man who deserts his best friend when he is unjustly attacked? What do any of us say about a fellow who joins hands with those who have tried to stab an honored chief, a friend and a benefactor, in the back?[54]

On several occasions during the rest of the 1952 campaign, Truman lashed out at Eisenhower for embracing Senators McCarthy and Jenner. Years later, when *Washington Post* correspondent Edward Folliard asked Truman what had caused his feud with Eisenhower, Truman answered:

Oh, Eddie, I wouldn't call it a feud. But I'll tell you what made Ike mad. It was a speech that I made at Colorado Springs. You go back and look up that speech, and you'll see that I skinned old Ike from the top of his bald head to his backside.[55]

The Issue of Corruption in Government

Corruption is a perennially hot political issue when it involves public officials. It always makes juicy news copy. Nothing infuriates a taxpayer so much as to see a government official lining his pockets, contributing to higher taxes and a general decline in public morality. District attorneys, investigative reporters, opposition political leaders, crime fighters, and congressional committees have made deservedly good reputations exposing corruption in government.

I remember calling many meetings of Capitol Hill and agency officials during 1951 and early 1952 to compile research materials for the 1952 campaigns. A number of influential participants shook their fists at me and proclaimed: "All the best research materials in the world aren't going to be worth a tinker's damn unless you guys at the White House do something dramatic to clean up corruption in the Bureau of Internal Revenue, Justice Department and the White House itself."

As a product of the Pendergast machine in Kansas City, President Truman was a natural target for charges of corruption. It mattered little that the record showed Truman to have been an honest, incorruptible official in the administrative post of county judge of Jackson County. Hadn't he been described as the "Senator from Pendergast" during his first term in the Senate? And hadn't he used an Army plane to fly to Boss Tom Pendergast's funeral, after the boss served a prison term for income tax evasion?

The White House staff and President Truman's associates were under constant scrutiny by reporters, congressional investigators, and opposition leaders who knew that the slightest breath of scandal would make political hay. I suspect there were those on the outside who were deliberately laying traps to catch the unwary, although I personally never encountered any such situations.

On October 5, 1947, the President delivered a radio-television address on food prices and shortages, during which he said that "the cost of living in this country must not be a football to be kicked about by gamblers in grain."[56] It embarrassed Truman when his personal physician,

Dr. Graham, as well as a close associate whom he had attempted to appoint as undersecretary of the Navy, Edwin W. Pauley, were on a published list of speculators in grain futures. Although the President denied any wrongdoing on Dr. Graham's part, Republican campaign orators frequently brought up the issue.

Five Percenters and Other Scandals

The Senate Committee on Expenditures in the Executive Departments, chaired by North Carolina Senator Clyde Hoey, published a report in 1950[57] that grew out of public hearings on the influence of "five percenters" in Washington—those ingratiating and somewhat oily "public relations" agents who received five-percent commissions for allegedly providing information on how to obtain contracts and other favors. Unfortunately for Truman, some of the testimony rubbed off on the White House, because several five percenters bragged about their close association with Vaughan. It was evident that Vaughan had not been very discriminating in the friends he tolerated or failed to discourage. Truman received a wave of criticism for defending Vaughan, but never wavered in supporting his military aide.

Another bombshell from Capitol Hill came with the publication of the report and hearings of the Senate Banking and Currency Committee,[58] in which two of the President's Democratic critics, Arkansas Senator Fulbright and Illinois Senator Douglas, figured prominently. The report carefully skirted the issue of the propriety of various influences on the Reconstruction Finance Corporation, but it did name Democratic National Chairman Boyle, former RFC personnel director and Truman administrative assistant Dawson, and E. Merl Young, whose wife worked in the White House as a secretary, as unduly active in connection with RFC loans. Even more damaging was the subsequent news that Mrs. Young had received a mink coat at a reduced price, a revelation that was cleverly linked with the Vaughan deep freeze as one of the big Republican issues of the 1952 campaign.

Dawson, immediately defended by the President, emerged from the RFC scandals as relatively clean. Not so Boyle and Mrs. Young. Although the President publicly defended Boyle's role as member of a law firm receiving a fee from a company that obtained an RFC loan, the heat on the President and his National Committee chairman intensified during the summer of 1951. At the July 26, 1951 staff meeting, Hassett referred to the Boyle case and commented, "Mr. President, your friends will destroy you." The President answered, "It's all right, Bill, things will straighten out."[59] But they didn't. By October, Boyle was out as national chairman.

I got into the RFC squabbles in the following way. The White House had obtained the letters written to the RFC by Senate and House members indicating congressional interest in pending RFC loans. Early in 1952, I constructed a tabular analysis through 1950 of the possible connection between congressional pressure on the RFC and granting of loans, along with data on campaign contributions from loan recipients to congressmen. In a memorandum to Murphy on April 23, 1952, I concluded that "it would be extremely difficult to make any kind of a general case on the basis of these letters, inasmuch as just as many Democratic Congressmen as Republicans were intervening on behalf of their constituents." I added:

> If a *general* use were made of this information here at the White House, singling out only the Republicans, such a use might backfire not only because it is known we have the letters, but also because it is well known that many Democrats are also authors of these letters.
>
> The letters themselves involve nothing very unusual or nefarious. A cursory search has not revealed any link between campaign contributions and support of RFC loans—although such a link may exist.[60]

Corruption in the Justice Department and Bureau of Internal Revenue

The situation with five percenters and the RFC was penny-ante stuff contrasted with full-blown scandals that erupted in the Bureau of Internal Revenue and the Department of Justice during 1951 and 1952. The President acted forcefully in removing those officials whose activities made it evident that they were engaged in receiving favors or payoffs, or other questionable practices. Unfortunately, the President was not served well here: His responsible appointees did not act vigorously to root out corruption in advance of its being publicized. These shortcomings were spotlighted in articles by enterprising journalists. At the outset Secretary of the Treasury Snyder perhaps could have done more to stave off the scandals in the Bureau of Internal Revenue. In Snyder's defense it must be conceded that most of the corruption occurred among

Internal Revenue agents appointed by prior administrations. Snyder seemed more interested in the general economic policies he frequently discussed with the President than in whether an Internal Revenue agent in Podunk was involved in questionable activities. Attorney General McGrath had risen through the political system of Rhode Island, and had been a senator and chairman of the Democratic National Committee during the 1948 campaign. Unlike Truman, whose political background and principles had schooled him to insist that honesty always produced larger majorities at the polls, McGrath was looser in his tolerance for political favoritism as the route to political success. Like McGrath, Truman believed that patronage was a useful tool to strengthen party organization, yet he was determined that patronage should not be used to reward incompetent or weak individuals with a tendency toward dishonesty.

Under the aegis of the House Ways and Means Committee, the Subcommittee on Administration of the Internal Revenue Laws started an investigation on March 19, 1951, the repercussions of which shook the Truman administration to its foundations. This subcommittee uncovered some shady and shoddy practices that reached beyond the Bureau of Internal Revenue into the Department of Justice. The subcommittee began to look into tax fraud cases that the Justice Department failed to prosecute. As the evidence piled up, Snyder acted aggressively to lop off the heads of some of the corrupt officials in the Bureau of Internal Revenue. The clerk of the subcommittee, Adrian DeWind, alerted special counsel Murphy concerning damning evidence. As early as May 24, 1951, the President, in an address to members of the Conference of United States Attorneys, warned that in the case of wrongdoing turned up by congressional committees, "it is your business to see that those things that affect the laws of the Federal Government are taken care of, that every man who has been breaking those laws is punished."[61] Still disturbed about false charges, McCarthyism and American freedoms, the President expressed himself pungently to Murphy about an extremely detailed conflict-of-interest questionnaire distributed to Bureau of Internal Revenue personnel: "Attached documents are totalitarian. If one was sent to me for answer, I'd tell the sender to go to hell!"[62]

On October 20, Bell, after analyzing the developing scandals, recommended that a special assistant to the attorney general be appointed as an investigator, that J. Edgar Hoover be brought into the act, and that

the President send a full-dress message to the Congress on the subject.[63]
The increasingly serious issues of scandals in the Justice Department and
the Internal Revenue Bureau were on everybody's mind when the President and his staff went down to Key West for their semi-annual vacation.

At this point, Murphy was getting more and more concerned over
the reports by Adrian DeWind. Before leaving for Key West, Murphy
asked Stowe to review the evidence compiled by the Ways and Means
Committee. Stowe discovered the situation was far worse than supposed, that there was wholesale evidence of bad judgment by Internal
Revenue officials, as well as failures to follow up by the Department of
Justice. After reading the transcript, Stowe felt it important enough to
call Murphy in Key West and report to him at length on what he had
found.[64] Murphy briefed the President, who moved quickly to get rid of
those officials whose integrity was clearly in question. It was evident
that Charles Oliphant, assistant general counsel of the Bureau of Internal Revenue, and T. Lamar Caudle, assistant attorney general in charge
of the Tax Division in the Department of Justice, were subject to criticism for their actions. Murphy discovered some reluctance on the part
of Attorney General McGrath and his assistant, Peyton Ford, to separate
Mr. Caudle, so the President quickly settled the issue by announcing the
firing of Caudle.

The scandals in the Bureau of Internal Revenue resulted in the firing
or resignation of 166 Internal Revenue officials during 1951, including
the collectors in Boston, St. Louis, San Francisco, and Nashville. Even
though the President was moving forcefully to clean up the situation,
and Secretary Snyder was actively trying to put the Bureau of Internal
Revenue on an honest, businesslike footing, at the end of 1951 McGrath
was still dragging his feet. Incoming Democratic National Chairman
Frank McKinney won praise by asking the President to take collectors of
Internal Revenue out of the patronage system and place them under
civil service, a suggestion the President himself prompted McKinney to
make.

Housecleaning

In his first news conference after his return from Key West, the President showed how keenly he felt about the scandals, and his determination to proceed with the housecleaning:

Q. Mr. President, did Mr. McKinney quote you correctly as saying that he said that you were very angry because you felt that some people had sold you down the river?

THE PRESIDENT. Well, who wouldn't feel that way? A man who has taken an oath to support and defend the Constitution of the United States, and who doesn't do it would make any executive angry. . . .

Q. Mr. President, Attorney General McGrath says he never knew anything about the Caudle thing.

THE PRESIDENT. Maybe so. I don't keep books for the Attorney General when he is Attorney General. I keep books for myself.

Q. Mr. President, as to the right sort of people, how did they get in the Government in the first place?

THE PRESIDENT. I don't know. How do you get people in banks that rob them sometimes? (Laughter). . . .

I expect to take action as promptly as possible and get the situation cleaned up, and whatever action is necessary for the Chief Executive to take, why he will take; because there is nobody believes more than I do in clean government. That has been my record and my theory ever since I became a public officeholder. You can go all the way back to 1922 when I was first elected to public office, and you will find that has been the policy I have pursued until this date, and I expect to continue to pursue it. Any wrongdoers have no house with me, no matter who they are or how big they are.[65]

The President realized he would have to move fast to provide an independent clean-up that would be respected by the public. He called together McGrath, J. Edgar Hoover and Robert Ramspeck, chairman of the United States Civil Service Commission. Here is what happened: "It was suggested that these three gentlemen form a commission and clean up the situation. There were loud outcries against the suggestion by all three of the gentlemen. Then I decided at their suggestion to set up an independent commission. . . ."[66]

The President next approached New York District Judge Thomas F. Murphy to head a three-man commission to handle the clean-up. Murphy had successfully prosecuted Alger Hiss, had served as New York City Police Commissioner, and had a reputation for independence. After accepting in mid-December, Murphy returned to New York, where he had second thoughts and backed out. Now the President decided on a new approach: to make McGrath ambassador to Spain, and bring in a person of unquestioned integrity to replace him as attorney general.

Truman offered Judge Rosenman the job on December 18.[67] Rosenman immediately declined, on the grounds that the public would never believe he would prosecute any member of the White House staff if the facts warranted it. As an alternative, Rosenman suggested that Truman appoint a prominent Republican, like Oregon Senator Wayne Morse, who would be above suspicion. The President called Morse in Rosenman's presence, and at a private interview with Morse offered him the job on December 21.

Morse thought at first that Truman was kidding, but indicated that Truman said to him:

> I mean it. Howard McGrath is a fine fellow but he can't do the job. You can write your own ticket. It isn't often that a President gives anyone an offer like this. I'm satisfied that 99.9 percent of our people are fine public servants. Apparently I've got a few rotten apples in the barrel. I want you to clean them out.[68]

In his letter of declination, hand-carried to the White House, Morse pleaded that "from your standpoint I think the job should be performed by a Democrat because you are entitled to the credit within your own party of cleaning up whatever fraud and corruption may have developed on the part of some officials within your Administration who have not kept faith with you."[69] Truman's handwritten response is not available, but in his notes for his answer to Morse, the President lamented:

> I appreciate your arguments and understand—but I wish you could have done the job—not for me but for the country. Political considerations were not a part of my suggestion. . . . What we need is an Isaiah or a Martin Luther to put us back onto the "straight and narrow path."[70]

In the waning days of 1951, special counsel Charles Murphy worried more about the problem of "corruption" than anything else. He appreciated that even though the President had seized the initiative by cleaning house in the Department of Justice and Bureau of Internal Revenue, there was a lingering feeling in the public mind that McGrath should have moved in more boldly to prosecute wrongdoing. Murphy also realized that as long as the image of laxity existed, the President's prestige and the fortunes of the Democratic party would suffer in 1952. Congressional committees were grabbing the headlines by appearing to be more aggressive in exposing corruption within the administration. The President decided on a two-pronged approach: to reorganize the Bureau of Internal Revenue, and to find an outstanding attorney general who had the integrity and public standing to accomplish a thorough clean-up job.

On January 2, 1952, the President announced he was making the Bureau of Internal Revenue "a blue ribbon civil service career organization," abolishing the Bureau collectors. He also pledged "to protect the Government from the insidious influence peddlers and favor seekers, and to expose and punish any wrongdoers." Murphy then negotiated with Justin Miller, one of the nation's most experienced and prestigious lawyers, and persuaded him to consider accepting the critical appointment to replace McGrath. The President was well-pleased with Miller's outstanding credentials, and after personally conferring with him in late December 1951 he offered him the appointment. Miller's acceptance lifted a big load of worry from Murphy's shoulders, for he was precisely the type of individual whose background and experience commanded widespread public respect.

Stung by the President's determination to kick him into an ambassadorship, McGrath desperately tried to sidetrack Miller's appointment. Connelly, who was not eager to have a man like Miller poking around in his own activities and those of his friends, enlisted FBI director Hoover in the effort. Hoover, who had voluminous files on every public figure, did not relish the prospect that Miller, who had made some critical comments on Hoover's *modus operandi*, might become his boss. Miller had pointedly expressed the thought that the FBI should concentrate on catching criminals instead of inquiring into the political beliefs of individuals, or collecting other personal data not relevant to the prosecution of crimes. Hoover also produced quotations that appeared to be criticisms of Truman's policies. These were assembled into a "dossier" used by McGrath, Connelly and Hoover to persuade the President that as a cabinet officer Miller would be so radical he would be detrimental. The offer to Miller was finally withdrawn. The outcome of these negotiations left Murphy despondent. Early in January 1952 the mood around the White House staff was dark and glum.

The Appointment of Newbold Morris and the Sorry Events That Followed

For the moment, McGrath was on "hold." All attempts to set up an independent commission, or find a new attorney general, had collapsed. Still, the message was getting through to McGrath that the only way he could keep his job was to do something substantial and dramatic to fight corruption. At a January 10 news conference, the President announced that after much thought he had come to the conclusion "that it is the business of the Office of the Attorney General to do the job,"[71] On a trip to New York, McGrath talked with Circuit Judge Learned Hand about the situation. Judge Hand mentioned his son-in-law, Newbold Morris,[72] who had been Republican president of the New York City Council and was a New York reformer of the Fiorello La Guardia stripe. "Who can you get purer than a guy like that?" McGrath later asked.

On February 1, with the President's approval, McGrath announced he was appointing Morris as "Special Assistant to the Attorney General." McGrath added that Morris "will have my complete, enthusiastic and unlimited cooperation, and that all of the facilities of the various agencies of the Government which I administer or which can be made available through the office of the President will be at his disposal."[73]

Morris, who traced his ancestry back to Gouverneur Morris of Revolutionary War fame, was "born with a silver foot in his mouth," according to a current New York saying. He was a compulsive talker before the news media and gloried in appearing on weekend television specials to expand on what he planned to do, despite his lack of experience as an investigator. Morris had several meetings with the President, at which the President pledged his fullest cooperation and made seven hundred fifty thousand dollars available from the President's Emergency Fund to help him get started. In a book reminiscing on his experiences, Morris had nothing but praise for the sincerity of the President in desiring to enhance the effectiveness of his efforts.[74] The President issued an executive order directing all federal agencies to cooperate fully with Morris. Truman also sent a message to Congress asking for legislation to give Morris the power of subpoena "to enable Mr. Morris to make a thorough and effective investigation of illegal or improper conduct in the transaction of Government business."[75] Although Congress denied him this and other powers, the President told a subsequent news conference that Morris would remain on the job, even though failure of the legislation "will hamper him in doing a bangup job." The President added, "We are going to give him every help we possibly can to do a good job. That is what we want. We haven't anything to cover up."[76]

Meanwhile, the President's plan to reorganize the Internal Revenue Bureau ran into some snags from senior senators like Arkansas's John McClellan and others who were reluctant to give up their time-honored patronage for a merit system. In the face of an adverse report from

McClellan's Government Operations Committee, Senators Hubert Humphrey of Minnesota, Blair Moody of Michigan and other Truman stalwarts, working closely with Murphy and his staff to obtain ammunition, finally won a bitter struggle for the reorganization.

When Morris discovered he really wasn't accomplishing very much in the spacious office that McGrath generously supplied him in the Justice Department, he decided to move out to the building on Pennsylvania Avenue once occupied by *The Washington Post*. The President supported him in this move. Murphy also asked Donald Hansen of his staff and Harold Seidman of the Budget Bureau to help Morris with any further problems. According to Seidman, and also according to Morris's book, the President in a private conversation at Blair House looked over a questionnaire Morris planned to send out to top federal employees, primarily to assess their incomes and outside interests.[77] The President expressed his approval of the questionnaire, and Morris announced he was going to submit the first one to McGrath.

About mid-March, relations between Morris and McGrath became tense when Morris left a huge batch of questionnaires at the Justice Department and sent word he wanted to see McGrath's appointment book, diaries, and all other private files. Lloyd and Hansen met with members of Morris's staff on March 28, when it was evident the investigation was stymied. Hansen predicted:

> If there is continued inaction on Morris' part, the press and congressional committees will soon learn of that and the whole operation very well may blow up. It is highly possible that there will be a blow up anyway, unless Morris obtains full cooperation from the Attorney General.[78]

McGrath subsequently explained how the President called him and said, "If you don't mind, I would like to have Morris come over to Blair House and we'll show him our complete cooperation." McGrath later reflected, with some sarcasm, "Well, that was wonderful for me; after that I couldn't do anything with the guy.... Morris took off on his own. He got up this questionnaire, which was anything but. I couldn't go for it."[79]

At a cabinet meeting, Secretary of Defense Lovett led the attack on the questionnaire and charged that "every man I have working for me will go home if he has to fill that out."[80] Snyder joined the chorus of opposition. Several cabinet members ruefully observed that it was a reflection on the President if he didn't know enough about his cabinet to pass on their qualifications and integrity without having them fill out personal questionnaires.[81] Steelman, the assistant to the President, suggested that Morris was the principal fly in the ointment and should get out.

Not only the questionnaire, but also other actions, statements and attitudes made it apparent that Morris was antagonizing a large segment of official Washington, making him ineffective in his assignment. Increasingly, he became infatuated with headlines he was making, despite his lack of accomplishment. Seidman reported: "To our horror, every time he appeared [on television] he was adding to the list of people to whom he was going to send the questionnaire. . . . I guess he was going to send it to every man, woman and child in the United States before he was through."[82]

When he threatened to send the questionnaire to every member of Congress, an entirely new area of opposition arose. Then he announced on the radio that if he had been President, he wouldn't have appointed William O'Dwyer (former mayor of New York) as ambassador to Mexico or Vaughan as military aide. These statements made it appear that he was getting pretty big-headed. The President, as expected, responded "No comment on that" when he was asked about Morris's statement on O'Dwyer and Vaughan.[83] But criticisms were pouring into the White House. Morris staff members were disillusioned and ready to quit. Some of them lined him up and "told him to raise his right hand and swear that 'I will not appear on any more television programs.' "[84]

On March 31, McGrath testified before a House Judiciary subcommittee chaired by Representative Frank Chelf of Kentucky. The attorney general was blunt. He told the committee that if he had to do it again, he would not appoint Morris. He said he opposed distributing the questionnaire to his subordinates in the Justice Department; he hadn't even decided whether he would answer his own. He left little doubt that he was contemptuous of Morris's whole operation. It appeared certain that Morris's April 1 deadline for Justice Department employees to complete the questionnaire would pass without action.

The White House immediately sent for a transcript of McGrath's testimony. The President summoned McGrath to come to his office April 2. Murphy reported to the President that "the relationship between the Attorney General and Newbold Morris has become so bad that it will be extremely difficult and probably impossible to continue the present situation."[85] The President appreciated that McGrath, by testifying that he would not respond to the Morris questionnaire, was in effect stating that he would not comply with a presidential executive order.

Meanwhile, Morris had read the morning papers concerning McGrath's defiance, and he was foaming at the mouth, eager to appear in front of the television cameras. With some difficulty, Murphy got Morris to "sit still and keep his mouth shut until further notice."

Just before noon on April 2, when McGrath went to see the President, he suggested that if Truman would only express his opposition to the questionnaire, as had many cabinet members, then Morris would turn tail and go home and everything would be peaceful. In later years, McGrath tried to put a somewhat different light on what was undoubtedly a stormy session in the President's office. A clue to what Truman may have told McGrath is contained in his attitude when he emerged. News reports described McGrath as "flushed, tight-lipped, taciturn" and "angry."[86] He told the press he was prepared to resign if directed to send the questionnaire to the top officials in the Department of Justice.

The President now faced a difficult dilemma. He asked Murphy to go over to the Justice Department and negotiate the resolution of the dilemma. When Murphy arrived at the Justice Department, he had an immediate disagreement with McGrath over differing interpretations of the instructions each had received from the President. McGrath argued that the President had not told him to resign, and there was disagreement over how to get rid of Morris. He then interrupted the discussion because he had to join the President and members of the cabinet assembling at the Military Air Transport Service Terminal for the arrival of Queen Juliana of the Netherlands.

Shortly before 4:00 P.M., while the President and his cabinet awaited Queen Juliana and her party, a heated discussion broke out at the airport. McGrath approached the President with a renewed suggestion on how to terminate Morris. Murphy, never disposed to air an argument as delicate as this in public, attempted to pour oil on the troubled waters. But press secretary Short, realizing that the longer the corruption issue festered, the more it affected the fortunes of the President, vented his anger on McGrath.

"What has the President got to do with this? You brought Morris down here," Short exploded.[87] According to Short's assistant Tubby, he added, "Howard, you think only of yourself, and not at all of the President. You ought to get out."[88] For emphasis, Short pounded the palm of his hand with his fist, in what was obviously an intense argument.

How did the President weather this crisis? He had a great deal on his mind, including the sticky issue of seizure of the steel industry as a result of a nationwide strike, a bombardment of requests from Capitol Hill for loyalty files and data to uncover suspected corruption, and the immediate prospect of several public addresses and a State Dinner for Queen Juliana. My notes for April 2 read:

At 4:45 P.M., I went out to the west portico of the White House to await the Queen's arrival. When the cars drove up, we were only about four feet from the President and Queen in one car, and Prince Bernhard and Mrs. Truman in the next car. The President was at his best in making them feel at home. The President made a very gracious little introduction, referring to the wonderful reception which Margaret had received in the Netherlands. The rains descended when District Commissioner John Russell Young presented the key to the City, and he made one of his usual goofs by saying: "I believe the Weather Bureau is under Dean Acheson." But the President rescued the situation and spoke once again with genuine warmth which more than made up for the coolness of the rain.[89]

About six o'clock, McGrath met with Murphy and Short in the east wing of the White House. Another violent argument occurred between McGrath and Short, with Short charging that the President was being made the victim of circumstances that McGrath had created by bringing Morris to the Justice Department. McGrath later said he told Short and Murphy, "Well, you sons of bitches, I'll get rid of him. Don't think you can pull this crap on me. I know what you're up to. I can handle this myself."[90]

McGrath continued the argument into the evening. According to Carroll, "Later, at the State Dinner for Queen Juliana at the Carlton, McGrath was bitterly talking with his friends about Murphy and the White House 'gang' trying to knife him. He was talking very indiscreetly, loudly, over the heads of several ladies to people some feet away."[91]

Events moved swiftly on April 3. I went up to the Capitol with the White House party to sit with Mrs. Truman in the House gallery as Queen Juliana addressed the joint session of Congress. Mrs. Roger Tubby and I rode back together, and as we entered the White House gate, the guard said in an awed tone, "Attorney General McGrath just fired Morris!" Carroll told Murphy that it was vital that McGrath be cut off quickly, "or the impression would circulate that as soon as Morris was finding something rotten in the Justice Department, he was being

bounced." Carroll also told Short and his assistants Tubby and Perlmeter, who all enthusiastically agreed with his analysis, that "this is a
time when [the President] must rise above personal friendship. The
President's greatest virtue is courage."

When the President and his staff assembled for their pre–press-con-
ference session, another element had entered the picture. Connelly,
knowing of the President's inclination to force out McGrath, had his
own candidate for attorney general. Given the number of people who
had turned down the job or declined to touch the clean-up operation,
the President evidently felt more disposed to listen to Connelly's recommendation—a retired Philadelphia congressman and federal judge
named James P. McGranery. It proved a tragic mistake, for McGranery
served out the closing months of the Truman administration as probably
the least distinguished of all of the President's cabinet members.

On April 3, Carroll made these observations: "At the pre-press session, convening at 3:30 P.M., most of the staff were silent, but Joe Short
spoke up in favor of firing McGrath. The clock ticked away, and the
press conference time got closer and closer. Finally, Roger Tubby put in
what was really the clincher."[92]

Murphy agrees that Tubby's little speech seemed to be a strong factor in the President's decision to act quickly. According to Tubby, as
Short spoke, "Mr. Truman listened thoughtfully, drumming his desk
lightly with his strong, quick fingers." Then Tubby recalls this sequence:

> I said there was a feeling among many of the President's supporters that
> McGrath had betrayed him, the President, in an effort to save face. John
> Steelman snorted at my left when I said "betrayed."
>
> I mentioned a phone call from a Mr. Malley of Springfield, Ohio, which
> had come in that morning. Mr. Malley had said that he thought McGrath
> was hurting the President, that Mr. Truman was an "honest man and a
> good man and should not be hurt by McGrath."
>
> The President said in a low voice that he guessed he'd have to let
> McGrath out.
>
> "What will you say at the press conference?" Short asked. "Do you still
> have confidence in McGrath? Are you going to ask for his resignation?"
>
> The President said he thought he couldn't say much of anything yet
> about McGrath.
>
> "Mr. President," I said, "if you don't take action on this matter this af-
> ternoon or early evening and put it off for some time, you will then be
> charged with acting only because of public pressure.
>
> "There will be, and already is, an outcry against McGrath's sacking of

Morris. You should take the action, sir, it seems to me, *now*, especially if you've already made up your mind."

Mr. Truman reached for the telephone.

"Get the Attorney General." A pause while we all sat with our turbulent thoughts, then:

"Howard, I've got to ask you to resign. I'm going to announce your resignation at my press conference this afternoon, in five minutes."

A few words from McGrath.

"I'm announcing it at the press conference," the President said again firmly but quietly, and hung up.

"Now, what's next on your agenda, Joe?"

Short brought up several items but the President interrupted him while we were talking about Korea and phoned Judge McGranery in Philadelphia, asking him to take McGrath's job. When he hung up he said:

"I hate to do what I did to Howard. I hate to do this to anyone. He was crying at the end."[93]

The President walked briskly into the Indian Treaty Room on the fourth floor of the Executive Office Building. It was the first time a press conference was filmed for television. I came in early, knowing there would be something of a crush, and it was lucky I did because the klieg lights and cameras took up space and people were almost hanging from the rafters. The President started with a routine three-sentence reaffirmation of his confidence in the United Nations negotiators at Panmunjom. My notes then read: "The whole assemblage gasped as the President announced simply: 'The Attorney General has resigned.' Much scurrying around for information on McGranery. I happened to have a complete voting record on him, compiled when he was in Congress from 1937 to 1943."

According to my notes,

Marty Friedman was disappointed in McGranery. "Just another machine politician," he said. I expressed surprise at Friedman's attitude, since he had always been such a firm advocate of organization politics. But Friedman pointed out that the situation called for a clean, new face. He said he had been up until 3 A.M. the night before compiling a suggested list of names, including Charles Murphy, Wilson Wyatt, John Carroll, Telford Taylor and Franklin D. Roosevelt, Jr., and several others.[94]

Carroll noted that when the President fired McGrath and then appointed McGranery, "the whole operation took less than five minutes." Vaughan, who often remarked that "anyone from the Justice Department in my book is out in left field without a fielder's mitt," looked highly pleased. "Just like changing your shirt," he said concerning the switch.

Less than a week after the axe fell on Morris, he returned to Washington to fulfill a commitment to address the National Press Club. I decided to go to this crowded luncheon, because I was interested in hearing his analysis of President Truman. In light of developments, it surprised me that his remarks sincerely praised the President.[95] His speech was interspersed with such comments as "I want to say that the President has given me complete cooperation from the start, and he really believes honestly in the fight against corruption," and "Harry Truman has plenty of guts."

Morris then said that of all the people in Washington, the President understood precisely what he was attempting and "this despite the fact that he was schooled in machine politics." Morris added that there were others around the nation's capital who looked upon a corruption fighter "as some strange man from Mars who was engaged on an impossible mission, but the President not only understood the nature of the fight against corruption, it is evident that he had been thinking about it for some time before I came, and he had some good ideas of his own."

At this point, Morris opened a new book entitled *Mr. President*, written by William Hillman, and read about the President's determination to extend the civil service merit system to marshals and United States attorneys and his recommendation that public officials reveal their sources of income.[96] He read this passage with gusto. He predicted that the President would send to Congress some reorganization plans putting marshals, United States attorneys, and postmasters under civil service. On the next day, April 10, the President did send up a special message and three reorganization plans embodying these recommendations; Congress, however, refused to give up its patronage and declined to approve the plans.

During the question period, Morris was asked who had recommended his appointment to McGrath. He shot back, "I don't know who recommended me to Mr. McGrath, but whoever it is, I'll bet he is in the doghouse now."

It is evident that McGrath never did appreciate the magnitude of the problem he faced. Several years later he observed, "I didn't see anything really to be alarmed about, but the President thought something dramatic had to be done. All these things that were happening were not related to him or the Department of Justice, but they finally convinced him to take some drastic action; then the people will quiet down and forget about it." The interviewer observed that the "mess in Washington" was "partly manufactured by the press and partly by people" in the President's own party. McGrath could not stomach that characterization, and responded: "There wasn't any mess. It was only the ordinary run of what goes on."[97]

In 1960 McGrath attempted a "last hurrah" by running for the Senate. He released to the press a letter written by President Truman some eight years earlier, less than two weeks after he had been fired. The letter referred to the President's March 29, 1952, announcement that he would not run:

April 14, 1952

Dear Howard:

I have been trying to write to you for several days. It seems as if my announcement of March 29 has made my days longer instead of shorter. The happenings in the Newbold Morris case were very disturbing to me. I want you to know that my fondness for you has not changed one bit. Political situations sometimes cause me much pain.

I am ready if at any time in the future you become interested in public service to do anything I can for you. I will go all out. I am most sincerely

Your friend

Harry Truman[98]

In the final months of the Truman administration, McGranery did little to remove the issue of "corruption" as a credible part of the triple-threat Republican campaign summarized in the phrase "Korea, communism and corruption." Newbold Morris faded away just as surely as did MacArthur, and he still maintained the same attitude toward Truman that he had after being removed. In a passage from the book he wrote in 1955, Morris related that since his return to New York from his two-month stint as a corruption-fighter in Washington, many people had asked him what he really thought of Harry Truman. Morris told the story of a leading industrialist who had served a tour of duty in Washington, and was given a welcome-home dinner by his silk-stocking Republican friends. When asked to give his personal opinion of Truman, the industrialist replied, "No, I can't possibly tell you. It would shock you."

When the ladies had retired to another room, one of the men again asked for an appraisal, without success. Finally, when all the other guests had departed, the host whispered in the ear of the honored guest that since they were all alone, he really wanted to know his candid opinion of Truman. The industrialist confided, "All right, I'll tell you then. *I like him*."[99]

11

Communicating with the Public

President Truman was always looking for ways to give a "down home" touch to his fireside chats. To prepare for a June 14, 1951, report to the people on the need to control inflation, he asked us to be on the lookout for letters that showed in human terms how rising prices were hurting American families.

We came up with a couple of good ones for the President's use. A seventy-nine-year-old retiree named J. A. Pels from Cincinnati wrote about his experience in 1946, when the "know-it-alls" had predicted the removal of controls would drive prices down, and instead they soared. A gray-haired, bespectacled teacher from Brooklyn named Mrs. David A. Green helped the President personalize his argument by illustrating a homemaker's struggle to make both ends meet. Her husband turned out to be a Truman critic, but it didn't hurt too much to have Mr. Green tell reporters "there is something wrong with American journalism when my wife becomes news."

The President also wanted to dramatize the heavy lobbying pressure against legislation by organizations like the National Association of Manufacturers. I recalled an interesting senior thesis I had supervised at Princeton University, entitled "The National Association of Manufacturers and Its Campaign Against Price Control," which included a number of full-page ads that the NAM had used in its effort to gut the 1946 controls. A hurry-up phone call to the Princeton Library produced a copy of the thesis, and Truman made reference to the full-page ads in his fireside chat.

The President invited several members of the staff and their families to be present in the Oval Office on the evening of June 14 when he delivered his address. About eight o'clock Murphy phoned to tell me that Keith's Theater had installed a special apparatus for telecasting the address live to the audience, and had asked the White House to send a representative. Although I went over to see what it was like, I didn't think much more about it until Murphy called the next morning and asked me for my reaction. He interrupted my account by saying, "Well, I guess you had better come over and tell the President that."[1]

I hot-footed it over to the west wing, trying to figure out how to cover up the button that had popped off my suit coat. Although the President had delivered his address at 10:30 P.M. and must have stayed up pretty late thereafter with his guests, he looked well-rested, healthy and vigorous. He joked that the theater visitors must have booed, because they came to see a movie and had to sit still to get some education instead. I told him about the master of ceremonies, who came onto the stage to say this was the first time in history a presidential address had been telecast in this way, that the screen was 320 square feet and the speech was about a subject that concerned their daily lives.

Truman began to grill me on audience reactions, saying, "I'm always hearing about communications from the experts in the field. Now I want you to tell me just how the audience reacted, and what you liked and didn't like. We're going to have to work some more on this business of communicating."

I told him I was surprised at the quiet attentiveness of the audience, and that I heard several people comment later that they liked the way he quoted from the personal letters. I told him I thought the most positive reaction came as he described how the lobbies were trying to get him to give in on price control, and he stuck out his chin and announced firmly that he was "not going to give in."

The President smiled broadly and shot back, "I put that in myself while I was delivering the speech; it wasn't in the copy."

I told the President I felt there was one flaw, and I had one suggestion. "It was a little distracting to see at the bottom of the screen that you were turning the pages of your manuscript. Also, I think it would lend a lot of force to your conclusion if you extemporized the last few paragraphs, instead of reading them."

The President listened carefully. I noted again that he was a better communicator one on one than in front of a camera. He talks very directly to you, and his mind is always on the subject. He never dodges an issue. He turned to Murphy and immediately said: "Murph, we'll have to do something about those pages that people can see turning. I wonder if we could experiment a little more with gadgets which will help improve this thing. We're always looking for improvements, you know."

Murphy talked about the use of cards during speeches, as the President had started to do with advance filming of speech excerpts for use by newsreels. Early in the President's first term, prior to the advent of television, newsreels were still the rage, and they customarily accompanied every full-length motion picture. Elsey had worked out a special procedure for filming portions of the final draft of a speech. Checking with Clifford to mark important passages, Elsey arranged with the Pentagon to have these excerpts printed on large four-foot by six-foot cards placed on an easel. The President then went to the special movie projection room in the east wing, and the resulting films gave the clear appearance of extemporaneous delivery.

At this point in our conversation that morning, the President mentioned he had been talking with the President of the Columbia Broadcasting System "about a new gadget he had which he calls a 'teleprompter.'" Although he brought up the subject himself, I could tell from the President's reaction that he was a little suspicious of any gimmick that made it appear he was faking his sincerity of communication. Cue cards for the newsreels were his limit with respect to props used while on camera.

The President always paid close attention to the mail and telegrams immediately after his speeches. When I saw him the morning after his anti-inflation fireside chat, I asked him what kind of public reaction he had received. He immediately reached across his desk. Even though it was fairly early in the morning after a late-night speech, the speed of communication was considerably faster in those days. The President handed me a stack of telegrams, as he noted, "Here, you read these. They are running 46–29 in favor, up to this minute. And when you read the ones in opposition you'll see they come from the kind of people whom I like to have opposing me—the lobby and special interest guys."

I couldn't resist making an observation about Grover Cleveland, about whom it was said that the people "loved him for the enemies he has made." As usual, the President startled me by relating a choice slice of American history—that Wisconsin General E. S. Bragg had used this phrase about Cleveland when he made a nominating speech in the 1884 convention. He warned me not to confuse this Bragg with the General

Braxton Bragg of Civil War fame, after whom Fort Bragg, North Carolina, was named. As I riffled through the telegrams, we talked unhur-
riedly for a few minutes. It came through loud and clear that although
the President was pragmatic about trying improvements in communication, he wasn't about to turn himself over to pollsters, soap salesmen or
advertising executives bent on using new-fangled methods emanating
from Madison Avenue.

The Truman Press Office

The news media are the best sounding board for any public figure,
and through a succession of press secretaries Truman expanded his communication with the public. His experiences in Missouri politics condi-
tioned him to resent the bitter opposition of most publishers, but his
personal relations with reporters were unusually frank and friendly. The
several press secretaries who worked for Truman had markedly different
approaches to the challenge of improving public communication.

According to Robert J. Donovan, a White House reporter and Truman biographer,

> Ross presided over a weak press office. He made little effort to coordinate
> the release of news throughout the government and seemed to have no par-
> ticular scheme for legitimately presenting Truman and his policies in the
> best light.... On the other hand, he exerted a good influence on Truman
> on the side of dignity, liberalism and good sense.[2]

Although Short, who took over the job after Ross's death in 1950, could
never hope to attain the same degree of intimacy that Ross had enjoyed
since childhood, Truman went out of his way to include Short in intimate policy discussions and put his full trust in him.

"The first thing he did, I remember, was to cut down the red velvet
cord which was like a gate to keep newspapermen out of the office of the
secretary to the press secretary. I think he did *that* practically within a
few minutes of being sworn in," recalls Mrs. Short.[3] Another important
move made by Short was to recruit two able assistants, Roger W. Tubby
from the Department of State and Irving Perlmeter from the Bureau of
Internal Revenue. At first, Tubby worked in the foreign relations area
and Perlmeter in the domestic, but gradually their fields overlapped.
Each man brought something new to the operation of the press office.
Noticing that there was sometimes a lengthy lag between the end of

news conferences and the completion of a stenographic transcript, Perlmeter had a stenographic recording machine attached to the public address system where news conferences were being held.[4] The Army Signal Corps installed a high-quality magnetic tape recorder, from which approved radio excerpts were released for rebroadcast.

At first, the physical arrangements for news conferences were quite primitive and informal. President Roosevelt's physical disabilities had confined him to his desk at news conferences, and Roosevelt also had loved the easy banter through which he controlled the flow of news from his desk. Truman continued the same system until April 27, 1950, when Ross moved the news conferences across the street to the Indian Treaty Room on the fourth floor of the Executive Office Building. Under the new arrangement, reporters did not have to jam the corridors outside the President's office, vying for position, then stand in packed dissarray writing their notes while leaning against the backs of those in front. Some of the "old fogies" among the reporters liked the old system better, because the senior wire service reporters could crowd around the President's desk and monopolize the questioning.[5] In the Indian Treaty Room, each reporter had a seat, the President could see everyone, and the acoustics were superior. Reporters jumped to their feet to get recognition; but those in the rear had a better chance to ask questions than in the President's office. Truman had a compelling private reason for moving the news conferences out of the Oval Office in 1950. He had just obtained a new rug, and the newsmen were making brown spots by grinding out their cigarettes. They were also standing on the expensive chairs in the Oval Office.

Tubby helped expand and regularize the briefing of the President prior to the news conferences. Building on his experience in the State Department, he began to collect possible queries and suggested answers from every federal department several days in advance. The night before a conference, he assembled this material, arranged in question-and-answer and memo form, in a black loose-leaf notebook, which the President studied that evening.[6] On the day of the conference, he updated this material and the staff would meet for a skull session, about forty minutes prior to the actual conference.

Short also established a much closer liaison with press officials in the federal departments, with whom he met frequently to exchange information. Short encouraged both Tubby and Perlmeter to see Truman often, and to attend the morning staff meetings to keep fully briefed.

Short was far more aggressive than Ross in organizing the press operation. There was an easy, old-shoe camaraderie with which Ross operated; reporters had free access to all White House offices. Short clamped down on this procedure, insisting that he control any press contact with White House staff. While I was compiling a simple chronology of developments concerning MacArthur, for release to Capitol Hill sources as a research tool, Short was unusually restrictive on releasing details of presidential statements and communications with MacArthur.

Every press officer serves two frequently conflicting clients, his boss and the news media. It takes a genius to ride both horses successfully. Short made his choice very specifically. As a result, Robert Nixon of the International News Service once stated:

> Ross was very light-hearted. . . . He let the President be himself. If the President got himself in trouble, Charlie was never particularly upset and didn't go around oh my godding. . . . Short would get angry if reporters or someone wrote a story which portrayed Truman in a poor light.[7]

Edward T. Folliard of *The Washington Post* observed: "Short lost all detachment once he became White House press secretary. He got emotionally involved." If a reporter "wrote something that Short thought was critical of President Truman, Short blew up. . . . He lost his cool."[8]

Televising News Conferences

The Truman staff had reservations about television. To begin with, the rules against direct quotation of the President were very strict at the beginning of Truman's presidency. The press corps occasionally persuaded the President to allow direct quotation of especially significant pronouncements, but generally the only direct quotations were contained in the prepared, mimeographed statements the President released at the start of his news conference. When Perlmeter instituted the system of radio recordings, additional excerpts were released for direct quotation. Then on April 3, 1952, the concept of excerpts for television was introduced for the first time.

There was a vigorous debate within the Truman White House staff concerning full TV coverage. I argued that Truman had everything to gain from projecting his views in the less formal, give-and-take atmosphere of the question-and-answer sessions. I felt that over the years

Truman had developed a better sense of when not to shoot from the hip, as he did too frequently in the early years, and when to respond "No comment" to loaded questions that might produce mistakes. He enjoyed the verbal fencing, and his personality and philosophy showed through very effectively in a news conference. Some staff members argued that there were so many journalistic prima donnas that they would be hamming it up in front of the cameras at the expense of the President. I doubt the President fell for this argument, although he certainly had pronounced likes and dislikes among the media representatives. In any event, it is unfortunate that he never had the advantage of utilizing fully televised news conferences, a practice which was not started until Eisenhower became president.

The pressures on the press secretary were very heavy, caught as he was between the competing demands of a wide variety of individualists and the effort to sort out the needs of the President. It came as a personal shock to Truman to lose two press secretaries to fatal heart attacks, both of them sudden. Short died in mid-September 1952. Perlmeter had a nonfatal heart attack while on duty and could no longer remain active. For a brief period, Defense Department press relations man and former newspaperman Clayton Fritchey was brought in to help, but the major burden fell on Tubby's shoulders. Tubby became acting press secretary during the fall of 1952 and was promoted to full press secretary for the final two months of the Truman administration.

Public Reactions and Press Relations

President Truman imposed another obligation on his press secretary, as well as other members of the White House staff, reflecting his thirst for facts and his determination not to become isolated from the public. He was genuinely curious to learn from both his staff and visitors how the public was reacting to various issues. He snorted at so-called "scientific polls" of public opinion, which had unanimously predicted his defeat in 1948. His attitude toward polls is best expressed in this passage:

> Some people think that public relations should be based on polls. That is nonsense.
>
> I wonder how far Moses would have gone if he had taken a poll in Egypt?
>
> What would Jesus Christ have preached if He had taken a poll in the land of Israel?

Where would the Reformation have gone if Martin Luther had taken a poll?

It isn't polls or public opinion alone of the moment that counts. It is right and wrong, and leadership—men with fortitude, honesty and a belief in the right that make epochs in the history of the world.[9]

Like all great presidents, Truman found solace in the unfair attacks that the press had made on his predecessors. In frequent letters, memoranda and diaries, he gained comfort from reflecting that nobody remembered the names of those who had attacked Washington for the Jay Treaty, Jefferson for the Louisiana Purchase, or Lincoln for use of his war powers. For every provocation prompting an angry response, like his famous letter to the music critic after Margaret's concert, Truman blew off steam with dozens of private diary notes or letters that remained in his files and were marked "unsent." He frequently dubbed Hearst, Pulitzer, McCormick and other opposition publishers as the "sabotage press." He took some satisfaction in making a private prediction: "To hell with them. When history is written, they will be the sons of bitches—not I."[10]

Truman and Personal Interviews

The regular White House correspondents had a proprietary attitude toward their right to obtain and print news about the President. Ross and his successors were sensitive to this strongly emotional feeling in the White House press corps, thus they always tried to discourage exclusive interviews. At times, Truman would overrule his press secretary, as in the case of a private interview that veteran columnist Arthur Krock had published in *The New York Times* on February 15, 1950. Krock convinced Truman that the *Times* was genuinely concerned about printing the truth on his private thoughts, and Truman invited Krock to the Oval Office for a frank conversation the day before the interview appeared. One of the items reported by Krock was that Truman would have followed through on his plan to send Vinson to Moscow had not the 1948 campaign been in progress.

At Truman's next news conference, the reporters expressed their anger with such volume that he fired back at them:

May I say to you gentlemen right now—you seem to be in a kind of disgruntled mood this morning—that the President is his own free agent. He

will see whom he pleases, when he pleases, and say what he pleases to anybody that he pleases. And he is not censored by you, or anybody else.[11]

Late in 1950, author John Hersey asked Ross if he could write a series of articles on everything Truman did or said from the time he went
on his early morning walk until he went to bed at night, including staff
meetings, appointments, speech freezing sessions and other private conversations. Obviously aware of the uproar caused by the Krock interview earlier that year, Ross immediately turned down the request. Fortunately, Hersey persisted and managed to persuade Truman that such
an account would be of lasting historical value. The result was a remarkable series of articles covering behind-the-scenes activities of Truman and his staff during the months of November and December 1950.
The articles were originally published in *The New Yorker* magazine, and
were later expanded into a book, along with a similar series concerning
President Ford and his staff and visitors.[12]

Truman also gave his fullest cooperation to Jonathan Daniels in the
research for his 1950 biography, *The Man of Independence*. Daniels was
a facile writer who had been a Roosevelt assistant and remained a few
months under Truman, later keeping in friendly touch with the White
House.

"Be sure and give Jonathan Daniels the right view point. His book
will be the historical basis for a lot of future statements both true and
false," Truman wrote to his cousins Nellie and Ethel Noland.[13] Some
years later, Truman told Merle Miller, "That book is filled with a lot of
bunk; I don't know what got into Daniels. He used to work for me when
I was President, and he worked for Roosevelt, and I liked him. But when
he wrote that book, he just seemed to go haywire in places."[14]

Far and away the most revealing "inside story" about Truman was
obtained by William Hillman, onetime foreign correspondent for the
Hearst newspapers, writer for *Collier's* magazine, and Mutual Broadcasting System reporter. During 1951, Hillman had a series of interviews
with Truman. He was surprised when Truman asked his private secretary Rose Conway to turn over to Hillman some of his personal diaries,
private papers and correspondence she kept locked in a private safe.
Both the President and Miss Conway looked on this material as "hot
stuff" and "dynamite." The President told Hillman:

The notes you have seen were never intended for publication and are written in simple words and are not polished up. I hope they will serve the

purpose of clarifying some things, just as they helped me to clarify my thinking as I wrote them.[15]

Hillman added:

The President himself had forgotten many of the handwritten memoranda which I found among his papers, turned over to me by his private secretary. Where they were used he requested that they not be changed nor edited in any way.[16]

The Last News Conference

At his three-hundred-twenty-fourth and final news conference, on January 15, 1953, the warmth and spirit of President Truman's relationship with reporters, photographers, newsreel, radio, television and magazine writers were evident. At the beginning of the conference, the President cordially shook hands with everybody, calling most of the representatives at the jammed conference by name. They showed their personal appreciation for Mr. Truman with prolonged applause and a sincerely expressed standing ovation that brought dampness to the eyes of the most hard-boiled cynics present. Since there had been rumors circulating about possible discontinuance of news conferences in the incoming administration, the President made a strong plea for keeping the informal give-and-take he had always relished: "This kind of news conference where reporters can ask any question they can dream up—directly to the President of the United States—illustrates how strong and how vital our democracy is."[17]

Raymond P. "Pete" Brandt of the *St. Louis Post-Dispatch* wanted to know what the President thought about written questions.

The President answered, "I don't know. I have never tried it, Pete. It might give you more chance to deliberate. But then I like this rough and tumble press conference we have right here. If I can't take care of myself, that's my fault."[18] The President reflected that in all his 324 news conferences, "I have never felt that I have been unfairly treated." He also elaborated on one hidden advantage: "By the questions you ask, I find out a lot of things that you don't think I find out." He concluded, "I get as much kick out of these things as you have."[19]

There were many occasions when members of the White House staff watched President Truman perform at a news conference and hoped that the public could see him just as we did. He displayed the dignity of the great office he held, yet never completely obscured those human traits that were pure Harry Truman—the occasional flashes of anger, the emotional attachment to his family, his humility and lack of pretense, the burning pride and patriotism that never dimmed, his stubborn refusal to be pushed around by pressure groups, his realization of his responsibility as lobbyist for all the people, and his determination to "follow the gleam" even should it occasionally flicker as he restlessly searched for his greatest goal: world peace.

Fireside Chats

In attempting to improve the quality of President Truman's major speeches, the staff agitated for techniques employed by President Roosevelt. The most obvious and basic of these was the "fireside chat," which Truman readily used, until some questions were raised about the frequency and nature of the occasions when this type of speech was used. There was concern that they would lose their impact if used too frequently. Stowe, one of the strong advocates of more fireside chats, even though he was not directly involved in the speech-writing process, asked me to review how often Roosevelt delivered fireside chats. Stowe summarized these results to Murphy as follows:

> I believe you will be interested in looking through the attached memorandum on fireside chats of 1940–1942 prepared at my request by Mr. Hechler. This memorandum of fireside chats bears out my feeling that the President of the United States does not have to have a special occasion to report to the American people beyond the fact that the American people are in need of such report.[20]

It is true that few of President Truman's major addresses included memorable, quotable phrases like Roosevelt's "arsenal of democracy," "the only thing we have to fear is fear itself," "the good neighbor," or "a date which will live in infamy." One critic characterized Truman's speeches as "like a musical comedy which doesn't have tunes you can whistle." Murphy tackled that comment by observing:

> A presidential speech is a different animal from a news broadcast. Its primary requirement is accuracy, not style. Those on the outside sometimes fail to realize this. When some of them have been asked to write a draft incorporating their suggestions, they have bogged down badly.[21]

Murphy was a genius at reducing stilted and complex language to the kind of clear and simple sentences that President Truman liked. The President expressed his philosophy that "People don't go to hear people

make speeches for entertainment any more. They have plenty of entertainment on the radio, and television and the movies. What they want
are facts and supporting data to prove those facts are correct, and that's
all there is to it."[22] Sometimes I would hear the phrase "Missouri
English" to describe the type of simple and direct phraseology that was
necessary for a speech draft to pass muster. Subjunctives, passives, poly-
syllabic words, foreign phrases, lengthy sentences, and a unique language called "State Departmentese" received a brutal blue penciling.
Anything that sounded like a diplomatic communiqué or an after-action
report of military operations was immediately tossed out. Bell sometimes referred fondly to "My Aunt Minnie" as an argument to defeat
some obscurely worded phrase he contended she would never compre-
hend. Murphy and Lloyd were lawyers, but I never met a pair as adept
at ruthlessly rejecting legalistic language. Even economists like Bell and
public administration specialists like Neustadt disowned the bureaucra-
tese with which their contemporaries peppered scholarly journals.

"It takes special talent to be a speaker," Truman once said. "But
everybody can tell whether a man is sincere or knows what he's talking
about without his having to have that special talent and that's what
counts."[23]

Although Truman gained confidence on the speaking platform, he
was never an accomplished orator. He had a tendency to botch up
speeches when he read, because he delivered them too fast, slurring over
words and phrases. His extemporaneous speeches were superior, particularly when they revealed his sincerity and emotion. In the Senate, he
was a pedestrian speaker.

During his conversations with Hillman, the President commented:

> But I follow the practice of many speakers and radio commentators by un-
> derlining certain sentences or phrases or even words which I wish to em-
> phasize.
>
> But all too frequently I can't resist making a penciled mark on the mar-
> gin of the text I am going to read from for an off the cuff remark.
>
> Sometimes I forget the microphone and the formality and really warm
> up. But you will note it's usually where I want to drive home some impor-
> tant facts and not just phraseology.[24]

Using her large-type speech typewriter, Rose Conway typed the
reading copy of the President's speeches to produce the best delivery.
Each line ended at a point where there was a natural pause, so that the

flow of remarks was uninterrupted when the President's eyes swept back to the left side of the page to start a new line. The bottom third of the page was left blank to insure that the audience, television cameras, or photographers did not get a view of the top of the President's head bending down to read the bottom lines. Finally, no sentence or paragraph was ever split at the end of a page, so that no interruption of a thought occurred when turning pages.

Humor in Truman Speeches

Truman had a wonderful sense of humor, laughed heartily at a good joke, and told some beauties himself. There was frequent staff discussion concerning how much humor to include in speeches. Many outsiders who felt that Truman's speeches could be spruced up through humor cited Roosevelt's 1944 campaign speech about "my little dog Fala" as the perfect example of effective humor. The point was not entirely persuasive, however, since this was one of the few Roosevelt addresses that used the technique. It was generally felt that humor injected into an otherwise serious address would detract from the dignity of the presidential office, a principle to which Mr. Truman was deeply wedded. He had already been criticized for "cronyism," the "Missouri gang," the poker sessions, and his use of barnyard language, which caused the staff to be sensitive about the dignity of the office. On rare occasions on the campaign circuit, the President would tell a story. At times they went over like the proverbial lead balloon. On his "nonpolitical" Western trip in June of 1948, Truman had a great time at the reunion of his World War I Thirty-fifth Division in Omaha. He surprised his listeners at North Platte, Nebraska, by repeating this story, told to him the day before by Major General Butler B. Miltonberger:

> He said he was going up to the front and they began to shell the road, and he got under a tank. And there was a private under the tank with his back to him. And after the shelling let up a bit, why General Miltonberger said to the young man, "That was worse in this war than it was in the last." And the boy whirled around and said, "Were you in the last war?" And the General said "Yes." And the boy said, "You are the damndest fool I have ever seen."[25]

Perhaps because it was a Sunday in North Platte the crowd reaction was not as raucous as at an Army reunion, and the President did not attempt to tell any more stories. His campaign humor scored more effectively when put into political terms, like the "doctor" and "shadow" metaphors he used in 1948 and 1952.

Truman was at his excruciatingly funniest in ad-libbed remarks on January 19, 1949, at a dinner of the Presidential Electors Association at Washington's Mayflower Hotel.[26] That was the famous time when he recalled waking up about midnight on election night in 1948 to hear H. V. Kaltenborn say—and here he imitated him with a perfectly clipped Dutch accent—"While the President is a million votes ahead of the popular vote, when the country vote comes in, Mr. Truman will be defeated by an overwhelming majority."

Lloyd's humor occasionally bubbled to the surface in Truman speech drafts. One of his best efforts was included in a dinner speech delivered by Mr. Truman at the national convention banquet of the Americans for Democratic Action on May 17, 1952. Since Dave had been the research director for the liberal ADA, he repeatedly tried to persuade the President to come to one of their big dinners. Truman declined on several occasions because he still was not too happy about the way the ADA had tried to dump him in 1948. During his speech, which received tremendous applause from the big assemblage at the Washington Statler Hotel, he kidded the ADA about its 1948 preconvention behavior with this little ditty:

> Between the Taft and the Dewey,
>   When defeat is beginning to low'r,
> Comes a pause in the ADA's occupation,
> That is known as the Eisenhower.[27]

The speech came at about the time when Senator Kefauver, never a friend of Truman's, was scrambling for primary votes in his bid for the 1952 Democratic nomination. Right after the ADA speech, I included these comments in a letter to Judge Rosenman:

> It was a brilliant performance from start to finish, and the crowd was perfectly attuned with the President and vice versa. Part of this was due to the uproarious ovation which the diners gave to the President when he walked into the hall with Mrs. Truman. I don't think I have ever heard a bunch of intellectuals give vent to so many ear-splitting shouts, even some things which sounded like Rebel yells. The demonstration lasted for several minutes, and Senator Kefauver, who was at the head table, exhibited considerable puzzlement on his face as the demonstration went on and on and he

vainly tried to summon up enough courage to applaud sufficiently. Each time he would slow down and stop applauding, a new surge of enthusiasm greeted the President.

I had a long talk with James Rowley, head of the White House Secret Service detail, at the ADA dinner, and also wrote to Judge Rosenman:

> Jim Rowley told me last night that he had never seen the President so relaxed, so full of good humor and so effective in his remarks as during the past ten days. Rowley said that unfortunately the audiences which the President has been addressing consist mainly of people who know and who have seen the President or who really don't have very much political influence. Furthermore, these informal speeches are naturally not covered as extensively in the press as a formal speech where an advance release is handed out to the wire services and other reporters. Rowley said that he hoped, under the circumstances, that the President would get out on the road and make some of this type of speech to audiences who do not know him or who have only read the propaganda of the opposition press. I certainly agree with this point, and I know that the President intends to follow it out—but probably not until after the Convention.[28]

Lloyd's humor showed through again in an address that Truman delivered at a Columbus Day Dinner in New York. The Republicans had been sending a "truth squad" to hold press conferences in every city and town after the President spoke. In his remarks, the President brought a big laugh by exclaiming: "I wonder if Columbus ever had a truth squad following him around, shouting at the top of his voice: 'The world is flat, I tell you. The world is flat.' "[29]

Truman Letters

Letters were one of Truman's favorite forms of communication. Every morning before most of the office staff arrived, the President would dictate a large number of letters to Rose Conway. Letters from members of the cabinet, Congress, members of his family in Missouri, a list of personal friends, letters about his military service, the history of Jackson County, and the National Old Trails Association would come to him first, unopened. Frequently, he would write very personal replies in longhand. On occasion he would mail these himself.

The President's correspondence secretary, from the time he took office until the summer of 1952, was Hassett. Some of the thousands of letters addressed to the President would be acknowledged over Hassett's signature; the better ones and those from influential people would either go directly to the President or be sent along after Hassett had drafted a suggested reply.

In addition to the personal letters funneled through Hassett's office, the tall, gray-haired Vermonter had the responsibility for "official greeting" letters to all kinds of organizations. As a general rule, he would parcel these out among Murphy's or Steelman's staffs, so that policy expressions by the President would mesh with those issue-oriented items that the President had high on his priority list. Frequently, these exchanges were made at the morning staff meetings. I made a point to get to know Hassett shortly after I came to the White House, because we shared an interest in history. We used to have an occasional Sunday dinner together, or take in a movie when the workload wasn't too heavy.

A short time after I started working at the White House, I got a note from Hassett asking if I would draft a letter to one of the labor organizations. Resolving to do a thorough job on my first assignment, I spent several evenings at the Library of Congress going through newspapers, magazines and books until I had mastered the complete history not only of the union, but also of the areas in which its members were strongest. Then I read the *Congressional Record* debates on the key issues in which this group was interested, and went to the union's international headquarters to interview everybody from the higher-ups to the janitor. My "masterpiece" went on and on about the aims, ideals, principles, hopes, and dreams of that organization, along with fulsome words of presidential inspiration.

I heard nothing from Hassett, until one day he phoned me and without a word about my "great" letter, he said he wanted a letter from the President to the General Federation of Women's Clubs. "As a bachelor, you are uniquely qualified to know how Women's Clubs operate," he said. When he sent over the background data, he included this sly hint: "Hereabouts we think that wisdom does not carry over to the second page of a letter. Thanks very much for your help." After getting over that hurdle, I found the letters were a lot of fun because they opened doors to interesting people. In this way, I helped greet the International Association of Firefighters, Communication Workers of America, Knights of Columbus, National Federation of Postal Clerks, International Typographical Union, Textile Workers Union of America, International Association of Public Employment Services and countless other organizations which, hopefully, were given a taste of Harry Truman's philosophy.

Hassett had attempted to retire on several occasions, but the President drafted him to stay. In the spring of 1952 he became ill and had to make his retirement permanent because of his age and health. Following the sudden and unexpected death of press secretary Short in September 1952, the President asked Short's widow, Beth, to take on the post of correspondence secretary. Although the President was out on the road whistle-stopping during the 1952 campaign, Mrs. Short attended presidential staff meetings when he was in town and answered correspondence, which one week reached a volume of twenty thousand letters. She also started answering previously ignored "con" mail—not the crank letters, but criticisms written with some feeling and logic, like the letter from a widow whose husband had been killed in Korea.

Truman relished the opportunity to write those letters that carried his very personal brand of bluntness. He mailed many of them himself without showing them to anyone. The famous Hume letter was written after an extremely trying week for the President. On the heels of the massive invasion of Korea by hundreds of thousands of Chinese troops, Truman at his November 30 news conference caused international confusion by his indiscreet remarks on the possible use of the atomic bomb. On December 5, his close friend and press secretary Charles Ross collapsed and died of a heart attack. That evening Margaret sang in concert at Constitutional Hall. Hume's panning review in the next morning's *Washington Post* triggered the injured outrage of a father already suffering personal grief and strain. Publication of the Hume letter stirred a storm over the expletives used by the President.

The White House staff was generally appalled by the letter. Correspondence secretary Hassett facetiously suggested that the President wasn't keeping him busy enough. The Hume letter was preceded and followed by numerous others—one vowing he "wouldn't appoint John L. Lewis dogcatcher"; one to Republican Congressman Gordon L. McDonough saying that the Marines "have a propaganda machine that is almost equal to Stalin's"; and one to former Secretary of State James F. Byrnes, saying "Et tu, Brute." Matt Connelly put a printed card on the President's desk, reading: "PUBLIC RELATIONS is the letter you don't write when you're mad and the nice letter you write the soandso after you've regained your sense of humor."

The President did not share his staff's reaction to the Hume letter. "Wait till the mail comes in. I'll make you a bet that eighty percent of it is on my side of the argument," he predicted. He was right; slightly over eighty percent of the letters favored the President. He told his staff:

"The trouble with you guys is, you just don't understand human nature."[30]

Jonathan Daniels concluded: "The clear fact is that Harry Truman would not be Harry Truman if he stopped speaking his mind, writing his letters, penning his postscripts, reaching for the telephone, taking his chances with his countrymen in the native—although not always the presidential—language."[31]

"Our Foreign Policy"

In addition to speeches, news conferences, letters, visitors and other public appearances, President Truman always looked for new ways to communicate with the public. In 1950, he decided it would be useful to have the State Department publish a simple, clear, brief, popular explanation of American foreign policy. One of my tasks was to keep after those who had reluctantly undertaken the work in the Department of State. Some officials complained that our foreign policy was so complex that it couldn't possibly be explained in less than one hundred pages!

Widespread misunderstanding about our aims and goals in Korea made it even more urgent after the summer of 1950 that such a pamphlet be rushed to completion.

When galley proofs of the brief pamphlet "Our Foreign Policy" were submitted to the White House, Elsey drafted a "Foreword" for the President's signature and submitted it to Truman. He not only took it home to read that night, but also wrote on the galleys suggestions on phraseology to express our foreign policy in human terms. Robert Thompson, head of State Department publications, then designed an attractive cover and readable format for the seventy-nine-page pamphlet. "Our Foreign Policy" received widespread, favorable editorial comment, was much in demand in educational institutions, and sold for twenty-five cents a copy. The 1950 edition sold out; in 1952 Lloyd helped write a new "Foreword" for an updated edition.

The President and his staff restlessly searched for additional ways to improve communication with the public. By the standards of today and with the perspective of history, President Truman looms larger as a great chief executive who communicated with the American people and the world far better than he knew or realized at the time.

12
"Cargo of Truth"—
The Anatomy of a Speech

On March 4, 1952, Truman boarded the United States Coast Guard cutter *Courier*, which had been refitted for use by the Voice of America. In welcoming ceremonies held on Municipal Pier on the Potomac River in Washington, D.C., he broadcast this message around the world, later translated into forty-five languages for rebroadcast: "This vessel will not be armed with guns, or with any instruments of destruction. But it will be a valiant fighter in the cause of freedom. It will carry a precious cargo—and that cargo is truth."[1]

Although this would not qualify as one of the President's major speeches, the process through which it was developed furnishes a case study of the vast amount of background work that precedes a presidential address, as well as the President's participation in the "freezing session," when he finally decides on the substance of his remarks. Notes that I made at the time enable me to furnish a play-by-play account of one of President Truman's more interesting and successful public addresses.[2]

Frequently, the President articulated his belief that military might was insufficient to protect the forces of freedom against aggressive communist threats around the world. In addition to strengthening the economies of developing nations through the Point Four program and saving western Europe through the Marshall Plan, the President stressed the need to combat communist lies with the truth. "Unless we get the real story across to the people in other countries, we will lose the battle for men's minds by pure default. . . . We must make ourselves heard round the world in a great campaign of truth," he told the American Society of Newspaper Editors on April 20, 1950.[3]

On January 18, 1952, Edward W. Barrett, the aggressive assistant secretary of state for public affairs, drew up a summary of the achievements during the twenty-month period of the Campaign of Truth.[4] Both the President and the secretary of state were searching for additional ways to dramatize this campaign. It was finally decided to commemorate the tenth anniversary of the Voice of America with an address by the President, to be delivered on February 22. This would occur just a week after the formal commissioning of a seagoing broadcasting station on the United States Coast Guard cutter *Courier*, refitted at the Bethlehem Steel Company's Hoboken, New Jersey, shipyard.[5]

Origins of the Speech

Background material reached the White House in a memorandum from Frederick C. Oechsner, who had the imposing title of "acting special assistant to the assistant secretary for public affairs." Oechsner's memorandum and draft speech,[6] dated January 31, suggested an afternoon ceremony geared to obtaining additional congressional appropriations.

Lloyd had central responsibility for drafting the remarks. On February 8, Dave handed me the Oechsner memorandum, with the comment that the State Department draft was "rather rambling and tepid." We spent a few minutes mulling over an old problem: Why, with all the high-priced talent available to formulate persuasive Voice of America broadcasts, were State Department personnel incapable of producing a first-rate speech draft in clear and simple English? We agreed that the draft emphasized the accomplishments of the Voice of America and told only briefly, at the close, about the nature and purpose of the vessel from which the broadcasts would emanate.

The idea for the floating transmitter had been developed under a project known as "Operation Vagabond," a program of psychological warfare approved in 1951 by the President and the Joint Chiefs of Staff. The *Courier* was a 5,800-ton, 338-foot, gray vessel, manned by a Coast Guard crew, including ten officers trained in radio. Voice of America engineers supervised the operation of the transmitting equipment. The transmitters were the most powerful ever to be installed on a ship, including one 150-kilowatt medium-wave transmitter (three times the power of the largest American broadcasting station), two 35-kilowatt short-wave transmitters and supporting equipment. The vessel was a floating base to rebroadcast messages to peoples behind the Iron Curtain. The project was developed to provide maximum mobility and twenty-four-hour, all-weather operation from movable bases. It provided new problems for the Soviet jamming apparatus. The diesel engines were capable of generating one and a half million watts of electrical power for the radio equipment.[7]

A Snag Develops

On Saturday, February 16, the day after the *Courier* was supposed to be officially launched in Hoboken, I received a telephone call from an agitated Ben Crosby of State's Office of Public Affairs. He said that because of strikes, lack of spare parts and several other excuses, Captain Oscar C. B. Wev of the *Courier* had told him he was not sure he could get his vessel to Washington in time for the February 22 ceremonies. This was a real rhubarb, and Crosby asked me to intervene with the President to change the date. I told Crosby the President had many engagements and requests for appearances and it was out of the question to leave open a "floating" date, to be filled when the ship arrived at its Potomac dock. When I would not give Crosby any satisfaction, he called Perlmeter with the same request.

Perlmeter called me on Monday the eighteenth and said that "so far as I am concerned the whole deal is off if the State Department can't produce the ship." He observed, "They really ought to fly the ship down piece by piece, since they had committed the President to a definite date for a speech." We both wanted to make sure that everybody understood it was a serious matter to commit the President to a definite speaking date when the details had not been well planned. The President initially decided to cancel the whole thing, but eventually he softened and agreed to reschedule his appearance for the morning of March 4.

On February 26, I had lunch with Murphy and Bell, and Bell asked, "Who is handling the *Courier* speech?" I reviewed the developments. Our interactions with the State Department indicated that they were scared of being too provocative in the speech. Bell immediately said: "What can a little ship do? It has no guns. It just has a radio. There's nothing provocative about that, for crying out loud!"

Hurry, Hurry!

We had been expecting a promised new draft from the State Department, reflecting our February 11 discussions in a meeting Lloyd and

I had with State Department aides to get the ball rolling. Days passed
and nothing happened. Finally, on Thursday, February 28, I phoned Joe
Phillips to say that unless we received something by the end of the day
we would not be able to incorporate their suggestions. Late Thursday
afternoon, State sent their draft, along with two other drafts that Phillips said he had rejected but which we might want to see anyhow.

Lloyd looked over the material and suggested we should start on a
new tack. He said we ought to use this opportunity to broadcast a message of peace and friendship to the peoples of the Soviet Union and
China. Lloyd emphasized that we had helped both nations when they
were invaded by Germany and Japan. He pointed to a 1951 congressional resolution of friendship with the peoples of the Soviet Union,
which had been transmitted to President Shvernik. Then he casually said
to me, "In the light of the shortness of time, would you have a new draft
by tomorrow morning?" I gulped an affirmative.

First White House Draft

After a quick dinner, I returned to the office about 8:00 P.M., and
settled down to do about an hour's research before starting to write. I
pulled out the 1951 congressional resolution sent to President Shvernik.[8]
There was little substantive inspiration here, but it did use the novel
technique of trying to pierce the Iron Curtain to reach the people rather
than their leaders in the Kremlin. Then I sifted out one or two ideas in
the State Department draft. But the central theme was still missing. In
desperation, I began to finger the "rejected" State Department drafts.
Buried in one draft that had been turned down I discovered a brilliant
phrase by a chap named Holder of the Eastern European Affairs desk,
that the ship did not carry weapons but only a cargo of truth. I decided
to salvage this concept and feature it in my draft. The "cargo of truth"
phrase not only stayed in every subsequent draft, but also became the
title of the address.

The draft started with a brief description of the mission of the vessel,
leading into the fact that it did not carry guns, but a "cargo of truth."
Then I worked in the idea that many peoples had contributed to building the ship. There followed a simple, direct message to the peoples behind the Iron Curtain. I tried to imagine both the President and those
listening by including this sentence: "I say to you with all my heart that
we yearn for peace, and we want to work with you to secure peace."

Then I added a portion about our help to Russia and China during the war and our aim to bring peace on earth and good will toward all men.

I tried again to picture the people listening to the broadcast, in their homes, at gathering places, or in isolated areas, and attempted to address them directly, extending "the hand of friendship across the seas" and adding, "although the future may look dark to you, have faith that all peoples will once again walk in the sunlight of peace and justice." At Lloyd's suggestion, I tried to work in a summary of our disarmament proposals, and ended with a "work together for peace" theme.

Lloyd liked the draft very much, and while he was smoothing out some phrases the next day—Friday the twenty-ninth—I took several calls from the State Department. They implored me to emphasize that the *Courier* was only one phase of the entire Campaign of Truth, and not to convey the impression that this constituted the bulk of the program. Lloyd worked this into my draft, and added that other free nations were doing their part. I also incorporated some suggestions from James Loeb, former director of the Americans for Democratic Action, who was doing some special work with the White House.

Just before lunch on the twenty-ninth, Lloyd and I spent an hour and a half reworking several sections of the draft. I readily agreed with his second thoughts that the disarmament material was not relevant. I got a little worried about the length of the draft as one or two other paragraphs were tossed overboard. We agreed to change the tone of the last section to make it sound less like we were working too closely with the Soviet Union and China.

Lloyd and I rarely had extended disagreements, and I realized that time was getting short, but we had what almost amounted to a shouting match over one little phrase. I had written toward the end that our aim was to "bring peace on earth and good will toward all men." Lloyd insisted that "this is not a Christmas speech" and took out "good will toward all men." When the speech was finally mimeographed and distributed to the press, this phrase was omitted, as it was in the reading copy. I protested to no avail that this was a perfectly natural phrase and it should remain. When the President delivered the speech, as he came to the phrase "peace on earth," he looked up from his manuscript to ad lib "and good will towards all men."

By now the speech was down to three legal-sized pages, which is a little short for a five-minute speech. But we had it typed and sent copies over to the State Department and to Murphy for review.

Murphy Additions

Murphy's reaction was that the three-page draft was a little too thin and could use some more affirmative substance. On the afternoon of Friday the twenty-ninth, he took a personal hand at revising the middle section, adding some stirring phrases about the meaning of truth and its relationship to peace. Just after lunch on Saturday, Bell, Loeb, Neustadt and I reviewed the redraft in Murphy's office. Since Lloyd had to make a train, he marked his suggestions on my draft and asked me to express them for him.

We worked over the draft for some time, then sent the changes to the White House staff room for retyping. Murphy said to me in his unhurried drawl: "When you get the draft back, maybe it would be a good idea to clear it with the State Department so we can have it ready for freezing by the President at noon on Monday."

That was a really tough assignment. It was about 4:00 o'clock Saturday afternoon when the speech was retyped and ready for clearance. By that time everybody except workaholics and White House staff had fled for the weekend. I made a few fruitless phone calls to try to locate somebody in the State Department. I finally reached Marshall Shulman at home, and he told me that since the key people who could clear the draft were simply not around, the best they could do was to give it a quick clearance early Monday morning. I knew that Murphy always wanted to be certain that the department centrally concerned should have a last crack at the semi-final draft of a speech. But secretly I hoped that the close deadline might cause the State Department not to quibble too much about a speech that was going to be frozen by the President less than twenty-four hours before it was to be delivered.

On Monday morning, March 3, agonized wails came over the telephone from the State Department. They were particularly upset by the omission of a paragraph stating that the *Courier* was only a small part of the Campaign of Truth. They insisted that this paragraph be reinserted, and that we also state we were carrying on the exchange of persons program to promote peace and good will. Lloyd agreed to write in the old paragraph about the work being done with libraries and information centers, but he harrumphed: "Unless and until the State Department gets a better word for exchange of persons, I refuse to have the President endorse something that sounds suspiciously like white slave traffic."

Finally, at 1:00 P.M., Lloyd and I finished our smoothing over and sent the draft off to the staff room for another retyping. Murphy called me while I was lunching at the White House mess, and said he wanted to do a "final" review with Lloyd and me immediately prior to the freezing session with the President. As soon as I finished lunch, I went up to the Cabinet Room where Murphy, Elsey, Bell, Lloyd and Shulman were working on the Mutual Security message and radio address, to be delivered March 6. Murphy and Lloyd quietly withdrew from the Mutual Security speech conference as I entered the Cabinet Room, and the three of us slipped into an adjoining room.

I told Murphy and Lloyd that the State Department had called again, objecting to the word "attacking" in a phrase I had written stating that in Russia and China the "rulers are now attacking us." They wanted to know why State objected. I responded, "I think they're probably right, because the United States is really not being attacked physically." They looked at their watches silently. I said, "I still have time to change that word to 'assailing'; is that OK?" They readily nodded assent.

Freezing Session

"I'll have them do a hurry-up retyping job on those two pages and send them over to the Cabinet Room for the freezing session," I said.

Just before 4:00 P.M., I walked into the Cabinet Room with the eight freshly typed copies of the speech in a big brown envelope. The door on the west side of the Cabinet Room suddenly opened. It was the door that led to the President's office, through Rose Conway's office. The President walked in quickly, and, of course, everyone rose. He took a seat at the west end of the cabinet table. Bell sat to the President's right, with Murphy beyond him on the south side of the table. As I started to sit down on the north side of the table, press secretary Short suddenly appeared from nowhere. He must have come in while I was watching the President. Short sat to the President's left and I sat next to Short. I quickly distributed my copies of the *Courier* draft.

Someone asked the President how his eighty-nine-year-old mother-in-law, Mrs. Wallace, was getting along. The President once wrote "When I hear these mother-in-law jokes I don't laugh. They are not funny to me, because I've had a good one."[9] He responded with feeling:

Well, she feels OK in the mornings, but not so good in the afternoons. I thought I ought to summon her sons, and they all came in. She appreciates it, but you know the old lady called them all in this morning and said, "Boys, I want you to know that I love you even more for coming to me this way, but I'm old enough to go, and you have big jobs to take care of back home; when I go, I'll know you've been here, so that's all that matters—you can go home now."

As the President picked up the *Courier* draft, he said,

This certainly has the virtue of brevity. That's more than you can say for the one I have to give next Thursday night [the Mutual Security speech]. I worked on that one last night, and the Madam says it's a darned good speech—and she's a good critic too. I'm going to work on the Tuesday speech this evening. By the way, can you get me a final of the Thursday speech by Tuesday, because I want to have at least two days to work it over before delivering it?

Murphy and Bell pursed their lips in silent whistles. They had counted on finishing the message to Congress first, and then going to work on the March 6 fireside chat on Mutual Security; now they knew they had to drop their work on the message, and shift their priority to the fireside chat.

Then the President looked at the *Courier* draft and started reading it aloud. While he was reading, Lloyd came in and took a seat at the cabinet table between Short and me, on the north side of the table.

Bell spoke up first:

Mr. President, it seems to me there were an unusually large number of "s" sounds in the first two paragraphs of that page. I see words like speaking, ship, special, ship again, mission, precious, to cite just a few. I'm just wondering if you won't have some trouble with that kind of combination.

The President laughed good-naturedly and responded, "That 's' sound doesn't bother me near as much since the dentist fixed my teeth. I don't whistle on 'em nearly as much as I used to, Dave."

When we got down to page three, Joe Short said, "Can't somebody get me a better and clearer page three so the girls in the staff room won't go blind retyping this?"

I made a hurried search and discovered to my horror that for some reason, the carbons were all faulty on page three. The President didn't seem to mind at all. He quipped: "Page three has pernicious anemia. Let's just go ahead."

Short asked that a colon be inserted at one point, to the approval of everybody. Suddenly, the President put the draft down, and a sad look crossed his face. I wondered what was troubling him. He merely said, "You know, Charlie Ross was the greatest guardian of the colon and the semicolon in days gone by." There was silence for a moment, and then the President asked, "Any other changes on that page?" I singled out the word "particularly" and deliberately stumbled over it to prove how hard it was to pronounce, adding, "I think you should change that word 'particularly' to 'especially' for obvious reasons." The President marked the change on his copy, adding, "I'm 225 percent in favor of that change."

Bell suggested changing a sentence reading "This ship is a small but important part of this campaign" to read, "This ship is an important part of this campaign." For emphasis, Murphy said "this" should be switched to "that" in the sentence just changed, and in one other place. The President accepted both changes readily.

The President then commented that the sentence about libraries, motion pictures, newspapers and magazines was very dull and sounded like a laundry list or a table of organization. He said, "Even my old Army field orders used to have more zip than this catalogue." Lloyd somewhat apologetically pointed out that although he agreed, the State Department had fought long and hard to have that sentence left in, and would feel terribly let down if it were not mentioned, dull though it was. The President leaned back and made a kindly, but somewhat derogatory remark about the ability of some people in the State Department to take a simple, declarative statement and stretch it out into something of extreme complexity.

After we finished page four, the President turned to Bell, who had a crease in his forehead, and asked, "What's the trouble over there, Dave?" Bell said, "Mr. President, you'll be talking to a big audience around the world. I just wonder how many of them will really understand the word 'assailing'?"

Short immediately leaped to the defense of "assailing." "That's a good old headline word which any newspaperman understands, and we like to use it. I think most people will understand it. I vote to keep it in there."

There was a little flutter of argument, back and forth. I then made a weak pun: "Since it's a ship, isn't it OK to have it assailing?"

There was an embarrassing silence for a moment, punctuated by the deep Mississippi drawl of Short, proclaiming in throaty disgust: "Oh, God, no!" I felt like slinking under the table, but the President rescued

240

me with a hearty, albeit slightly forced, laugh. He said, "Let's keep assailing," and that's the way he delivered it.

After he had finished the last page, the President laid aside the draft
and said quietly, "Well, that's a fine statement. I'll work on it some more
tonight." He arose to return to his office, and we picked up our papers
and adjourned.

The Public Ceremony

On March 4, there was a cold drizzle and a bite in the air as I headed
down to the Potomac. The *Courier* was docked along Maine Avenue, in
Southwest Washington. I reflected that on that date, exactly nineteen
years earlier, Roosevelt had delivered his first inaugural address in the
midst of a banking crisis. Not until later did I learn that on that same
fourth of March, 1952, an actor named Ronald Reagan, who had been on
the platform in Los Angeles during Truman's 1948 campaign address,
was marrying an actress named Nancy Davis.

There was a gangplank from the dock onto the Coast Guard cutter,
but those without invitations were being turned away. A Secret Service
man spotted me, nodded affirmatively to a man who had temporarily
blocked my access to the gangway, and I went up to the top deck. A
canopy protected the speaker's stand, decorated with red, white and
blue bunting, from the rain. Metal folding chairs were provided for some
250 guests. It was obvious that some guests had decided they would not
come because of the rain, but the small crowd was enthusiastic.

Voice of America Director Foy D. Kohler said he was sorry he
couldn't do something about the weather, "but I have an idea that the
Courier in its travels will go through much worse weather both literally
and figuratively."[10] The program was carefully timed to broadcast a
thirty-minute segment, starting at 10:30 A.M., including the President's
remarks and comments by Secretary Acheson, International Information
Administrator Wilson Compton, and other officials. Truman delivered
his address in clear and measured tones. He showed that his heart was in
the speech by ad libbing several additional lines. At one point, when he
said, "Our arguments, no matter how good, are not going to influence
people who never hear them," he paused, looked up and said, "I'll re-
peat that."[11] He drove the point home again for emphasis. The entire
address was inspiringly delivered. The audience reaction was warm,
positive and enthusiastic. There was a genuine ring of conviction in the
President's delivery. The chilled crowd gave him a rousing ovation.

Within an hour of my return to the White House, I received three separate telephone calls from Crosby, Phillips and Knox of the State Department. They all offered congratulations and said that the Department of State was pleased with the entire ceremony and in particular the delivery and substance of the President's address.

Lloyd told me the President was pleased with the speech and had commented to him favorably on several occasions since its delivery. I asked Park Armstrong, State Department's intelligence assistant, to run a survey abroad to gauge the reaction in foreign countries. Domestically, the newspaper and editorial reaction was very positive. Messages, letters and telegrams, most of them favorable, came in from all over the nation, and even from a ship in the middle of the Atlantic.[12]

Following the President's March 4 address, the *Courier* put to sea for a successful shakedown cruise to Latin America and the Caribbean to test its broadcasting equipment. The ship carried a number of barrage balloons, sixty-nine by thirty-five feet in size, along with one hundred fifty thousand cubic feet of helium to inflate them. These balloons were hoisted from the flight deck of the vessel to give additional range for the antennae.[13] During extended tests in the Canal Zone, the medium-wave transmitter was heard clearly throughout the Caribbean, and the two short-wave transmitters as far away as Europe and New Zealand. On July 17, 1952, the *Courier* sailed for the island of Rhodes in the eastern Mediterranean, where it operated a floating relay base for programs beamed to the Soviet Union and to the Near and Middle East,[14] and on September 7, the *Courier* commenced successful broadcasts to these areas.[15]

Although Truman's address from the *Courier* on March 4 was not regarded as one of his major efforts, it was widely hailed for its significance and effectiveness in the President's continuing search for world peace.

13
The Last Campaign as President: 1952

On several public occasions the President noted that he had made up his mind early not to run in 1952. "Long ago, shortly after I was inaugurated in 1949, I decided that I ought not to run for office," he told a St. Louis audience at the climax of the 1952 campaign.[1]

"One of the most amazing things I recall from all my years in Washington" is the way Hassett characterized the well-guarded secret that President Truman did not plan to run in 1952.[2] Truman first wrote of his determination not to run in a diary entry on April 16, 1950.[3] He informed members of his senior staff of this decision on November 19, 1951[4] (contrary to his own statement in his *Memoirs*, which inaccurately fixes the date as March of 1951[5]). Truman wanted to give his staff the opportunity to adjust future personal plans. Aside from Hassett's retirement and Short's death, none of Truman's staff left after 1951.

After his unsuccessful attempt in January to induce Chief Justice Vinson to succeed him, Truman tried to persuade Illinois Governor Adlai E. Stevenson to run. The President got the impression that he said yes, but Stevenson told others he had said no. When the period of uncertainty set in, there were many attempts to get the President to change his mind about not running. Finally, Truman announced his final, irrevocable decision at the Jefferson-Jackson Day dinner at the National Guard Armory in Washington on March 29, 1952, shocking hordes of assembled Democrats.[6]

Reasons for Decision

The decision and his reasons for it were set forth in his April 16, 1950, diary notation: "In my opinion eight years as President is enough and sometimes too much for any man to serve in that capacity. There is a lure in power. It can get into a man's blood just as gambling and lust for money have been known to do."[7] He wrote that "by a quibble I could say I've only had one term," but he added that the two-term tradition, although broken by Roosevelt, should continue.

As a great politician, Truman realized his influence with Congress would wane once he became a "lame duck" President. Hence there was a long delay before he made his intentions public on March 29.

Present at the November 1951 meeting at which he announced his decision to his staff were Admirals Leahy, Dennison and Souers; Murphy, Short, Tubby, Hassett, Steelman, Dawson and Vaughan. The meeting started about 3:00 P.M. and went on until 5:00 P.M., as there was difficulty in assembling everybody because they had scattered around the Naval Base.

According to Dennison, the President read from a memorandum written in 1950, indicating his determination not to run, and Dennison recalls, "I was sitting next to him and when he got through with it I had a hard time believing it. I asked if I could see it and he handed it to me and I read it."[8]

It couldn't have been more than an hour after the President told his senior staff about his plans that some of us on the junior staff arrived at Key West. Our group included Russell Andrews, Dallas Halverstadt, Milton Kayle, Richard Neustadt and I.[9] We were housed close to the President's quarters. It was a muggy evening, with the mosquitoes out in force and the huge sprayers fogging everything up to treetop height so it would be more comfortable when venturing outside to get a full taste of our semi-tropical surroundings. Following the style set by the President we hurried into the most outrageously colored sport shirts available and savored the opportunity to spend ten enjoyable days with wonderful company and absolutely nothing to do.

There was clearly an air of tension among the senior staff the night we arrived. We concluded that the excitement was caused by the President's pending departure to speak at the Women's National Democratic Club dinner in Washington, D.C. There was no inkling of the momentous announcement just made. But I do have a sharp recollection of the completely relaxed mood displayed by the President on the evening of our arrival. We saw him before dinner, and joined him in chatting and swapping stories with several staff members. Truman joined a spirited argument concerning military commanders back to Alexander the Great. Bell was the only staff member who could keep up with the President's knowledge of the relative merits of Genghis Khan and Tamerlane. Many times since that evening I have thought of the conversation. Truman glided from his surprise decision, to ancient history and then, as the door suddenly opened, to a first-class ribbing of a dripping and bedraggled Dr. Graham, just returned from a long fishing jaunt with a paltry catch.

In his address to the Women's National Democratic Club on November 20, the President intrigued his listeners with this account of where he stood on the 1952 nominee:

> Down at Key West, I have also had more time than usual to think about some of the things that lie ahead of us.
>
> One of the things I have been thinking about is next year's election. I am sure that is a matter of considerable interest to all of you people here tonight. It's a matter of considerable interest to me, too, and that's what I want to talk to you about.
>
> I'm not going to make any announcement about who the candidate will be, although I do have some ideas on that subject.[10]

Murphy's Reaction

One of the most interesting reactions to the President's November 19 announcement came from Murphy, who accompanied Truman on his November 20 trip back to Washington, and then wrote the President this letter:

> Dear Mr. President:
>
> I want you to know some of the thoughts that are in my mind about this memorandum you read to us Monday afternoon.
>
> In the first place, I accept your decision without question, although there are many important reasons why I believe the public interest would be served by your continuance in office. But, if this is the way you want it, I will do all I can to help make it work out with the desired results. On the other hand, if circumstances should perchance require you to change your decision, I will be very happy to do all I can to help make it work out on that basis.

In either event, I will be right here until January 20, 1953, if you want to keep me around. I am not particularly worried about my own personal future, as I am satisfied I can get along reasonably well. That, of course, is due in large part to the opportunity you have given me to make a reputation by working on your staff.

It is a great privilege to work here for you as I do. It has given me opportunities to be of service such as come to few men—and many rich and thrilling experiences. This is probably the high point of my life. But no matter what happens from here on out, I will have much to remember and much to be thankful for.

I deeply appreciate all the consideration you have shown me. I cannot contemplate the end of this association with you, even some distance in the future, without a very heavy heart.

With great respect,
Charles S. Murphy[11]

The President
The Little White House
Key West, Florida

Truman and Stevenson

In the early months of 1952, the White House was beset with serious problems. The war in Korea dragged on, the Democrats in Congress were turning tail in the face of McCarthy's scattershot attacks, and the corruption problem worsened. The misunderstanding that grew out of the first meeting with Stevenson troubled the President, because he thought he understood human nature. Having worked for both men at different times, I could easily surmise why they sometimes thought at cross-purposes. Truman had an instinctive, visceral feeling about issues that concern the common man, and his reactions were basic, immediate and forceful. Stevenson had an intellectual, many-faceted knowledge of world problems and sought intelligent solutions to every issue. To Truman, Stevenson seemed indecisive; to Stevenson, Truman overlooked certain problems—like corruption, for example. Truman wanted to solve the corruption issue and get it behind him with one stroke; Stevenson recognized that the moral climate could not be altered by one or two firings. Then Stevenson made the mistake of allowing a reporter to draw him into using the phrase "mess in Washington." The coolness between the two men intensified when Stevenson removed Truman's appointee, McKinney, as chairman of the Democratic National Committee and replaced him with an amateur, Stephen A. Mitchell.

On February 18—forty days before his public announcement that he would not run in 1952—Truman asked six of his closest advisers to dine with him and discuss the campaign ahead. The President's hitherto-unpublished personal notes on this secret meeting follow:

> February 18, 1952
>
> Had a grand meeting tonight from 6:40 to 11:25 P.M. Dinner and a discussion of the Presidential Campaign. Present were the Chief Justice Fred Vinson, Sam Rosenman, William D. Hassett, Clark Clifford, John R. Steelman, Charles Murphy.
>
> The discussion was about possible candidates for President, including the present occupant of the White House.
>
> The Chief Justice opened the discussion by saying that while he did not believe in the indispensable man he did not see how the President could refuse another term. Sam Rosenman came to the same conclusion. Mr. Hassett thought the President should do what he wanted to do and retire and let the conditions work out the result. Dr. Steelman thought that someone could surely be found to work out the succession. Clark Clifford thought Robt. Kerr might qualify. Mr. Murphy discussed Adlai Stevenson pro and con. No real conclusions were reached. Every one made a contribution.[12]

The President wrote on March 4 that Stevenson had advised him that "he had made a commitment to run for reelection in Illinois and that he did not think he could go back on that commitment honorably."[13] According to the President's diary, Stevenson then "argued that only I can beat any Republican be he Taft, Eisenhower, Warren, or anyone else! My wife and daughter had said the same thing to me an hour before. What the hell am I to do? I'll know when the time comes because I am sure God Almighty will guide me."

According to Murphy, a further discussion by the President with all the members of his senior staff, plus Vinson, McKinney and several others, resulted in a nearly unanimous decision that the President should not run. Murphy expressed the thought that a new Democratic president "would clear away a lot of deadwood in his Administration that ought to be cleared out." Vinson emerged from the meeting, shaking his head in wonderment and saying, "That was the frankest meeting I ever heard in my life." He was surprised so many people close to Truman advised him not to run, which according to Murphy "was quite different from the popular conception at the time—that the President's staff, his hangers-on, would be urging him to run again, so they could keep their jobs."[14]

Harriman's Candidacy

In the spring of 1952, the President and his supporters, rebuffed by Stevenson, cast around for a candidate who could head off Kefauver and also prevent the Democratic party from falling into the hands of the Southern conservative wing led by Georgia Senator Richard B. Russell. Oklahoma Senator Robert Kerr was supported by Clifford, but in Truman's eye Kerr was tied too closely to the oil and natural gas interests. A true-blue Roosevelt-Truman Democrat, Harriman, all but convinced Truman that he deserved to be the rightful heir. As ambassador to the Soviet Union under both Roosevelt and Truman, and secretary of commerce as well as top foreign policy adviser for Truman, Harriman had a record of strong support for Truman's policies. Although he had never run for office and his experience had been primarily in foreign affairs, he had strong backing among labor and liberal groups.

During this political turmoil in the spring of 1952, the White House staff was split down the middle, with most of Murphy's group, myself included, wholeheartedly for Harriman. Harriman's lack of political experience certainly figured in the President's reluctance to give him an all-out public endorsement.

As a strong supporter of Harriman, I was concerned that he was not projecting a forceful image of leadership, nor was he articulating with sufficient personal fervor the liberal philosophy that he radiated in small gatherings. He appeared nervous in making his early political speeches. One of his staff remarked that he "almost peed on the floor" before making a public speech. But Harriman displayed a remarkable reversal of form in an address to the National Press Club that I attended on May 13.

Several people spoke with me about Harriman after this speech, knowing I was one of his supporters. One was the venerable Louis Brownlow, a renowned expert in public administration, who had helped coin the phrase "passion for anonymity" as qualification for a good White House staff assistant. Brownlow remarked to me, "I used to be for Adlai Stevenson, but this speech really sets me back on my rocker and I have changed my mind completely."

Harriman mobilized sufficient support to sweep the Democratic primary in the District of Columbia, and picked up a scattering of delegates in New York, Utah (where his Sun Valley enterprises operated) and several other areas. At the Democratic convention, his tally on the first ballot was 123½—well behind Kefauver, Stevenson and Russell, in fourth place. By this time, Stevenson had informed an impatient Truman that he would accept if nominated. A breakfast arranged by labor leaders with Barkley finally convinced him that his "last hurrah" was over. Truman then sent word to Harriman asking him to release his delegates, which he immediately did, to Stevenson's advantage.

Truman Insists on Smooth Transition

After his March 29 announcement, Truman frequently repeated his desire for a smooth transition of power after January 20, 1953, no matter who was elected. The very day after the Jefferson-Jackson Day dinner speech, Truman earnestly underlined his strong feelings on this issue to a small staff group working in the Cabinet Room. My personal reaction at the time was "let's get the 1952 campaign won to put a Democrat back in the White House" before concerning ourselves with such far-off projects as the "orderly transition." But the President's mind always worked that way—looking into the long future and taking advantage of his experience and knowledge of history. During the eighty-two days he served as Vice-President he had felt the lack of briefing by Roosevelt keenly. He expressed one further thought: With the spread of atomic power to aggressor nations, the world had become too dangerous to allow any nation to be uncertain about the continuity of American policy. During this period I had the honor of developing a seven-year review of the President's role in the establishment of the United Nations and the high points of United States participation in the UN.[15] In this document, transmitted to Congress and cited by the President in his July 3, 1952, news conference, Truman stressed that the fabric of international cooperation had been strengthened through bipartisan support and required that type of consistent support to be effective.

At the Bureau of the Budget, it came as no surprise that Truman was looking beyond 1953, insisting that his successor receive the baton of power in a smooth transfer. The Bureau revealed that even in 1948 Mr. Truman had sanctioned discussions with Dewey's representatives about future policy considerations.[16]

1952 Democratic Convention

In preparation for the 1952 Democratic convention, Murphy parceled out various staff assignments. Neustadt was given responsibility for preparing the first draft of the platform. All of us provided bits, pieces and comments, but the final handiwork was Neustadt's. Murphy observed, "He had a long time to work on it and did an excellent job. I think it was a far better document from a literary standpoint, and probably from the standpoint of content, than the one which came out eventually."[17] In this and other instances, the platform committee naturally felt some pride of authorship, which is the reason they switched around certain sections drafted by Neustadt.

The President's liaison with the 1952 Democratic national convention in Chicago was Dawson, an administrative assistant. When it became known that the President, although officially a delegate, did not plan to attend the convention until after the selection of the nominee, attention naturally focused on what the President's alternate would do when casting his ballot. Interest intensified when the President announced that his alternate was Thomas Gavin of Kansas City. It was Dawson's unique responsibility to be the conduit between the President and Gavin, just as soon as the word came down whom the President would support. That decision was made easier following Stevenson's phone call to the President asking if it would embarrass the President to have his name placed in nomination. The President's response, as recorded in his *Memoirs*, was "I have been trying since January to get you to say that. Why would it embarrass me?"

Coal Mine Safety Legislation

Extensive preparations for the convention did not occupy all of the President's time during the summer of 1952, because the regular flow of business continued unabated. Congress was hurrying to adjourn before the conventions, and as usual a pile of last-minute legislation was rushing through. One of these bills was the effort to strengthen the Federal Coal Mine Safety Act. History indicates that most mine safety legislation follows a disaster in the mines. The President was shocked when 119 coal miners were killed in a major accident on December 21, 1951, at West Frankfort, Illinois. In strong letters to Barkley and Rayburn on January 22, 1952, Truman called for strengthening existing mine safety laws.[18] He specifically indicated that many accidents "could surely have been avoided if the Department of the Interior had had authority to enforce compliance with Federal standards of mine safety." West Virginia Senator Matthew M. Neely introduced a strengthened mine safety bill. But as so frequently happens, by the time the coal operators and their lobbyists had pawed over the bill it had been amended, weakened and watered down. When the legislation reached the President's desk, he had a difficult choice to make. A veto would mean that no improvements would be made in existing law. To sign it would mean accepting weak enforcement provisions.

Finally, the President decided to write a strong statement condemning the numerous shortcomings in the bill. Among his criticisms were these:

> The broad phase of accident prevention in general remains the responsibility of the States in which coal is mined, despite the record to date indicating either the inability or unwillingness of the States to meet this responsibility. . . . The measure contains complex procedural provisions relating to inspections, appeals, and the postponing of orders which I believe will make it exceedingly difficult if not impossible for those charged with the administration of the act to carry out an effective enforcement program.[19]

The President had no illusions that the legislation he was signing would sharply reduce mine accidents. He warned the Congress:

> We will do our very best to prevent mining disasters with the authority granted in this bill but the Congress eventually will have to meet its responsibility for enacting legislation which provides tools fully adequate to prevent the great loss of life and the thousands of crippling injuries due to mine accidents.[20]

Unfortunately, Congress did not heed the warning. No thoroughgoing effort was made to correct the shortcomings that President Truman pointed out in his 1952 message to the Congress, until the disaster at Farmington, West Virginia, on November 20, 1968, in which seventy-eight coal miners lost their lives. Only then did Congress respond with the passage of the tough Federal Coal Mine Health and Safety Act of 1969.

Local Color and "Props" for 1952 Campaign

One day in August 1952, Murphy sauntered into my office. He gazed with puzzlement, mixed with disapproval, at the huge pile of newspapers, magazines, books and papers of all shapes and sizes scattered around my desk, chairs, sofa, windowsill and in assorted heaps on the floor. Murphy always maintained a neat desk and wondered aloud what all this junk was and how I ever managed to find anything among the mass of materials. I showed him a couple of samples of "props" I was collecting for the campaign—newspaper and magazine stories that helped highlight local issues. Many of these were drawn from daily and weekly newspapers from communities around the country that we were likely to visit on the campaign train. As we began to get hints of a tentative schedule, I would enter a three-month subscription to local newspapers. This provided useful articles on federal projects or what was on the minds of the local people, and frequently included editorials, cartoons, or special articles to dramatize the issues that concerned the President.

With Bell in Springfield helping Stevenson, and Elsey working as Harriman's assistant in directing the Mutual Security program, Murphy and Lloyd were the only people left from the highly successful 1950 whistle-stopping team of writers. Just as soon as the President's schedule was fixed for a Labor Day swing through Pennsylvania, Ohio, Wisconsin and West Virginia, I began to churn out two-page outlines of the economic, political, historical and other features of the cities and towns. This background information, compiled by the same method used in 1950, furnished some good clues for the issues the President wanted to stress in each area.

The Atmosphere on Campaign Trips

One of the first things I discovered on the campaign train was that I was cut off from my customary sources of information and intelligence. I couldn't switch on radio or television to find out what was happening in the world. There is scarcely time during a ten-minute stop to jump off and get a newspaper. If the President wanted a fact or figure checked before using it, I couldn't pick up a telephone and go right to an accurate source—I had to take enough material along to supply the answer immediately. At some stops, I jumped off the train, made a beeline for a shop that might have a pay telephone, and made a quick long-distance call to double-check some obscure fact we had to verify. In such circumstances, it was essential to listen carefully for the "beep-beep" signal that sounds just before the train is to pull away from the station. Fortunately, the train always moved at a slow speed for the first few hundred yards, to enable laggards to hop aboard at the last minute. This practice saved me on several occasions from being left behind. I still shudder and break out in a cold sweat when I recall the worst example, at a town whose name I cannot remember. For a speech on small business I made an unusually lengthy phone call to my friends in the Department of Commerce and other agencies who had up-to-date economic records. I heard the warning signal, but the phone was located a little distance from the train, and by the time I had run down the track, the train was already pulling out. The President and the governor of a state I cannot even remember were still waving to the crowd, when down the track came this staff assistant huffing and puffing with a look of desperation. A football-muscled Secret Service man reached down and helped pull me up onto the rear platform, where the President got a great kick out of the genuine burst of speed I had mustered in the final fifty-yard sprint.

Being out of touch with the outside world produced embarrassing situations also, despite the up-to-date communications system maintained by the United States Army Signal Corps in a railroad car filled with elaborate equipment and coding devices for classified messages.

"Cordell Hull Is Dead!"

The President delivered a warm, effective little talk to a sundrenched noontime audience in Crestline, Ohio, on September 1;[21] the train then thundered west toward Milwaukee, where he was scheduled to give his evening Labor Day address. Murphy, Lloyd, Short and I sat together in one of the train compartments in what seemed like a relaxed moment. The Milwaukee speech had been frozen; the text already had been released to the reporters on the train. The respite was soon over, however, as we started to get out the long yellow pads and pencils for some serious drafting work.

Suddenly we heard the pounding of hurrying footsteps down the aisle, and the chief of the Signal Corps team, Captain Harvard Dudley, breathlessly thrust a message into Short's hand, yelling, "Cordell Hull is dead!" We stopped our other work immediately. We all knew this had been expected. Roosevelt's long-time secretary of state was eighty-one years old. He had just suffered a stroke, was confined at Bethesda Naval Hospital, and before we left Washington the news accounts indicated his condition was grave. Short immediately said the President would want to issue a news release and also send Mrs. Hull a message of condolence. Lloyd asked me if I would work on both of these.

Short handed me the message Captain Dudley had brought him. It was headed: "THIS IS THE STATEMENT PROPOSED BY THE STATE DEPARTMENT AND APPROVED PERSONALLY BY SECRETARY ACHESON: THE PEOPLE OF THE UNITED STATES AND INDEED THE WORLD TODAY LOST ONE OF THEIR MOST NOBLE SONS. ALL AMERICANS JOIN WITH ME IN MOURNING THE PASSING OF CORDELL HULL. . . ."

The statement went on for several pages, and I felt it was rather vague and did not detail some of Hull's great achievements. While I was redrafting the statement, someone else composed and sent a comforting telegram to Mrs. Hull.

The statement was mimeographed for immediate release, headed "ABOARD TRAIN EN ROUTE TO MILWAUKEE," and distributed to the press. About an hour later, while our train was still rattling across the Middle West on its way to Milwaukee, gray-haired, bespectacled little Anthony Leviero, the White House correspondent for *The New York Times*, suddenly stuck his head into our compartment. This was unusual because the compartment was by custom off-limits to the press. Evidently Leviero had something serious on his mind, because he said it was very important that he talk to Short. He revealed his mission right away: "My desk tells me that Cordell Hull is still alive and didn't die."

I regret to say that, as I thought of the implications of that piece of startling news, I expressed absolutely no joy whatsoever that Hull had survived.

Somehow everything got straightened out, a follow-up message of explanation and apology was sent to Mrs. Hull, and the incident was quickly forgotten. The sequel to this story is that, despite his grave illness, Hull lived on for several years, until July 23, 1955.

The President's Labor Day address, broadcast nationally, was well received by an enthusiastic crowd in the Milwaukee Sports Arena. Before an audience including eleven thousand cheering workers turned out by both AF of L and CIO unions, the President delivered a hard-hitting attack pointing out the differences between Eisenhower's statements and the Republican record in Congress on labor and other issues.[22] The crowd interrupted the speech forty-two times with applause.

Snollygosters and Smokehouses

Coming across West Virginia the next day, September 2, Truman enjoyed tremendous crowds. By this time we had worked out a division of labor on the speech-writing staff; Murphy and Lloyd handled the major addresses and I had the responsibility of preparing the whistle-stop outlines. At the first stop in West Virginia, at Parkersburg, thirty-five hundred people turned out at the railroad station, where the President delivered a serious foreign policy address denouncing recent efforts of Republicans to claim they would liberate the captive peoples behind the Iron Curtain.[23] It was intended more for national than local consumption. But two parts of the speech in particular delighted the local crowd.

Just before we pulled into Parkersburg, Truman asked me for a Bible.

"Anything special I could find for you, Mr. President?" I asked.

"Thank you very much. I know exactly where it is: Gospel according to St. Matthew, Chapter 6." He flipped the pages quickly and started reading the verses with feeling:

> And when thou prayest, thou shalt not be as the hypocrites are: for they love to pray standing in the synagogues and in the corners of the streets, that they may be seen of men. . . .
>
> But thou, when thou prayest, enter into thy closet, and when thou hast shut thy door, pray to thy Father which is in secret; and thy Father which seeth in secret shall reward thee openly.

Then he added that some Republican campaign orators like John Foster Dulles were posing as self-righteous defenders of the captive peoples of Eastern Europe. He read the Bible passage to his Parkersburg audience, adding that his grandfather used to tell him that when you heard someone praying loudly in public, "you had better go home and lock your smokehouse." Then Truman sent reporters scurrying for their dictionaries when he denounced Republican "snollygosters." He turned to the puzzled press corps, chewing their pencils at trainside, and quipped, "Better look that word up, it's a good one." Later in the speech he suggested, "I wish some of these snollygosters would read the New Testament and perform accordingly." Short explained that the word meant "a pretentious, swaggering, prattling fellow." John Edwards of the American Broadcasting Company took a particular interest in the word, which the President said his father had used many years before.

An uproarious crowd of six thousand greeted the President in Clarksburg. Writing in the *Fairmont Times*, veteran correspondent William D. Evans, Jr., used this lead for his enthusiastic front-page story: "President Harry S. Truman yesterday proved to the complete satisfaction of thousands of cheering West Virginians that he has lost none of the mastery which four years ago made him the world's champion 'whistle-stop' campaigner."[24]

At West Virginia whistle stops in Grafton, Clarksburg, Keyser, and Martinsburg, the crowds were large and enthusiastic. The President was in fine fighting form and was pleased with the entire trip. I had a feeling that despite a few "bugs" the whistle-stopping was going to be almost as enjoyable as it would have been if the President had been a candidate. It proved to be even better than I imagined. At a news conference following his return, the President remarked, when asked about his whistle-stop trip, "To tell you the honest truth, I always enjoy it. I had a good time coming across West Virginia the other day." A reporter answered, "We enjoyed it, too. Thank you, sir."[25]

In the few days that he had between trips to reflect and catch up with his paperwork, the President discovered, in a report from his executive clerk Bill Hopkins, that for the first time since he had taken office the incoming mail had fallen below the five thousand mark. He quietly recorded this in his diary:

> It is fortunate that I've never taken an attitude that the kudos and kowtows are made to me as an individual. I knew always that the greatest office in the history of the world was getting them and Harry S. Truman as an individual was not. I hope I'm still the country man from Missouri.[26]

The Western Trip

One of the most strenuous trips of the 1952 campaign started ten days later. It stretched to California, Oregon, and Washington and required two weeks on the road. On his first day out, in Fargo, North Dakota, the President faced up squarely to the corruption issue:

> Betrayal of the public trust is damnable, and those who are guilty of it ought to be prosecuted to the full extent of the law. And as long as I am President they will be. The people who gave the bribes and the people who took them should all be behind the bars.[27]

He contrasted the number of bank embezzlements with the record of the Bureau of Internal Revenue, which he found to be "a great deal better." On a more positive note, he pointed to the reorganization plans he had sent to Congress "to improve the Government's machinery for preventing corruption in the future." Then he attacked congressional Republicans for voting "against every reorganization plan I have proposed to take Government jobs out of politics and put them under civil service."

At Grand Forks, North Dakota, the President used a copy of the *Wall Street Journal* that I had brought along, quoting proposals by the Republicans "to crack down on the unions" if they gained strength in Congress. Truman brought howls from the crowd when he remarked, "That is one time I agree with the *Wall Street Journal*. It is very seldom I ever agree with them."[28]

At Minot, North Dakota, the President waved a copy of the *Fargo Forum* with the headline "1951 North Dakota Farm Income the Third Highest on Record."[29] He contrasted his record with that of the Republican Congress on farm programs.

At every stop, the President included strong plugs for the election of Stevenson, defining him as one who "will fight for the plain people of this country," and "a man of peace" who "has made a great and progressive record as Governor of Illinois." But the crowds really warmed up to his jabs at the Republicans and their presidential candidate, about whom he said "the best thing for you to do is send him back to the Army where he belongs."

On September 30, the President moved west across Montana. Once again, he delighted local residents with comments about their towns. In Chinook, Montana, he mentioned the warm winter winds after which the town was named and then said, "I wish we could get a Chinook wind into the Republican Party." Truman then added, "You know why I wish that? It would melt the ice around the Republican hearts and get them to show some warmth toward the common people."[30]

I couldn't resist dragging in the old acorn analogy the President had used so successfully in Missoula in 1950. Here is what he told the crowd in Chinook:

> When I spoke here in Montana 2 years ago, I said that most Republicans could look and look at an acorn and all they could see were the little old acorns. But people like Mike Mansfield, with vision for the future, can see that acorn as a giant oak tree. So I say as I did 2 years ago, don't vote for the little men with acorn minds, but vote for the people like Mike Mansfield who have the broad vision to carry us forward to peace and prosperity.[31]

At Havre, Montana, the President used one of the quotes included in my collection entitled "Lest They Forget"—statements that leading

"Where Did Everybody Go?"

Copyright 1952 by Herblock in the *Washinton Post*

Republicans had once made about the friendly intentions of the Soviet Union. Noting that Governor Stevenson was one of the first people to warn that the Russians were becoming a threat to peace, the President quoted an Eisenhower statement before a congressional committee in November 1945: "There is no one thing that guides the policy of Russia more today than to keep friendship with the United States." Truman added that he was tired of hearing the contention that Republicans first awakened the nation to the Soviet threat, and Democrats had been taken in by the belief we could get along with the Soviets.[32]

At the dedication of the Hungry Horse Dam on October 1 the President made the biggest hit of his trip across Montana. It was a major address, studded with facts and figures about the benefits of public power projects throughout the nation. But what attracted the attention of the audience, the news media, and everybody else was a classic phrase that Murphy inserted in the President's remarks: "All of you who are here today had better go over and take another good look at that dam, because if the Republicans win this election, it will be a long time before you see another new structure of that kind."[33]

The next day, the President made effective use of a copy of *The Farm Journal* for September 20, 1952. At the little town of Snohomish, Washington, the President waved the *Journal*, which he characterized as "a very nice slick Republican magazine." He read an editorial denouncing the Truman administration as "helplessly lost, groggy and inept," and then turned to an article on page forty-six of the same magazine headed "What To Do With Surplus Money." The article started off by stating, "For farmers as for many others, the question of what to do with surplus cash is often a problem."

The President had a lot of fun with that one: "Now that certainly sounds like we have got the country in a terrible fix. We have created a new problem for the farmer: what to do with his surplus money."[34] Then he had the crowd in stitches by relating: "I heard a story over in Montana, told to me by the Governor. He said the farmers over there were in somewhat of a fix. He said he had met one farmer who was in such a bad fix that he had to wash his own Cadillac!"

On October 3, the train moved through Oregon and down into California's Central Valley. In many of his speeches, he had been talking about the five different jobs the President had to perform—chief executive, Commander in Chief of the Armed Forces, ceremonial head of state, maker of foreign policy, and leader of his political party. One day as I was wandering through the press car, John Davies of the *Newark News* showed me a piece he had written, and I liked it so much that I showed it to the President. He got a good laugh out of it, and when we reached Gerber, California, he told his whistle-stop audience:

> Now one of the newspapermen along on this trip has heard so much about my five jobs, as President, that I hear he wrote a little piece for his paper saying: "President Truman keeps talking about jobs all the time—five for himself and 62 million jobs for the rest of the American people." I like that description, because that is just what the Democrats have done for the last 20 years—we have brought jobs to 62 million people.[35]

When we arrived at Davis, California, the site of the Agricultural College of the University of California, the audience was belligerently unruly. Many students were out with "I Like Ike" signs, and there was an organized effort to disrupt the rally. Governor Earl Warren was scheduled to introduce the President, but there was a chorus of boos and catcalls when the President appeared on the platform, along with chanting from the "I Like Ike" sign-wavers. I was afraid that some fist-fights would break out between the local Democrats and the students. Finally, the governor raised his hand for silence, and delivered an adroit introduction. He reminded the audience that he had run as the Republican candidate for vice-president in 1948. He added that he cared not which party the audience was supporting, but as Californians they should behave with the dignity and courtesy due the high office of President of the United States. He noted that as long as he was governor of California, he was going to show respect for the office of President that he felt all Californians shared. By now, there was a noticeable reduction in the raucous chants from the crowd. Warren made them feel a twinge of conscience and the crowd quieted as he introduced the President. Truman was deeply moved; he began his rear-platform speech by saying, "I want to say to you that I think you have one of the greatest Governors in the United States. He has always been my friend, and I have always been his—and I shall always be."[36] The audience listened respectfully throughout the rest of the speech.

In San Francisco at the Palace Hotel next day, Truman used a clipping sent by the National Committee. It was a news story in the *Nashville Tennessean* concerning a Nixon rally, for which a local doctor had used a gimmick he hadn't dreamed would be publicized. The newspaper published a photostat of a letter written by a doctor to his fellow doctors, asking that they come out to a Nixon rally, adding: "In order to make the best impression on the general public, we are asking you to use a small car if that is at all possible." The President accused the top Republican candidates of surrendering to the "dinosaur" wing of the Republican party, in contrast to Republicans like Paul Hoffman, Wayne Morse, and Governor Warren. At Oakland auditorium that evening, he scorched Eisenhower for attacking the bipartisan foreign policy that he had helped to formulate.[37]

Swinging east into Utah, Truman noted the "Give 'em hell, Harry" cries he received at many whistle stops. He responded: "Well now, I don't strive for a reputation of that kind. I tell the truth on them, and that's a lot better for the country than giving them hell, because they can't stand the truth."[38] At Brigham Young University in Provo, Utah, he brought out a clipping from the *San Francisco Chronicle*, pointing out that job offers to college graduates were so plentiful they could choose between five to ten offers—indicating prosperity in the area.[39]

On October 6, I had great fun with the President's speech at Helper, Utah. I had talked with several railroad people on the use of helper engines in the rugged mountains of Utah. The President told his audience at Helper:

> I have always been interested in the way your good town got its name. They tell me that Helper was named for the helper engines that pull the train up these wonderful mountains you have around here. You know, I think the Republican Party needs some helper engines. It would take a whole roundhouse full of these helpers to get them elected this fall, with their terrible record holding them back.
>
> As for their candidate for President, I don't think helper engines can get him out of the trouble he is in now. With the crew he has got around him, I don't think he will ever be elected. I just don't think the people are going to elect a President who has surrendered to Taft and McCarthy and Jenner and Kem.[40]

At Grand Junction, Colorado, Murphy turned a local project into a humorous thrust against the Republican party. Referring to water storage on the Upper Colorado River, the President said: "I think that Dinosaur National Monument ought to be preserved. In fact, it ought to be enlarged. After this election, we will enlarge it to accommodate the dinosaur wing of the whole Republican Party. We will fill it up with the old Republican fossils."[41]

Roaring east across Iowa and Missouri, Truman continued to spread the gospel about Democratic prosperity and how it could continue under Stevenson, but possibly be sabotaged if a Republican were elected. He held up a copy of the *St. Joseph News-Press* in that town, showing the headline "BUSINESS IS LOOKING UP ALL OVER THE COUNTRY."[42]

By October 8, the President and his party had been on the road for eleven consecutive days. Starting sometimes before 7:00 A.M., and frequently not giving his last speech until shortly before midnight, the President thrived on the rugged pace. Even without his customary two-mile brisk early morning walks, he still managed to feel fit, and he was able to drop off to sleep quickly despite the swinging and swaying of the train. For the major speeches, we received a supply of fairly good first drafts from Washington, and Murphy and Lloyd were hammering them into shape in time to enable the release of an average of one major prepared speech per day. Meanwhile, Neustadt and I fed whistle-stop drafts to Murphy for final clearance. Sometimes the drafts for the following day were not completed until the small hours of the morning, after which Murphy would work them over and meet with the President early in the morning before the first whistle-stop speech. If Murphy got more than two or three hours of sleep a night, he was lucky. The rest of us worked well into the early morning hours and then got up about 8:30 A.M.

In preparing the two-page background summaries for the President and for the other speech-writers, I furnished the names of the congressional incumbents and Democratic candidates. We had just passed through Democratic territory in Missouri where the congressman in office was also the Democratic candidate. We then entered Indiana, having Republican congressmen and Democratic challengers.

Unfortunately, one of the other speech-writers, in his zeal to rush a draft to the President, had incorrectly copied the name of the Republican incumbent instead of the Democratic candidate in Anderson, Indiana. Because of the lateness of the hour, the customary process of checking and rechecking the draft was short-circuited and the error went directly into the President's speech draft.

About 8:15 or 8:20 A.M. on October 9, Murphy appeared at the compartment door where one of the other speech-writers and I were snoozing away. We woke up pretty fast when he said, "The Boss is a little upset. He just endorsed the Republican candidate for Congress, in fact it was the present Republican congressman!"

I was shocked to discover that although my copy of the background data on Anderson, Indiana, was correct, it had not been transmitted accurately to the President. I wondered how the Democratic candidate must have felt to hear Truman urge his audience to vote for a Republican congressman who opposed nearly every one of the President's policies. I shuddered to think how the press would handle this goof.[43]

Staggering into the dining car shortly after 9:00 A.M., I listened closely to the newspeople discussing the President's speeches. I wondered how long it would be before they discovered the slip. I was amazed to find out that not a single one of them had bothered to get up that early to listen to the President. They ribbed me with comments like: "When are you going to stop making every whistle stop so full of meat that we have to cover them all?" Most of them seemed a little groggy from a dozen straight days of early-to-late concentration on highly newsworthy, interesting speeches.

None of the wire services covered the mistake at Anderson. When we got back to Washington a few days later, I made it a point to order the local papers in Anderson and surrounding territory. Not one of them mentioned the error. Apparently it was too early in the morning for any news or radio correspondent to cover. The incident was quickly forgotten. But you can be sure that from that point forward, I muscled in to take a last-minute look at every speech draft that went to the President. Characteristically, neither the President nor Murphy said anything further, in keeping with their gentle forbearance toward their staff.

In Buffalo, New York, on October 9, James L. Sundquist joined the speech-writing group. I had worked with him on the 1950 whistle-stop campaign, one of the quarterly reports we prepared for Director of Defense Mobilization Charles E. Wilson, and other speeches. He was a fast writer, and helped considerably.

On October 10, the President whistle-stopped through New York. In Batavia, he pulled out a copy of the local newspaper, stating the "Batavia area industries are in urgent need of manpower."[44] In Utica, near Hamilton College, he praised one of Hamilton's most illustrious graduates, Philip C. Jessup, ambassador-at-large, who had been viciously attacked by McCarthy.[45] At Hudson, Truman produced another *Wall Street Journal*, which charged that Eisenhower's campaign was as vague as Dewey's had been in 1948.[46] In Harlem to receive the Franklin Delano Roosevelt Award, the President made a rousing speech about Stevenson's accomplishments and record on civil rights.[47]

New England Trip

With only a few days' rest, he was out again at 9:00 A.M. on the North Haven Green at the start of a four-day swing through New England, which ran from October sixteenth through the nineteenth. In Middletown, Connecticut, Acheson's birthplace, he talked about the accomplishments of his secretary of state.[48]

It was glorious Indian Summer weather as we campaigned through Connecticut, Massachusetts, and New Hampshire, partially by train, with frequent side trips by motorcade. The foliage was in full color, the crowds were warm and usually friendly, and the President was in top form. In the Connecticut River Valley, the glories of nature reached their peak. At occasional college or prep school towns, we would meet loud groups of "We Like Ike" fans who sometimes tried to drown out the President, but usually subsided when he gently reminded them about the courtesy of most New Englanders.

Even though much of the President's campaign was keyed to the prosperity his administration and the Democratic party had brought to the nation, the largest crowds were in the areas with the highest unemployment—Lowell and Lawrence, Massachusetts. Addressing twenty thousand people jammed into streets around Middlesex Depot in Lowell in the early evening of October 16, he showed the value of social security. Using a copy of the *Lowell Sunday Sun*, he mentioned that in the week past $307,000 in social security checks had been mailed to eight thousand people in greater Lowell. A funny thing happened when the President mentioned the local newspaper; a chorus of boos went up. He was more than equal to the occasion and ad libbed, "I see you have the same opinion of the *Sunday Sun* that I have of the *Kansas City Star*. But sometimes, my friends, sometimes these awful newspapers have to print the truth, and this is one time it did."[49]

When the President arrived in Exeter, New Hampshire, on the morning of October 17 he had trouble with a group of boys from the prep school. They were out in force, pushing their way to the front of the crowd at the railroad station with their Ike signs, brooms, and cries for a "clean-up." I cringed as I watched the turmoil at the railroad station. I had given Truman a Walter Lippmann quotation and I sensed that Lippmann's prescient prose could scarcely tame those youngsters determined to raise some cain. The President led off with some petulance, as he surveyed the disruptive coterie of trouble-raisers:

Now I see that a great many of you young people are out here to have a good time, and I am glad to have you have a good time. But I have something to say to you that will cause you to think, I am sure, and I would like for you to listen so you can do a little thinking. And then if you want to holler for Ike, I will be glad for you to do it, because I like Ike too—but I like him in the Army.[50]

Despite harsh glances from academy teachers, the boys booed. "You yourselves will be running the country in the next generation," the President told them, and even this failed to sink in. The Lippmann quote praising Stevenson was completely lost on the younger members of the crowd. Truman finally asked the academy boys to do "some studying for citizenship." They listened a bit more silently when he warned them, "In order that the Government shall continue to be yours when you come to the point where you can take it over, you must prepare yourselves. You must do some thinking for your own benefit and welfare."[51] Finally, he almost had to give up what he intended to say to the voting audience, and fired a parting sally at his tormenters: "Go home and talk to your daddy and your mother. . . ." It was not a very comfortable meeting.

In contrast the President mounted a platform above Compagnone Memorial Common at Lawrence, Massachusetts, two hours later, to look out upon the hugest crowd in Lawrence's history—a warm and friendly outpouring of fifty thousand people. Margaret added color and warmth to the ceremony as she was showered with gifts of orchids and a bolt of cloth made in Lawrence mills.[52] The President showed emotion as he greeted the parents of the three Compagnone sons who lost their lives in World War II overseas combat. I watched his face closely as he turned to the crowd and began to appreciate the acres of humanity stretched out as far as his eye could see. He began, "I don't think I have ever seen so many people in one place in my life, and I have been a good many places where there have been big crowds."[53] After, the President told a reporter, "This has been the greatest reception yet accorded me on my New England campaign."[54] His address denounced isolationism as the road to war, and was well received. A young Congressman named John F. Kennedy, running for the Senate, presented the President with a Lawrence-made suit of clothes, courtesy of the Amalgamated Clothing Workers. The warmth of the entire affair wiped out the unpleasantness of Exeter.

That night in Boston they had a barn-burner of a rally in Symphony

Hall. In addition to his remarks in support of Stevenson and senatorial candidate Kennedy, the President put in a plug for a forty-year-old Democrat running his first time for the House of Representatives—Thomas P. O'Neill, Jr. He spoke eloquently of his battles to thwart communism abroad and at home. He leveled his strongest attacks against McCarthy and denounced Eisenhower's toleration of the slanders against Marshall.[55]

After an overnight and restful stop in Boston's South Station, the President's campaign special sped out to Brockton, arriving at the depot at 8:00 A.M. on October 18. We drove to Legion Parkway, where there was a platform decked with red-white-and-blue bunting. The President was wearing a blue serge suit, he had a healthy tan, and I remarked to one of the Secret Service men that I had never seen him look so refreshed. There must have been thirty thousand people lining the streets on the short ride to Legion Parkway. I did not go up on the stand, because I wanted to stay back in the crowd where I could hear comments of spectators on an outline I had worked up. I especially wanted to observe the reaction to the opening line of his speech: "I am happy to be here this morning in this city which is famous for its shoes, and for its great boxing champion, Rocky Marciano."[56] A powerful response rippled across the big and friendly crowd. Then he brought another roar with a solid hit: "This reception at this time of day, however, is a real knockout. And this makes me feel that we are going to knock out the Republicans just as we did in 1948." The balance of the speech went swimmingly. The crowd was with the President all the way.

The rest of the day was one of the most strenuous of the campaign. Before it was over, the President had made fifteen major and minor speeches, in Rhode Island, Connecticut and Massachusetts, winding up with a 9:30 P.M. address at the Eastern Parkway Arena in Brooklyn, New York. By the end of the day, the many stops almost became a blur as the crowds faded into each other in our memories.

Hitting the Campaign Trail Again

The President was able to rest for one day in Washington, on October 19, but then it was off again on Monday the twentieth for a campaign tour of Delaware, New Jersey and Pennsylvania, returning through West Virginia and Maryland on the twenty-third. A group of only about three hundred, smaller than expected, was at the Wilmington railroad station, and although there were eight thousand at Jersey City, local Democratic machine organizers were disappointed. But on a hundred-mile motorcade through New Jersey to Philadelphia, the crowds were bigger and friendlier than those that had greeted Eisenhower the week before. "I am overwhelmed by this magnificent turnout," the President told a noontime crowd of seventy thousand in Newark, where he drew four times the assemblage addressed by Eisenhower. At both Newark and Elizabeth, he hit hard on the differences between the parties and the candidates on civil rights. Before a gathering of twelve thousand in front of the steps of the Middlesex County Courthouse in New Brunswick, Truman attacked the Republican party for its "big lie and smear technique." The audience spiced the speech with cries of "Give 'em hell, Harry!"[57] Before he left the platform, the President drew happy shouts by announcing with obvious pride, as he did on many other occasions, "I have my daughter with me. She is my greatest asset, with the exception of her mother. Here is Margaret."[58] The speech-writers pondered whether the crowds were more interested in these human touches than in Truman's campaign argument.

Hitting hard on the fact that Stevenson's positions on issues were identical in all parts of the country, Truman tried to drive a wedge into the Republican party by pointing out that Eisenhower was a liberal in the Northeast and an isolationist conservative in the Middle West. Still smarting over differences with the former secretary of state, the President asked a Trenton audience to speculate on a recent Eisenhower visit to South Carolina: "I just wonder if he and Jimmy Byrnes discussed civil rights when they had lunch together in South Carolina? I'll make you a bet they did not discuss it."[59]

In the early evening of October 21, the President addressed twenty-five thousand people crowded into Reyburn Plaza, Philadelphia. Not content to end his day at 6:00 P.M., he continued his restless efforts as he reboarded his campaign train, heading west into Pennsylvania. In a slam-bang, shoot-from-the-hip speech at Bridgeport, Pennsylvania, he dubbed the Republican platform "the lousiest platform that has ever been presented to the country."

At Reading, he referred to the military mind and the fact that he had to relieve a general "when he got too big for his britches." He then went into a theme that was a Truman favorite—naming all the generals supporting the Republican ticket, including "General Electric, General Motors, General Foods," climaxed by this thrust:

The only general that we have got working in the Democratic Party is general welfare. He has always been with the Democrats. Between you and me and the gatepost, I am perfectly willing to let the Republicans have all the generals they want, but I will take the corporals and the privates and we will win the election.[60]

Coal miners from the hard-coal regions were bused in to Pottsville, where the President finally ended his long day on October 21 by leaving the train to address an audience of ten thousand at the high school stadium. High school bands and cheerleaders added to the spirit. The speech would have been better for a serious group of news editors and economists than this spirited partisan audience. There were extensive quotations and statistics compiled by economics professor Simon Kuznets of the University of Pennsylvania, along with a commentary from the *American Economic Review*.[61] The crowds sat in the football stands, literally on their hands. I returned to the campaign train very discouraged with the reception. Maybe all this material about inflation, the economy, purchasing power, and per capita income had to be talked about for the record, but why couldn't it be done in terms of pork chops instead of "productivity"?

At the public square in Wilkes-Barre on October 22, Truman used the Washington Bulletin of the National Association of Manufacturers to predict that if the Republicans won, the Taft-Hartley Act might be used to help break unions.

The noontime crowd at the train station in Northumberland was dominated by youngsters intent on out-yelling the President. It was Exeter all over again. My outline mentioned that the famous British scientist Joseph Priestley had lived in Northumberland between 1794 and 1804. This fact was of no interest whatsoever to the "I Like Ike" chanters. The President said that Priestley would be amazed if he could see the miracles of the twentieth century. The chants became derisive. Truman viewed them coldly and observed, "And I think he would also be amazed if he could see the courtesy of the young men and young women of this great day and age."[62] The distractions increased, until finally the President became exasperated and told them that "nine-tenths of you can't vote," and turned his attention to the older section of the crowd.

At Williamsport, Altoona and Johnstown, the crowds again were big and friendly. I contributed two lines to the Altoona whistle stop that seemed to delight the proud local people: "The General has contradicted himself on so many issues that you can't tell exactly where he does stand. He meets himself coming back—worse than a train going around Horseshoe Curve."[63] The next day, the *Altoona Mirror* commented editorially on the Horseshoe Curve remark and the introduction of Margaret as the high points of the President's visit.[64]

Arriving in Pittsburgh on the evening of October 22, the President left the train to drive through the Hill District with Mayor David Lawrence and CIO and Steelworkers President Philip Murray. At the Syria Mosque, four thousand people interrupted his speech thirty-two times with applause—so much, in fact, that the last part of his address was cut off the telecast. Irked that Eisenhower had indicated he could end the war by going to Korea, Truman interjected in his Pittsburgh speech, "If he knows of any panacea by which we can win the Korean war, it is his business to tell me, and not make a political football out of it."[65]

At Wheeling, West Virginia, the next day, the President was greeted by a cheering crowd of three thousand. He gave them a little history, telling them how Andrew Jackson put his stagecoach on an Ohio River boat at Louisville, debarking at Wheeling for the long ride across the mountains to the nation's capital via the old National Road—a thirty-day trip.[66] He then pulled out copies of *Business Week* and the *Wall Street Journal* to read predictions of how the Republicans might curb organized labor if elected.

Whistle-stopping across Pennsylvania, the President delighted a crowd of five thousand at Connellsville by telling them of a bankers' poll indicating that the banking profession was twelve to one in favor of the Republicans, but he predicted a Democratic win because "life has been too easy and comfortable" to make a change.

In Cumberland, Maryland, on October 23, the President displayed a 1951 Senate report denouncing the 1950 "back street" campaign against Senator Tydings. He then charged that McCarthy, the ringleader of that campaign, was being welcomed as part of the national Republican effort in 1952.[67] He ended this phase of the campaign with a rousing speech in Harpers Ferry, West Virginia, that evening before returning to Washington.

The Last Lap

On October 27, the President set out through Ohio, Indiana, Minnesota, Iowa, Michigan and Illinois to wind up his campaign the Saturday before election with the traditional speech at Kiel Auditorium in St. Louis. The crowd of eight thousand that greeted his early speech at Waterloo, Iowa, was intrigued to hear him tell that as a farmer, along with his brother and sister, "we bought our first manure spreader from Waterloo, Iowa, in 1906." He then retold the old story of how William Jennings Bryan, speaking atop a similar machine, "said that was the first time he ever made a speech from the Republican platform."[68] But it was dead-serious politics as Truman repeated, at many stops, that it was "the most important election since the Civil War." He urged farmers, workers, and housewives not to trust the "Old Guard," but to support the enlightened leadership of Stevenson. Before ninety-five hundred people in the municipal stadium in Davenport, Iowa, the President warned about Republican threats to grain price supports. A local reporter indicated that Truman "never looked more fit or pleased with the rigorous job of 'giving 'em hell.' "[69]

At Moline, a friendly crowd of three thousand cheered as the President quipped, when presented with a miniature plow, "Y'know what I'm going to use this for? I'm going to use this to plow under Republicans!"[70] On a more serious note, he reminded his audience that "world peace and the welfare of our country hang in the balance" of the election. Later in the day, at the Negro War Memorial in Chicago, he reviewed the positive steps he had taken to achieve integration of the Armed Forces.

Some twenty thousand noisy partisans greeted the President's early morning appearance at Muskegon, Michigan, in mild temperatures and clear air on October 30. It was the first time a President had ever visited Muskegon, and Mr. Truman modestly proclaimed:

> You know, it's very, very hard for me to understand what is taking place in this campaign and in the country. I have never in the history of the country—and I am rather familiar with it—known of a "has been" drawing so many people to hear what he has to say.[71]

He noted that he had made two hundred speeches while traveling seventeen thousand miles during the preceding two months. At Grand Rapids, the hometown of the late Senator Vandenberg, Truman praised Vandenberg's role in cementing bipartisan foreign policy and suggested that policy was being undermined by the Republicans. Throughout the day, he drew big and friendly crowds in Michigan, climaxed with a roaring welcome at the State Fair Coliseum in Detroit. There he contrasted the records of the two parties on three "great issues of our day—prosperity, civil rights, and world peace."[72]

Blazing across Ohio on the last day of October, the President met more attentive and enthusiastic crowds. At Troy three thousand people were at the train depot.

Eisenhower had charged in Boise, Idaho, that the government did "everything but come in and wash the dishes for the housewife." Since Troy had a company that manufactured dishwashers, I thought this would be a good opportunity to win over the dishwashing vote. As the President pointed out, "We have made it possible for many housewives to get cheap electricity so they can afford to have electric dishwashers to do the dishes." The spoof proceeded:

> The Republicans are more interested in the problems of the big corporations than they are in the problems of people who have to wash their own dishes. They are too busy trying to open up loopholes in the tax laws for the special interest lobbies to spend much time trying to make life easier and better for the ordinary citizen. I am afraid that the Republican candidate is going to lose the dishwasher vote. I think he will lose the vote of the KP's who have had to wash dishes in the Army, too.[73]

Then the President went through his routine about the generals and the fact that the Democrats work with general welfare. He wound up saying the Republicans could have all the generals, "but we will take the corporals and the privates and the KP's—and the housewives who wash dishes—and we will win the election." Even if the prediction proved wrong the following Tuesday, I was pleased to see that the change of pace went over well with the crowd. The next day the local paper had a headline: "Says Progress Has Made It Possible for Housewives to Buy Locally-Made Dishwashers."[74]

The President delivered a real gem on the night of October 31 at the Music Hall in Cincinnati. It was one of his most humorous speeches, tailored to Taft's hometown. Comparing the Republican campaign to a soap-selling drive, the President said,

> Now I honestly think they ought to have let Bob Taft have the nomination. He was the best representative of their party, and what it stands for, and he deserved that nomination. But the advertising experts said no. . . . Then they had to have a slogan for a sales drive. "Back to McKinley"? No, that may be an honest slogan but it doesn't have the right kind of ring to it. . . . "Ninety-nine and 44/100 percent pure"? Well, they were using that for a while; and then somebody started asking questions about their vice-presidential candidate, and some of the other great crusaders, so they dropped it. . . . So they decided on this one: "It's time for a change." Whatever soap

you are now using, they tell you, switch to our new brand. If you do that, you will have no more problems. Use an entire package, and you can clean up all the fears of depression and unemployment. You can wash away the whole problem of Korea with one simple application.[75]

On the last day of his campaign, the President started at 7:20 A.M. at Vincennes, Indiana, and delivered seven speeches across Indiana and Illinois. At Danville, Illinois, the President used a copy of the October 26 *Danville Commercial-News*, a Republican newspaper, which called for support of the Republicans on the grounds that "it's time for a change." Holding up the newspaper, the President pointed out that in the column right next to the editorial was a "Do you remember" column with events from twenty years ago. One of the items was that "the lowest price for wheat in the history of the Chicago Board of Trade" had been recorded in 1932 at forty-four cents a bushel. The President of course asked if that was the kind of change being demanded.[76]

The Last Whistle Stop

At Litchfield, Illinois, the President read from an editorial in the *Litchfield News-Herald* endorsing Stevenson.[77] At 3:40 P.M., the President's train pulled into Granite City, Illinois. Milton Kayle prepared the outline for Truman's last whistle-stop speech. It was a good summary of the President's long campaign on behalf of Stevenson, as well as a capsule statement of his philosophy of campaigning:

My experience in 1948 proved something I have always known in my 40 years of politics. If the people get the truth, they can be trusted to look out for their own welfare, and the welfare of their great country. That is the basic principle I have followed in my 7 years as President of the United States.[78]

The President autographed the speech for Kayle following its delivery.

For Truman's final speech of the campaign, at the Kiel Auditorium in St. Louis, I had an interesting assignment. The main address had been completed and just about "frozen" for mimeographed release when the President decided that he wanted to dramatize the manner in which Republican candidates jump on the bandwagon of Democratic issues just before the election. He wanted to do a parody of the poem "Just before Christmas I'm as good as I can be." To do so, he wanted to verify the original wording of that poem. None of the materials I had along for research purposes, including Bartlett's *Familiar Quotations,* included the poem.

When the train arrived in St. Louis, we had only a few hours before the speech. I tried a few libraries, which were closed on Saturday afternoon, but finally located one where I could check the precise dialect used in Eugene Field's poem. The President wowed the crowd with his rendition, which included the lines, "Jest 'fore election I'm Fair Deal as sure as sure can be," and "Just 'fore election I'm fer the people as strong as strong can be."[79]

He wound up his address with an attack on Eisenhower for deserting his former principles and contrasted his behavior with Stevenson's "courage and dedication to duty," which led him to interrupt his campaign to quell an Illinois prison riot. The President based his appeal on checking aggressive communism, preventing another world war and preserving and developing "the ideals of democracy and civil liberty."[80]

Luncheon at the Muehlebach

On the day before election, the White House campaign staff were Truman's guests at his suite in the penthouse of the Muehlebach Hotel in Kansas City. It was a spirited luncheon, filled with fond reminiscences about our wonderful times together. There was no pessimism about the next day's election. From the President on down, as we went around the table, I was surprised to hear everybody say that Stevenson would certainly score an impressive victory.

I am sure that the President, despite his doubts about Stevenson's method of campaigning, felt that the Democratic party would eventually regain the confidence of the people. His candid remarks to us in private, as well as his letters to his most personal friends, revealed a buoyant optimism about the 1952 outcome. On September 24, he wrote to Henri L. Warren in Corpus Christi, Texas: "I am starting out on a round the country trip next Saturday and when I get back I think you will find that there will be some pretty big patches in the fur of the enemy on which they can't grow hair."[81]

Then in mid-October, he exuded a confident attitude in writing his old friend "Shay" Minton, whom he had appointed associate justice of the United States Supreme Court: "I believe we are going to hang the hide of the Republican Party on the tree to dry on November fifth. We will do the hanging on the fourth but it won't dry until the fifth."[82]

As the staff voiced their sentiments at the Muehlebach luncheon, I kept my mouth shut. If I had any doubts the day before election, they certainly would have been dispelled by the unanimity expressed around the table. After all, in 1948 President Truman had turned out to be the smartest political analyst in the nation.

Perhaps we should have read the signs better—the strong feeling expressed by critics at some of the rallies, the lingering doubts about corruption, the general unpopularity of the Korean war, and the inroads made by the McCarthy smears. But none of us really measured the towering respect and admiration that the nation accorded to Eisenhower, primarily because of his leadership in World War II. Running against Eisenhower was like running against George Washington.

Notes I made at the time indicated some of my own thinking before I got caught up in the swirl of the campaign and began to hope that maybe Stevenson had a chance. When Massachusetts Senator Henry Cabot Lodge, Jr., announced that Eisenhower would enter the Republican presidential primary in New Hampshire, Rosenman asked for my reaction. I wrote the judge on January 9, 1952: "I think he will be a powerful candidate who will be almost impossible to beat, even if there is a knock-down and drag-out fight with Taft at the convention. In my days of sin, at Princeton, I was supporting Eisenhower in 1947 and 1948."[83]

During a period when I was keeping a sporadic diary in the spring of 1952, I included this note:

> *April 1, 1952:* Harry Schwartz, a young, ex-Columbia statistics professor—now with *The New York Times* as an expert on Russia—dropped in. . . . He suggested we might get some good dope on Ike's regime at Columbia from the files of the *Spectator* [student newspaper] and by interviewing a few Democratically-minded faculty members like Harry Carman, who had some hair-raising stories about Ike's academic naiveté. I'm skeptical about any efforts by the Democrats this year to blemish Ike's personal life; I believe the Democratic campaign should be entirely against the GOP record in Congress.
>
> I said this in a memo to the research director of the National Committee. I cannot understand the way people at the White House minimize the hold Ike has on the American people. They seem to feel that all the Democrats have to do is to ask positive questions, like they did to Dewey in 1948, and Ike will collapse.[84]

That was a note to myself, but my discussions with the National Committee took a somewhat sharper turn. On June 3, 1952, I sent the following memorandum to Bertram M. Gross, the research director of the National Committee, concerning a rather biting document he had prepared on Eisenhower:

> I do not think that you should waste your time trying to attack Eisenhower's qualifications as a military man or as a leader. I think I know General Eisenhower and his capabilities well enough to say that he is one of the greatest leaders and one of the greatest military strategists that this country has ever produced. All right-thinking people appreciate this fact, and I do not think that any purpose would be served in trying to criticize those qualities. There may be some point, however, in indicating the extent of the split in the Republican Party by what the Taft people are saying about those qualities, but my point is that we should dissociate ourselves from this type of irresponsible criticism.
>
> I hope that you will give attention to General Eisenhower's qualifications not only as a politician who can deal with Congress and with political leaders everywhere, but also as a politician who can or cannot control the isolationist element within his own party.[85]

As the Republican national convention approached, I became fearful of how Taft's nomination might affect the nation and the world. At the same time, I found little to argue with in Eisenhower's statements on key issues of foreign policy and national security. My friendly feeling toward Eisenhower was again expressed in a June 26, 1952, letter to Rosenman, an excerpt of which follows:

> I heard General Eisenhower's foreign policy speech the other night, and you could close your eyes and imagine that it was made by a strong supporter of the Administration. The President might easily send a telegram of congratulations to General Eisenhower thanking him for his support of the Administration's foreign policy, and wish him luck, success, health and happiness; an information copy might then be sent to Senator Taft's headquarters and the whole thing released to the press. I would be serious about this, were it not for the fact that I am now convinced that Senator Taft is a more dangerous candidate, and for the sake of both the country and the Democratic Party and the peace of the world, I hope that General Eisenhower is the Republican nominee.[86]

Suffice it to say, I did not raise my voice at the pre-election luncheon in the Muehlebach, nor did I raise any objections as we went through the campaign and the attacks on Eisenhower became more strident. I personally doubt that the campaign results would have changed had these presidential attacks been less personal or less explicit.

Transition

The President followed through on his determination to make the transition a smooth one. He asked each of us to instruct the incoming "team" on pending problems and on where the minefields and booby traps might be located, and to offer any other helpful hints that we could on operating procedures. The Bureau of the Budget was centrally responsible for taking the lead in issues relating to the transition. The day after the election, Frederick J. Lawton and Elmer B. Staats, director and deputy director of the budget, called on the President and stressed the importance of having "someone work with us in developing the new budget." According to Staats:

> He called President-elect Eisenhower immediately, and eight days later Joe Dodge was on the scene. Our instructions from President Truman were to give Dodge every bit of information bearing on the budget and to treat him just as if he were part of the present administration. . . . Because of the confidence built up by virtue of the trust President Truman placed in the incoming budget director, by the time Dodge was ready to take over he was prepared to keep all the bureau's staff without any change at all.[87]

The President noted on November 15, "Since Nov. 4 things have moved very fast. The office work of the President has almost doubled."[88] There did not seem to be any slowdown in the work of the White House staff either. Executive clerk Hopkins, a career man who remained, was busier than most in preparing for the change-over—the thousand and one details that needed attention to insure that the White House would continue to operate smoothly with a new chief executive after January 20, 1953. Steelman offered to be available after January 20 to explain the background of administrative problems. Dawson's phone rang off the hook with questions from people with civil service status and Truman appointees speculating what they should do about their own futures. Murphy and his staff could not rest on their oars, because the President still had to fill many speaking engagements in the interim. More and more people wanted to squeeze in appointments with the President while he was still in office; hence Connelly certainly did not find any letup in his work. Lloyd was giving thought and attention to plans for the Truman Library, for which he would coordinate fund-raising and other administrative details after leaving the White House. Neustadt worked on the first draft of the President's farewell address, to be delivered January 15. Mrs. Short found that many people were writing their appreciation of what President Truman meant to them. These letters were much too personal to leave them unanswered. Tubby and the press office were busy arranging exclusive interviews with the President for many newsmen.

Postelection Assignment

I had an interesting assignment that occupied nearly all my time until Truman left office, and I even spent some time updating my work after Inauguration Day. On November 10, the President, always thirsty for facts, asked for a number of items in the following handwritten note:

Memo for the staff:—

An analysis of Eisenhower's campaign speeches. A complete copy of every one of them in booklet form.

Reference index to his statements on foreign policy:—Europe, Asia, Korea, Middle East and Iran. Statements on domestic policy:—Federal Employees, State Dept., Defense Dept., Agriculture, Labor, Commerce, the Vatican, Social Security.

The Republican Platform and its relation to Eisenhower speeches.

All his statements—about McCarthy, Jenner, Korea, Vatican and all other subjects, national and international. His messages to France, Churchill and other foreign countries.

An analysis of Nixon talks. His attacks on the President. His soap opera speech, the facts about his income, who the people are who support him.

Obtain the files of the McCarthy-Benton hearing in the Senate.

Statements of Tabor [sic], Wolverton, Fulbright, Smathers, Byrd et al. about the election results and the part they took in the campaign.

Analyze Trumanism.[89]

I decided if the President of the United States wanted this tremendous collection of material, he deserved the best effort I could make to get it all together and analyzed before he left office. When I first looked at the memorandum, I felt I might be able to finish the job by Thanksgiving Day. After two or three days of hunting for the Eisenhower and Nixon speeches, I realized it would take at least until Christmas. Actually, it took a little longer.

First, I made copies of all the speech texts available in *The New York Times*, which generally covered only the major speeches. Then I conned the Washington Bureau of the *Times* into letting me rummage through its files. I picked up a number of speeches from the Washington offices of various interest groups. I went to see correspondents of newspapers in the states Eisenhower and Nixon had visited. Allen Dulles, whose son had been in a class I taught at Princeton, sent me a few speeches he had. Those news correspondents who had been on Eisenhower's train were very cooperative in turning over what they had. Some friends in various federal offices provided copies when the speeches related to policies in their departments. After a few long-distance calls, I got newspeople in numerous localities to supply copies they had obtained from the Eisenhower campaign train. Some Republican offices on Capitol Hill provided missing texts. I made a deal with Dr. Floyd McCaffree, Republican National Committee research director, saying, "I'll tell you what, Floyd, I'll give you copies of the ones you haven't been able to find if you'll give me copies of the ones I couldn't get." He agreed to the trade. Then we pooled our information on how to locate a few missing speeches, and before long we each had a nearly complete file.

Excerpting, analysis, categorizing, indexing, and cross-indexing were the next big job. By the time the document on Eisenhower was finished it was more than six hundred pages long, and included more than anybody would ever want to know about Ike, arranged so that the reader could find anything within a few seconds. We mimeographed twenty-five copies. Since this was before the days of mechanical assemblers, I spent Inauguration Day in the White House bowling alley, the only place other than the main ballroom where I could spread out and assemble six hundred pages. The Democratic National Committee promptly labeled the Eisenhower collection the "Iklopedia."

In compiling the material on Nixon's attacks on Truman the most difficult to find was Nixon's characterization of Truman as a traitor. The best verification I could obtain was an Associated Press dispatch of one of Nixon's speeches at Texarkana, Texas, on October 2, 1952. According to the Associated Press, Nixon charged that Truman, Acheson, and Stevenson were "traitors to the high principles in which many of the nation's Democrats believe." He was then quoted as saying that "real Democrats" were "outraged by the Truman-Acheson-Stevenson gang's toleration of and defense of communism in high places." It was impossible to locate a copy of the text of Nixon's Texarkana speech. The closer I came to it, the more sensitive I found were the friends and associates of the 1952 Republican vice-presidential nominee. They argued the speech must have been delivered extemporaneously. It could be contended that

Nixon was charging Truman, Acheson, and Stevenson with being traitors to their party, rather than traitors to their country. Yet one could
certainly conclude that "toleration of and defense of communism in high
places" was a form of treason. If indeed Nixon did not intend to brand
the President a traitor, his choice of words nonetheless conveyed that
impression.

There was a small sequel to the "traitor" story. When I sent the hundreds of pages of answers to the President's November 10 memorandum,
I made no special effort to flag the data on the Texarkana speech. As
time went on and the Republican National Committee began to deny
that Nixon had called Truman a traitor, I suspected that perhaps my
quotation from the Associated Press story might have become buried
with all the other material. Then in 1956, Leonard Hall, Republican
National Committee chairman, issued a public statement offering one
thousand dollars to anybody who could prove that Nixon called Truman
a traitor. I sent Mr. Truman a photostat of the Associated Press article,
along with these comments:

> By the way, you may be interested in the attached photostat with a direct
> quote from Nixon concerning his 1952 "traitor" charge. Of course, he will
> claim that he only said you were a traitor to Democratic principles, but in
> the very next sentence he refers to "defense of communism in high places"
> which pins him down on exactly what he was trying to convey. If you col-
> lect $1,000 from Leonard Hall, I'd like to get a cut out of it.

Shortly thereafter, Truman wrote to Hall as follows:

> Some time ago you made a statement to the press that you would contrib-
> ute one thousand dollars to any charity I might name if it could be proved
> that the Vice President had called this former President a traitor.
>
> Because it has been proved rather conclusively, may I suggest that this
> contribution be made to the Red Cross of Korea, a country in which the
> Republicans have professed such a deep interest during the past few
> years.[90]

Hall subsequently declined to send the contribution, stolidly contending
that Nixon had not meant to call President Truman a traitor.

The Last Dinner

I received a letter dated December 12 from Connelly, which read:

> The President hopes that you can come to the White House on the evening
> of December 18th at 7:30 P.M. at which time he is giving an informal dinner

(black tie) for the men who have served him in various capacities on a staff level since he first took office in April 1945.

Please let me know if you can attend.

The gathering on December 18 brought together many old friends and also some of the early Truman assistants who had not been around recently. It was a joyful occasion, tinged with some sadness, as we assembled for the last time that everybody, past and present, had a chance to get together with the President. Going through the spacious main lobby, past the grand staircase, we were ushered into the Blue Room, where cocktails were served and we rubbed elbows with the key White House staff members who had served since 1945. After about thirty minutes, we filed into the Red Room, where the President shook hands and engaged in small talk with each of us. From this point, we moved into the great State Dining Room. Instead of the usual individual tables for dinner, there was a long rectangular table at which each of us had a designated place. We were all equals at one head table, with no special ranking. I recall reflecting that it was characteristic of the President to treat every human being as an equal.

The President had indicated that this was just to be a quiet dinner among friends, with no speeches. With his back to the fireplace and mantel, in the center of one of the long sides of the rectangular table, the President arose after dinner with a few simple words of appreciation to those who had been privileged to work for him. The evening was marred by Connelly and Daniels, both of whom had too much to drink and engaged in a loud and disruptive argument. The President, although not amused, accorded both of them their First Amendment rights to spout off angrily at each other. But despite this minor flaw, the majesty of the occasion was not lost on anyone present. I am sure we all felt a tremendous pride in having been fortunate enough to work and travel with President Truman as we reflected on the contributions we had made.

14

Mister Citizen

On the afternoon of January 20, 1953, while thousands lined Pennsylvania Avenue to view Eisenhower's inaugural parade, Truman and some of his old friends and staff lunched at the Georgetown home of Dean Acheson. A large crowd of well-wishers waited outside the old red brick house, hoping to get a glimpse and possibly a word from the outgoing president. He did not disappoint them. Standing at the top of the steps of Acheson's front porch, Mr. Truman addressed the demonstrative crowd, which quickly hushed when he spoke: "May I say to you that I appreciate this more than any enthusiastic meeting I have ever attended as President, or Vice President or Senator. This is the greatest demonstration that any man could have, because I'm just Mr. Truman, private citizen, now."[1]

Later that day, as five thousand emotional supporters sang and cheered a farewell at Union Station, Mr. Truman stood with Mrs. Truman and Margaret, waving from the rear platform of the *Ferdinand Magellan* as of old, this time on the way home to Independence.

When I was asked to "analyze Trumanism," I despaired at the thought that to answer that question adequately would require a full-blown history of the Truman administration. I finally settled on two simple paragraphs as the best I could do without spending a lifetime supplying an adequate answer:

> Trumanism is the policy which has successfully strengthened the free world and rolled back the threat of communism. It is the Truman Doctrine, which extends military and economic aid to Greece, Turkey and other nations, thereby saving those free nations from communist subversion and armed aggression. Trumanism is Point Four—the bold, new program

"Independence Day"

From The Herblock Book (*Beacon Press,* 1952)

which has given life and hope to millions of people in underdeveloped countries, through economic and technical assistance and capital improvements. Trumanism is the electrifying speed with which the United Nations, backed up by the full power and influence of the United States, stood up and met the communist armed challenge in Korea.

Trumanism is the policy which has brought this country the greatest prosperity this country has ever known, with a Fair Deal to all groups of the population. It means extended social security, civil rights, aid to education, better housing, inflation control, development of our great natural resources for all the people, high wages and better working conditions for labor, the greatest prosperity farmers have ever had, and scores of other policies for the benefit of the average man.[2]

An editor who once wrote that he "hates Trumanism" inspired Mr. Truman to confide to his diary:

Let us define Trumanism.

One, we have found by hard experience that the Soviets respect only force. So we have built up our armed forces. . . .

Two, we have held the economic front in balance at home. The farmer, the laboring man, white collar workers, industry and industry management are in the midst of the most prosperous era in the history of the world.

Three, the public interest comes first in the mind of the present occupant of the White House.

Four, we prevented Tito from taking Trieste right after the German foldup, we forced Stalin out of Iran, we saved Greece and Turkey, we stayed in Berlin, and we knocked the socks off the communists in Korea, we gave the Philippines free government, we gave Puerto Rico its first native governor, we gave that beautiful island a constitution and home rule, we appointed the first native governor of the Virgin Islands. If that's Trumanism, I confess judgment and I'm proud to have my name attached to that program by the lousy, unfair, controlled press even if that controlled press tries to make me look like a dub![3]

After observing this remarkable human being at close range, John Hersey made an astute analysis of what contributed to Truman's greatness:

President Truman seemed to think of himself sometimes in the first person and sometimes in the third—the latter when he had in mind a personage he still seemed to regard, after nearly four years in office, as an astonishing tenant in his own body: the President of the United States. Toward himself, first-personally, he was at times mischievous and disrespectful, but he revered this other man, his tenant, as a noble, history-defined figure. Here was a separation of powers within a single psyche, and a most attractive phenomenon it was, because Harry Truman moved about in constant wonder and delight at this awesome stranger beneath his skin. And to some extent this wonder and delight must have elevated and purged the mere man.[4]

If I had to pick Mr. Truman's one trait that made me proudest of all to work for him, it was that he never lost the common touch and was determined to use the awesome power of the presidency to help bring peace and justice to the average people all over the world.

Notes

Abbreviations

AP   Dean Acheson Papers
AYP   Eben A. Ayers Papers
CP   Clark M. Clifford Papers
EF   George M. Elsey Files
EP   George M. Elsey Papers
FH   Francis H. Heller, *The Truman White House*
HF   Ken Hechler Files
HP   Ken Hechler personal papers and diaries (to be turned over to Truman Library)
HST, Vol. I   Harry S. Truman, *Years of Decision*
HST, Vol. II   Harry S. Truman, *Years of Trial and Hope*
LP   David D. Lloyd Papers
MF   Charles S. Murphy Files
MP   Charles S. Murphy Papers
MT   Margaret Truman, *Harry S. Truman* (Pocket Books edition)
NeP   Richard E. Neustadt Papers
NP   Mary Ethel Noland Papers
OF   Official Files, Papers of Harry S. Truman
OH   Oral History
PPF   Postpresidential Files, Papers of Harry S. Truman
PPT   U.S. National Archives and Records Service, *Public Papers of the Presidents of the United States—Harry S. Truman* (with designation by year)
PSF   President's Secretary's Files
VP   Major General Harry H. Vaughan Papers
WH   William Hillman, ed., *Mr. President*
WP   Stanley Woodward Papers

Except as noted, all of the files and papers listed above are housed in the Harry S. Truman Library in Independence, Missouri.

1   *"What Kind of a Person?"*

1. The story of Winthrop Aldrich's visit to President Truman is based on personal conversations I had with the President on the 1952 campaign train, the recollections of

several White House staff members, and a letter the President wrote to his cousin, Ethel Noland, on February 2, 1952. The Ethel Noland letter is handwritten and located with NP.

A much different version of an Aldrich visit with the President is included in OH, Joseph Feeney, a White House assistant. (The Feeney version is repeated in MT, p. 485.) Several White House staff members have disputed the Feeney version, as well as pointing out other serious discrepancies in Feeney's other recollections.

2. Dennison, OH, pp. 203–204.
3. Guests of the President at the Blair House dinner on the evening of June 7, 1950, were press secretary Charles G. Ross, correspondence secretary William D. Hassett, special counsel Charles S. Murphy and assistants David E. Bell, George M. Elsey, David D. Lloyd, Stephen J. Spingarn and myself.
4. HP.
5. For reference to early poker games on the third floor of the White House Mansion, see McKim, OH, pp. 127–128.
6. Personal observation at Key West, Florida, President's quarters, November 1951.
7. PSF, Box 333, 1945.
8. PSF, Box 333, 1952, Memorandum, July 6, 1952, "The Republicans."
9. PSF, Longhand Notes, Folder 1, 1952, dated December 25, 1952.
10. Tubby, OH, p. 25.
11. HP, notes on 1950 meeting in Cabinet Room.
12. Murphy, OH, p. 116.
13. FH, p. 144.
14. Friedman, OH, p. 23.
15. AP, Box 166, "Acheson-Truman Correspondence," copy of article in "The Tailor and Cutter & Women's Wear," December 22, 1950.
16. AP, Box 166, "Acheson-Truman Correspondence," Truman to Acheson, January 27, 1951.
17. *Ibid.*, Acheson to Truman, February 1, 1951.
18. *Ibid.*, Truman to Acheson, February 2, 1951.
19. *Ibid.*, Truman to Acheson, May 28, 1954.
20. *Ibid.*, Truman to Acheson, April 20, 1955.
21. Farley, *Jim Farley's Story.*

2   *Truman Selects His Staff, 1945–1948*

1. WH, p. 111.
2. PPT, 1945 Volume, p. 8.
3. *Ibid.*, pp. 16–17.
4. *Ibid.*, p. 119.
5. MT, p. 233.
6. HST, Vol. I, p. 327.
7. FH, p. 37.
8. Rosenman, OH, p. 62.
9. Rosenman, OH, pp. 76–77.
10. Diary, June 5, 1945; see WH, p. 120.
11. Rosenman, OH, p. 67.
12. *Ibid.*, p. 49.
13. MT, p. 316.
14. Clifford, OH, p. 3.

15. *Ibid.*, p. 10.
16. Elsey, OH, *passim;* also personal observation, and interview with Elsey, June 18, 1981, HP.
17. Elsey, OH, p. 224.
18. *Ibid.*, p. 264.
19. MT, p. 379.
20. PPT, 1945 Volume, p. 414.
21. PPT, 1946 Volume, p. 491.
22. FH, p. 66.
23. PPF, Memoirs File, December 18, 1954, discussion with Mr. Truman, William Hillman and David Noyes, pp. 1–2.
24. *Ibid.*, p. 4.
25. FH, p. 69.
26. *Ibid.*, p. 187.
27. Murphy, OH, p. 42.
28. *Ibid.*, p. 45.
29. FH, p. 70.
30. *Ibid.*
31. *Ibid.*, p. 84.
32. Murphy, OH, p. 63.
33. Bell, OH, pp. 12, 82.
34. Dennison, OH, p. 48.
35. *Ibid.*, pp. 5–6.
36. FH, p. 138.
37. Dennison, OH, pp. 50–52.
38. HP.
39. Daniels, OH, pp. 113–114.
40. PSF, Ross Diary, February 27, 1946.
41. Vaughan, OH, p. 105.
42. Dennison, OH, pp. 39–40.
43. *The New York Times*, February 23, 1949, p. 1. Note that the official report of the address includes a bowdlerized version, with "any S.O.B." altered to read "anyone." See PPT, 1949 Volume, p. 143. The official reporter-stenographer, Jack Romagna, explained that he had made the change on his own initiative.
44. PPF, Vaughan to Truman, July 26, 1967.
45. Tubby, OH, pp. 65–66.
46. HP.
47. *Ibid.*

3   *Planning the 1948 Campaign Strategy*

1. PSF, Box 333, 1945, Diary, May 22, 1945.
2. PPF, Memoirs, Box 47, Set 1, January 23, 1946.
3. Clifford, OH, p. 190.
4. Quoted in Ross, *The Loneliest Campaign*, pp. 55–56; see also "Summary of Remarks by George M. Elsey," Princeton University, January 11, 1949, EF.
5. Rowe, OH, appendix.
6. Al Larkin, "The Campaign and the Presidency," *The Boston Globe Magazine*, November 2, 1980.
7. Interview with Charles S. Murphy, June 11, 1981, HP.
8. Rowe, OH, p. 25.

9. PSF, James Roosevelt to J. Howard McGrath, October 29, 1947.
10. PSF, Truman to James Roosevelt, November 4, 1947. Roosevelt wrote to me on February 16, 1982: "I've no personal recollection of receiving that letter from President Truman." Roosevelt then suggested that a search should be made among his letters at the Franklin D. Roosevelt Library in Hyde Park, New York. Director William R. Emerson of the FDR Library informed me on March 2, 1982: "Our archivists have made a thorough search of Mr. Roosevelt's papers and do not find the item you mentioned—or anything remotely approaching it. Their search would seem to bear out your surmise that this was one of those letters Mr. Truman never sent!" See HP for this correspondence.
11. PSF, Eleanor Roosevelt to Truman, March 26, 1948.
12. Daniels, *The Man of Independence*, pp. 347–348.
13. WH, p. 135.
14. MF, Memorandum, Box 1, "Speech—May 6, 1948."
15. PPT, 1948 Volume, p. 259.

4 The "Nonpolitical" Tour

1. PPT, 1948 Volume, p. 284.
2. *Ibid.*, p. 286.
3. MP, Box 50, "Some Aspects of the Preparation of President Truman's Speeches for the 1948 Campaign," December 6, 1948, p. 5.
4. EF, "Summary of Remarks by George M. Elsey," Princeton University, January 11, 1949.
5. *Ibid.*
6. CP, Speech File, Batt to Clifford, June 8, 1948, and Bell to Clifford, undated.
7. PPT, 1948 Volume, p. 290.
8. PPT, 1948 Volume, p. 301.
9. *Ibid.*, p. 335.
10. Kent, OH, p. 48.
11. Nixon, OH, p. 557.
12. Murphy, OH, p. 23.
13. Webster's *Third New International Dictionary*, p. 2606, includes definitions of "whistle stop" used as both a noun and a verb to connote the type of grass-roots campaign initiated by President Truman in 1948.

5 The 1948 Convention

1. HST, Volume II, p. 190.
2. MT, p. 9.
3. PPF, Memoirs, diaries, Box 3, July 12, 1948.
4. *Ibid.*
5. EP, Box 9, Speech File, July 15, 1948.
6. Quoted in Ross, *The Loneliest Campaign*, p. 124.
7. PPF, Memoirs, diaries, Box 3, July 14, 1948.
8. PPT, 1948 Volume, p. 406.
9. *Ibid.*, p. 409.
10. AYP, Ayers, Diary, July 13, 1948.
11. PPT, 1948 Volume, p. 409.
12. Clifford, OH, p. 237.

13. HP, Elsey to Hechler, August 24, 1981.
14. PPF, Memoirs, Box 3, diaries, July 15, 1948.
15. *Ibid.*, July 16, 1948.
16. PPT, 1948 Volume, p. 417.

6 *The Greatest Political Upset of All Time*

1. PSF, General File, Clifford Folder.
2. MF, "Suggestions for Preparing Outlines for Brief Platform Speeches," Box 1.
3. PPT, 1948 Volume, p. 477.
4. MF, Box 50, "Some Aspects of the Preparation of President Truman's Speeches for the 1948 Campaign," pp. 13–14.
5. *Ibid.*, p. 15a.
6. *Ibid.*, p. 17.
7. PPF, Memoirs, Box 3, diaries, September 13, 1948. Clifford recalls that the President was "under extreme pressure because of the campaign," but he does not remember Truman admonishing him in the terms indicated in Truman's diary. See HP, Clifford telephone conversation with Hechler, March 9, 1982.
8. MF, Box 50, "Some Aspects of the Preparation of President Truman's Speeches for the 1948 Campaign," p. 18.
9. *Ibid.*, p. 19.
10. PPF, Memoirs, Box 3, diaries, September 13, 1948.
11. PPT, 1948 Volume, p. 484.
12. *Ibid.*, p. 485.
13. PPF, Memoirs, Box 3, diaries, September 13, 1948.
14. *Ibid.*, September 14, 1948.
15. MT, p. 23.
16. *Bill Moyers' Journal*, "A Conversation with Clark Clifford," February 27, 1981, p. 10.
17. PPT, 1948 Volume, p. 508.
18. MT, p. 24.
19. *Ibid.*
20. PPT, 1948 Volume, p. 518.
21. Quoted in Ross, *The Loneliest Campaign*, p. 189.
22. PPT, 1948 Volume, pp. 550–551.
23. Folliard, OH, p. 9.
24. PPT, p. 572.
25. *Ibid.*, p. 601.
26. *Ibid.*, p. 660.
27. *The Herald-Dispatch*, Huntington, West Virginia, October 1, 1948.
28. HP, Elsey to Hechler, August 24, 1981. See also HP, Clifford telephone conversation with Hechler, March 9, 1982. According to Clifford, who was with Truman when he exchanged messages with Marshall in Paris, Marshall's opposition was couched in such strong language that Truman immediately agreed to back off from the proposal.
29. PPT, 1948 Volume, p. 724.
30. Cited in Ross, *The Loneliest Campaign*, p. 214.
31. PPT, 1948 Volume, p. 828.
32. *Ibid.*, pp. 824–827.
33. Rosenman, OH, p. 87.
34. PPT, 1949 Volume, p. 11. In actual fact, Carter did have breakfast alone with the

President one morning on the train. Murphy urged the President to arrange the breakfast in the closing days of the campaign. With a strong sense of self-importance, Carter even lobbied the White House staff to support him for undersecretary of state. See HP.

35. John E. Hopkins, "An Investigation of the Speech and Statement Preparation Process During the Presidential Administration of Harry S. Truman," pp. 109–110.
36. PPT, 1948 Volume, p. 839.
37. *Ibid.*, pp. 851–852.
38. *The New York Times,* October 26, 1948, p. 1.
39. PPT, 1948 Volume, p. 909.
40. Murphy, OH, p. 458.
41. PPT, 1948 Volume, p. 935.
42. *Ibid.*, p. 936.
43. MF, Box 50, "Some Aspects of the Preparation of President Truman's Speeches for the 1948 Campaign," p. 86.
44. PPT, 1948 Volume, p. 937.
45. Kent, OH, p. 48.
46. PPT, 1948 Volume, pp. 938–939.
47. *Ibid.*, p. 939.
48. Quoted in *New York Herald Tribune,* September 9, 1948.
49. *Bill Moyers' Journal,* "A Conversation with Clark Clifford," February 27, 1981, p. 9.
50. Elsey, OH, pp. 65–66.
51. PPF, Memoirs, Box 47, Set 1, October 5, 1948.

7 *A New Mandate: 1949*

1. FH, p. 141.
2. Hamby, *Beyond the New Deal,* p. 267.
3. *Ibid.*, p. 268.
4. PPF, Memoirs, Box 47, Set 1, Truman to Mary Jane Truman, December 13, 1948.
5. *The New York Times,* December 12, 1948, p. 58.
6. AYP, Diary, January 28, 1950.
7. PPF, Memoirs, Box 47, Set 1, November 7, 1948.
8. MT, p. 430.
9. *Ibid.*, p. 439, see CP, Elsey to Clifford, November 16, 1948.
10. Clifford, OH, p. 350.
11. EP, "Memorandum on Origins of Point Four," September 12, 1963, p. 2.
12. Russell, OH, p. 29.
13. *Ibid.*, p. 34.
14. EP, "Memorandum on Origins of Point Four," September 12, 1963, p. 3.
15. EP, longhand notes on January 10, 1949, meeting with Clifford and Lloyd, quoted in Elsey, September 12, 1963, Memorandum, p. 4.
16. PPT, 1949 Volume, p. 114.
17. *Ibid.*, pp. 118–119.
18. HST, Volume II, pp. 235–236.
19. PPF, Memoirs, Box 2.
20. Neustadt, in FH, p. 112.
21. PPT, 1949 Volume, p. 584.
22. Connelly, OH, pp. 162–163, 445.
23. Clifford, OH, p. 439.

8 *Whistle-Stopping in 1950*

1. FH, p. 217.
2. MT, p. 470.
3. *Ibid.* NSC-68 programed a vast increase in American military forces in the face of aggressive communist threats.
4. FH, p. 217.
5. *Ibid.*, p. 99.
6. Murphy, OH, p. 85.
7. FH, p. 164.
8. PPT, 1950 Volume, p. 36.
9. MP, Bell memorandum to Murphy, March 6, 1950.
10. *Ibid.*
11. HF, Memorandum, July 20, 1951, "Future Whistle Stops," a twelve-page memorandum that examines the Northwest trip in detail, incorporating the comments of White House staff members on earlier drafts of this memorandum.
12. EP, Elsey Memorandum for the President, subject: "Whistle-Stop Talks," May 6, 1950.
13. PPT, 1950 Volume, p. 296.
14. Harry La Cossitt, "He Takes the President on Tour," *The Saturday Evening Post,* June 16, 1951, p. 162.
15. PPT, 1950 Volume, p. 299.
16. *Ibid.*
17. "Washington Scene," by George Dixon, Aboard President Truman's Non-Political Campaign Train, May 10, 1950, King Features Syndicate.
18. PPT, 1950 Volume, p. 300.
19. MT, p. 474.
20. HP, Hechler to Rosenman, May 19, 1950.
21. PPT, 1950 Volume, p. 377.
22. *Ibid.*, pp. 377–378.
23. *Baltimore Sun,* May 13, 1950.
24. *The Washington Post,* May 13, 1950.
25. *New York Daily News,* May 13, 1950.
26. Murphy, OH, p. 178.
27. PPT, 1950 Volume, p. 412.
28. The wind that flipped the pages at Cumberland led to an innovation; thereafter, we suggested that a transparent plastic covering be used, which cured the problem and also protected against rain.
29. PPT, 1950 Volume, p. 416.
30. *Ibid.*, p. 421.
31. Anthony H. Leviero, "A 'G.O.P. Operator' Reports on Truman's Tour," *The New York Times,* May 14, 1950, Section IV.
32. Ray Brennan, "Truman's GOP 'Shadow' Eats a Lonely Lunch," *Chicago Sun-Times,* May 16, 1950.
33. Murphy, OH, pp. 177–178.
34. PPT, 1950 Volume, p. 426.

9 *The Politics of Congressional Relations*

1. WP, Truman to Stanley Woodward, June 24, 1950, correspondence with Harry S. Truman, 1950–1953 (handwritten).

2. *Ibid.*
3. Ayers remained as assistant press secretary until the death of Ross six months later. Thereafter, Ayers worked primarily on compiling the historical background of some of Truman's decisions.
4. FH, pp. 12–13.
5. *Ibid.*
6. MT, p. 499.
7. AYP, Ayers, Diary, July 3, 1950.
8. PSF, Box 333, September 11, 1950.
9. PPT, 1950 Volume, p. 492.
10. *Ibid.*, p. 496.
11. MT, p. 507.
12. *Congressional Record*, June 28, 1950, p. 9320.
13. *Ibid.*, June 27, 1950, p. 9229.
14. FH, p. 13.
15. *Ibid.*, p. 229.
16. Connelly, OH, p. 222.
17. NP, Truman to Nellie Noland, March 11, 1950.
18. PPT, 1946 Volume, p. 479.
19. HP, Memorandum on Bipartisanship in Connection with Foreign Policy, February 13, 1951.
20. Eighty-second Congress, First Session, Senate Document No. 87, "Review of Bipartisan Foreign Policy Consultations Since World War II," Presented by Mr. Sparkman, October 20, 1951.
21. *Ibid.*, p. 1.
22. PPT, 1952 Volume, p. 518.
23. Murphy, OH, p. 113.
24. Quoted in Richard E. Neustadt, "Presidency and Legislation: The Growth of Central Clearance," *The American Political Science Review*, September 1954, p. 658.
25. *Ibid.*
26. FH, p. 226.
27. *Ibid.*, pp. 227–228.
28. Neustadt, *op. cit.*, p. 661.
29. PPT, 1946 Volume, p. 351.
30. Truman to James M. Pendergast, May 21, 1946, PSF, Box 320, Pendergast, James (handwritten).
31. PPT, 1950 Volume, p. 13.
32. *Ibid.*, p. 700.
33. *Ibid.*, p. 713.
34. LP, Lloyd to Murphy, November 16, 1950.
35. PSF, Box 333, 1950, Diary, November 30, 1950.
36. Hersey, *Aspects of the Presidency*, p. 27.
37. MP, "Memorandum for the President," April 13, 1951 (unsigned).
38. MP, Murphy memorandum to the President, April 16, 1951.
39. MP, Murphy memorandum to the President, May 19, 1951.
40. MP, Hechler to Murphy, June 20, 1951.
41. EP, Lloyd to Elsey and Hechler, June 17, 1951.
42. HP.
43. *Ibid.*

10   *Korea, Communism and Corruption: MacArthur, McCarthy and McGrath*

1.   HST, Volume II, p. 442.
2.   Tubby, OH, p. 40.
3.   PSF, Box 278, Diary book, April 6, 1951.
4.   *Ibid.*
5.   MT, page 561.
6.   HST, Volume II, p. 447.
7.   PSF, Box 278, Diary book, April 9, 1951.
8.   FH, p. 156.
9.   Tubby, OH, pp. 42–43.
10. Quoted in Manchester, *American Caesar*, p. 770.
11. HST, Volume II, p. 449.
12. FH, pp. 156–157.
13. HF, "Lincoln and Gen. McClellan."
14. Lincoln to McClellan, Carl Sandburg, *The War Years*, Volume I, p. 600.
15. HST, Volume II, p. 443.
16. Tubby, OH, p. 135.
17. FH, p. 148.
18. Tubby, OH, p. 135.
19. Perlmeter, OH, p. 56.
20. Tubby, OH, p. 135.
21. *Ibid.*, p. 136.
22. FH, p. 148.
23. Tubby, OH, p. 136.
24. HP, William J. Hopkins, Memorandum for the President, May 8, 1951.
25. HP, Hechler memorandum to Carroll, April 17, 1951.
26. PPT, 1951 Volume, p. 227.
27. PSF, Box 333, 1951, Diary, June 21, 1951.
28. PPF, Memoirs, Major General Robert B. Landry, recorded interview with William Hillman and David Noyes, January 7, 1954.
29. "A Study of 'Witch Hunting' and Hysteria in the United States" (Hechler revision), copy in HF.
30. PPT, 1950 Volume, pp. 260–264.
31. *Ibid.*, p. 269.
32. PPT, 1950 Volume, p. 561.
33. *Ibid.*, p. 572.
34. *Ibid.*, pp. 645–653.
35. EP, Letters to Vice-President Barkley, Senator Scott Lucas, Speaker Sam Rayburn, and Representative John W. McCormack, August 28, 1950, Internal Security File.
36. EP, Ethridge to Matt Connelly, August 31, 1950, Internal Security File.
37. EP, Elsey to Mark Ethridge et al., September 2, 1950, Internal Security File.
38. "President Pleads for Tolerance," Washington Merry-Go-Round, by Drew Pearson, *The Washington Post*, September 14, 1950.
39. PPT, 1950 Volume, p. 451.
40. *Ibid.*, 1951 Volume, p. 119.
41. HST, Volume II, p. 287.
42. Hersey, *Aspects of the Presidency.*
43. *Ibid.*, p. 138.
44. *Ibid.*

45. Eisenhower News Conference, Abilene, Kansas, June 5, 1952.
46. PSF, Box 333, 1952, Memorandum, July 6, 1952.
47. NP, Truman to Ethel Noland, July 11, 1952.
48. See also *The New York Times*, May 18, 1950.
49. Eisenhower News Conference, Denver, Colorado, August 22, 1952.
50. *Ibid.*
51. Eisenhower address, Appleton, Wisconsin, September 3, 1952.
52. Eisenhower address, Green Bay, Wisconsin, October 3, 1952.
53. Eisenhower, *Mandate for Change,* pp. 386–387.
54. PPT, 1952–1953 Volume, p. 740.
55. Folliard, OH, p. 53. Sundquist assisted on Truman's Colorado Springs address.
56. PPT, 1947 Volume, p. 457.
57. U. S. Senate, Committee on Expenditures in the Executive Departments, Eighty-first Congress, first session, *Report,* January 18, 1950.
58. U. S. Senate, Committee on Banking and Currency, "Study of Reconstruction Finance Corporation Favoritism and Influence," Senate Report 76, Eighty-second Congress, first session, February 5, 1951.
59. Tubby, OH, p. 137.
60. MF, Hechler to Murphy, April 23, 1952.
61. PPT, 1951 Volume, p. 314.
62. MP, H.S.T., "Memo to Mr. Murphy," *circa* August 24, 1951.
63. MP, David E. Bell, memorandum, October 20, 1951.
64. Murphy, OH, p. 306.
65. PPT, 1951 Volume, pp. 643, 646–647.
66. PSF, Box 333, 1951, Memorandum, December 26, 1951.
67. Rosenman, OH, pp. 93–94. Although the context of Rosenman's oral history statement would seem to indicate these events took place after February 1, 1952, it is obvious that the conversation occurred during a Rosenman visit with Truman on December 18, 1951; see the correspondence with Senator Wayne Morse cited below.
68. A. Robert Smith, *The Tiger in the Senate,* p. 133.
69. PSF, Folder "M," Senator Wayne Morse to Truman, December 22, 1951.
70. PSF, Folder "M," Truman notes for response to Senator Morse, December 23, 1951.
71. PPT, 1952–1953 Volume, p. 24.
72. PPF, Memoirs File, J. Howard McGrath, statement for Truman memoirs pp. 24–25.
73. MP, copy of statement by J. Howard McGrath, February 1, 1952.
74. Morris, *Let the Chips Fall.*
75. PPT, 1952–1953 Volume, p. 156.
76. *Ibid.,* p. 166.
77. Seidman, OH, p. 86; see also Morris, *Let the Chips Fall.*
78. MP, Donald S. Hansen, Memorandum for Mr. Murphy Re Newbold Morris Investigation, March 28, 1952.
79. PPF, McGrath, *op. cit.,* p. 26.
80. *Ibid.*
81. *The New York Times,* April 1, 1952, p. 23.
82. Seidman, OH, p. 88.
83. PPT, 1952–1953 Volume, p. 209.
84. Seidman, OH, p. 88.
85. MP, Murphy to the President, April 1, 1952.
86. *The New York Times,* April 3, 1952, pp. 1, 31.
87. PPF, McGrath, *op. cit.,* p. 29.
88. Tubby, OH, p. 142.

89. HP, Notes, April 2, 1952.
90. PPF, McGrath, *op. cit.*, p. 30.
91. HP, Notes, April 2, 1952.
92. *Ibid.*
93. Tubby, OH, pp. 143–144.
94. HP, Notes, April 2, 1952.
95. MP, Hechler to Murphy, "Newbold Morris Speech at Press Club," April 9, 1952.
96. WH, pp. 61–62.
97. PPF, McGrath, *op. cit.*, pp. 24, 25, 31.
98. *The New York Times,* July 5, 1960, p. 21.
99. Morris, *Let the Chips Fall,* p. 40.

11   Communicating with the Public

1. The account of my experiences with the President's June 14, 1951, address is drawn in large part from a letter I wrote to my parents and brother Charles on July 26, 1951; copy in HP.
2. Donovan, *Conflict and Crisis. The Presidency of Harry S. Truman, 1945–1948*, p. 23.
3. Short, OH, pp. 19–20.
4. Perlmeter, OH, p. 11.
5. PPT, 1950 Volume, p. 327.
6. Tubby, OH, p. 13.
7. Nixon, OH, p. 388.
8. Folliard, OH, p. 5.
9. WH, p. 11.
10. PSF, Box 333, 1952, Diary, December 6, 1952.
11. PPT, 1950 Volume, p. 159.
12. Hersey, *Aspects of the Presidency.*
13. NP, Truman to Nellie and Ethel Noland, September 8, 1949.
14. Miller, *Plain Speaking,* p. 60.
15. WH, p. 3.
16. Hillman did not follow these instructions. A comparison of his book with the original documents in the Truman Library reveals that Hillman frequently edited and changed the Truman memoranda.
17. PPT, 1952–1953 Volume, p. 1189.
18. *Ibid.*, p. 1191.
19. *Ibid.*, p. 1196.
20. MF, Hechler to Stowe, August 29, 1950; Stowe to Murphy, September 20, 1950.
21. MF, Murphy, Memorandum for the President, September 13, 1950.
22. WH, p. 65.
23. *Ibid.*
24. *Ibid.*
25. PPT, 1948 Volume, p. 297.
26. PPT, 1949 Volume, p. 110.
27. PPT, 1952–1953 Volume, p. 341.
28. HP, Hechler to Rosenman, May 23, 1952.
29. PPT, 1952–1953 Volume, p. 804.
30. MT, p. 548.
31. Jonathan Daniels, "How Truman Writes Those Letters," *Collier's,* February 24, 1951, pp. 13, 65. For a collection of some of Truman's many unsent letters, see Monte M. Poen, ed., *Strictly Personal and Confidential: The Letters Harry Truman Never Mailed.*

12   "Cargo of Truth"—The Anatomy of a Speech

1. PPT, 1952–1953 Volume, p. 178.
2. A somewhat abridged account of the preparation of this speech, which does not include new material from the Truman Library and other sources, appears in FH, pp. 128–135.
3. PPT, 1950 Volume, pp. 262, 264.
4. LP, Edward W. Barrett, internal memorandum, Department of State, January 18, 1952.
5. LP, Department of State, Release No. 107, February 11, 1952.
6. LP, Frederick C. Oechsner to Roger Tubby, January 31, 1952.
7. LP, Department of State, Release No. 107, February 11, 1952.
8. PPT, 1951 Volume, p. 377.
9. PSF, Box 333, 1952, Diary, December 6, 1952.
10. A stenographic transcript of the entire ceremony, including the preliminaries, was placed in the Appendix to the *Congressional Record*, March 10, 1952, pp. A 1575–1578, by Representative A.S.J. Carnahan (Democrat of Missouri).
11. PPT, 1952–1953 Volume, p. 178.
12. OF, Cable from S.S. *Frederick W. Galbraith*, March 4, 1952, Box 20-E, "Voice of America."
13. LP, Department of State, Release No. 107, February 11, 1952.
14. HF, Department of State, Releases Nos. 206, 569, March 19, 1952, and July 19, 1952.
15. *Ibid.*, No. 698, September 5, 1952.

13   The Last Campaign as President: 1952

1. PPT, 1952–1953 Volume, p. 1039.
2. Quoted in MT, p. 575.
3. PSF, Box 333, 1950, Diary, April 16, 1950.
4. See Dennison, OH, pp. 193–195; Tubby, OH, p. 100; Rigdon, OH, pp. 53–57; HST, Volume II, p. 489.
5. *Ibid.*
6. PPT, 1952–1953 Volume, p. 225.
7. PSF, Box 333, 1950, Diary, April 16, 1950.
8. Dennison, OH, p. 193.
9. Log of President Truman's Trip to Key West, Florida, tenth visit, November 8–December 9, 1951, p. 57.
10. PPT, 1951 Volume, p. 633.
11. PSF, Murphy to Truman, November 23, 1951.
12. PSF, Box 333, 1952, Diary, February 18, 1952.
13. PSF, Box 333, 1952, Diary, March 4, 1952.
14. Murphy, OH, pp. 354–356.
15. PPT, 1952–1953 Volume, pp. 464–467.
16. FH, pp. 157–158.
17. Murphy, OH, p. 369.
18. PPT, 1952–1953 Volume, p. 117.
19. *Ibid.*, p. 480.
20. *Ibid.*, p. 481.
21. *Ibid.*, p. 542.
22. *Ibid.*, p. 543–548.
23. *Ibid.*, p. 549–552; note that the text as printed in PPT is the advance release only; the

full text as delivered is included with official reporter Jack Romagna's files at the Truman Library, Box 34.

24. *Fairmont Times*, September 3, 1952, p. 1.
25. PPT, 1952–1953 Volume, p. 584.
26. PSF, Box 333, 1952, Diary, September 9, 1952.
27. PPT, 1952–1953 Volume, p. 599.
28. *Ibid.*, p. 603.
29. *Ibid.*, p. 611.
30. *Ibid.*, p. 631.
31. *Ibid.*, pp. 631–632.
32. *Ibid.*, pp. 634–635.
33. *Ibid.*, p. 660.
34. *Ibid.*, p. 679.
35. *Ibid.*, p. 699.
36. *Ibid.*, p. 700.
37. *Ibid.*, pp. 707–711.
38. *Ibid.*, p. 712.
39. *Ibid.*, p. 723.
40. *Ibid.*, p. 714.
41. *Ibid.*, p. 716.
42. *Ibid.*, p. 744.
43. The transcript of the Anderson, Indiana, remarks as distributed to the press charitably deleted the President's endorsement of the Republican congressman. Therefore, the official account in PPT, 1952–1953 Volume, p. 758, is also silent on the subject. Even official reporter Romagna's files at the Truman Library include no mention of this slip.
44. PPT, 1952–1953 Volume, p. 775.
45. *Ibid.*, pp. 784–785.
46. *Ibid.*, p. 793.
47. *Ibid.*, pp. 797–801.
48. *Ibid.*, p. 813.
49. *Ibid., p. 825; Lowell Sunday Sun*, October 17, 1952.
50. PPT, 1952–1953 Volume, p. 842.
51. *Ibid.*, p. 844.
52. *Lawrence Evening Tribune*, October 17, 1952.
53. PPT, 1952–1953 Volume, p. 847.
54. *Lawrence Evening Tribune*, October 18, 1952.
55. PPT, 1952–1953 Volume, pp. 854–859.
56. *Ibid*, p. 863.
57. *Perth Amboy Evening News*, October 22, 1952.
58. *Ibid.*
59. PPT, 1952–1953 Volume, p. 901.
60. *Ibid.*, p. 905.
61. *Ibid.*, pp. 910–913.
62. *Ibid.*, p. 920.
63. *Ibid.*, p. 923.
64. *Altoona Mirror*, October 24, 1952.
65. PPT, 1952–1953 Volume, p. 930.
66. *Ibid.*, p. 931.
67. *Ibid.*, pp. 939–942.
68. *Ibid.*, p. 978.

69. *The Rock Island Argus,* October 29, 1952.
70. *Ibid.*
71. PPT, 1952–1953 Volume, p. 994.
72. *Ibid.,* pp. 1008–1012.
73. *Ibid.,* pp. 1017–1018.
74. *Troy Daily News,* October 31, 1952.
75. PPT, 1952–1953 Volume, p. 1023.
76. *Ibid.,* pp. 1031–1032.
77. *Ibid.,* pp. 1036–1037.
78. *Ibid.,* p. 1037.
79. *Ibid.,* p. 1041.
80. *Ibid.,* p. 1044.
81. PSF, Truman to Henri L. Warren, September 24, 1952.
82. PSF, Truman to the Honorable Sherman Minton, October 15, 1952.
83. HP, Hechler to Rosenman, January 9, 1952.
84. HP, April 1, 1952, notes.
85. HP, Hechler to Gross, June 3, 1952.
86. HP, Hechler to Rosenman, June 26, 1952.
87. FH, p. 158.
88. PSF, Box 333, 1952, Diary, November 15, 1952.
89. MP, Truman to Murphy, Memorandum, November 10, 1952.
90. PPF, Name File, Box 35, Hall, Leonard W., Truman to Hall, September 11, 1956.

14 Mister Citizen

1. *The New York Times,* January 21, 1953, p. 1.
2. HP.
3. PSF, Box 333, 1952, Diary, May 15, 1952.
4. Hersey, *Aspects of the Presidency,* pp. 9–10.

Sources

The list that follows is not exhaustive, but merely covers those sources most frequently consulted.

Documentary Materials

All of the documentary materials consulted are on deposit in the Harry S. Truman Library at Independence, Missouri, with the exception of those personal papers, notes and diaries that were generated by the author while he was a member of the Truman White House staff. The mammoth collection of Truman files and papers is unbelievably rich in content and scope. In recent years, a vast amount of previously restricted material has been opened to researchers, including a great deal of valuable Truman handwritten memoranda, diaries, appointment sheets on which President Truman made personal notations, the more personal President's secretary's files, as well as postpresidential files. This last includes a great deal of material originally assembled by Mr. Truman for inclusion in his memoirs, but not used in the two published volumes; this material added a great deal to a fuller understanding of the inner workings of the Truman White House staff.

The following manuscript collections, including files accumulated during the Truman years and papers donated thereafter, were consulted at the Truman Library:

Acheson, Dean (secretary of state) Papers
Ayers, Eben A. (assistant press secretary and special assistant) Papers
Bell, David E. (administrative assistant) Files and Papers
Boyle, William M., Jr. (chairman, Democratic National Committee) Papers

Chapman, Oscar L. (secretary of the interior) Papers
Clark, Tom C. (attorney general and associate justice) Papers
Clifford, Clark M. (special counsel) Papers
Connelly, Matthew J. (appointments secretary) Files and Cabinet summaries
Daniel, Clifton, and Margaret Truman, Papers
Daniels, Jonathan (press secretary) Notes
Davidson, C. Girard (assistant secretary of the interior) Papers
Democratic National Committee Records and Clippings
Dennison, Rear Admiral Robert L. (naval aide) Files and Papers
Edwards, India (vice-chairman, Democratic National Committee) Papers
Elsey, George M. (administrative assistant) Files and Papers
Enarson, Harold L. (special assistant) Papers
Friedman, Martin L. (special assistant) Files
Hassett, William D. (correspondence secretary) Papers
Kayle, Milton P. (special assistant) Papers
Landry, Major General Robert B. (Air Force aide) Files
Lloyd, David D. (administrative assistant) Files and Papers
Loeb, James I. (consultant) Files
McGrath, J. Howard (attorney general) Papers
Murphy, Charles S. (special counsel) Files and Papers
Nash, Philleo (administrative assistant) Papers
Neustadt, Richard E. (special assistant) Files and Papers
Noland, Mary Ethel (President Truman's cousin) Papers
Rigdon, Commander William M. (assistant naval aide) Papers
Rosenman, Judge Samuel I. (special counsel) Papers
Ross, Charles G. (press secretary) Papers
Short, Joseph H. (press secretary) Files
Snyder, John W. (secretary of the treasury) Papers
Souers, Rear Admiral Sidney W. (executive secretary, National Security Council) Papers
Spingarn, Stephen J. (administrative assistant) Files and Papers
Stowe, David H. (administrative assistant) Files and Papers
Vaughan, Major General Harry H. (military aide) Papers
Woodward, Stanley (ambassador to Canada) Papers

The following oral history interviews were consulted at the Truman
Library:

Allen, George (White House assistant and chairman of Reconstruction Finance Corporation)
Ayers, Eben A. (assistant press secretary and special assistant)
Batt, William L., Jr. (director, Research Division, Democratic National Committee, 1948)
Bean, Louis H. (secretary of agriculture staff)
Bell, David E. (administrative assistant)
Bell, Jack (Associated Press)
Biemiller, Andrew J. (U.S. representative from Wisconsin)
Birkhead, Kenneth M. (Research Division, Democratic National Committee, 1948)
Brandt, Raymond P. (St. Louis Post-Dispatch)
Bray, William J. (Democratic National Committee staff)
Brightman, Samuel C. (director of publicity, Democratic National Committee)
Carter, John Franklin (journalist and speech-writer; pen name "Jay Franklin")

Clark, Tom C. (attorney general and associate justice)
Clifford, Clark M. (special counsel)
Connelly, Matthew J. (appointments secretary)
Daniels, Jonathan (press secretary)
Davidson, C. Girard (assistant secretary of the interior)
Dennison, Rear Admiral Robert L. (naval aide)
Edwards, India (vice-chairman, Democratic National Committee)
Elsey, George M. (administrative assistant)
Ewing, Oscar R. (administrator, Federal Security Agency)
Feeney, Joseph G. (administrative assistant)
Folliard, Edward T. (White House correspondent, *The Washington Post*)
Fox, Joseph A. (White House correspondent, *Washington Evening Star*)
Friedman, Martin L. (special assistant)
Fritchey, Clayton (administrative assistant)
Gentry, Sue (reporter, Independence, Missouri, *Examiner*)
Hansen, Donald (special assistant)
Hassett, William D. (correspondence secretary)
Hopkins, William J. (executive clerk)
Jones, Roger W. (assistant director, U.S. Bureau of the Budget)
Keech, Richmond B. (administrative assistant)
Kent, Carleton (correspondent, *Chicago Daily Times* and *Chicago Sun-Times*)
Keyserling, Leon H. (chairman, Council of Economic Advisers)
Lawton, Frederick J. (director, U.S. Bureau of the Budget)
Leva, Marx (assistant secretary of defense)
Louchheim, Katie (vice-chairman, Democratic National Committee)
Lowenthal, Max (counsel to U.S. Senate Interstate Commerce Committee)
Lowry, W. McNeil (Washington Bureau, Cox Newspapers)
Mara, Brigadier General Cornelius J. (assistant military aide)
McKim, Edward D. (chief administrative assistant)
Murphy, Charles S. (special counsel)
Nixon, Robert G. (Washington correspondent for International News Service)
Noland, Mary Ethel (cousin of President Truman)
Pace, Frank, Jr. (secretary of the Army)
Perlmeter, Irving (assistant press secretary)
Pruden, Edward H. (pastor of First Baptist Church, Washington, D.C.)
Reinsch, J. Leonard (White House radio adviser)
Rigdon, Commander William M. (assistant naval aide)
Riggs, Robert L. (Washington Bureau, *Louisville Courier Journal*)
Rosenman, Judge Samuel I. (special counsel)
Rowe, James H., Jr. (attorney and Democratic party adviser)
Russell, Francis H. (director, State Department Office of Public Affairs)
Seidman, Harold D. (U.S. Bureau of the Budget staff member)
Short, Mrs. Beth C. (correspondence secretary)
Snyder, John W. (secretary of the treasury)
Spingarn, Stephen J. (administrative assistant)
Strout, Richard L. (reporter, *Christian Science Monitor*)
Sundquist, James L. (administrative analyst, U.S. Bureau of the Budget)
Trohan, Walter (Washington Bureau of *Chicago Tribune*)
Tubby, Roger W. (press secretary)
Vaughan, Major General Harry H. (military aide)

Published Sources

Books

Abels, Jules. *The Truman Scandals.* Chicago: H. Regnery Co., 1956.

Acheson, Dean. *Present at the Creation: My Years in the State Department.* New York: Norton, 1969.

Allen, George E. *Presidents Who Have Known Me.* New York: Simon and Schuster, 1950.

Allen, Robert S., and Shannon, William V. *The Truman Merry-Go-Round.* New York: Vanguard Press, 1950.

Anderson, Patrick. *The President's Men.* Garden City, New York: Doubleday, 1968.

Bailey, Thomas A. *Presidential Greatness.* New York: Appleton-Century, 1966.

Barber, James D. *The Presidential Character.* Englewood Cliffs, New Jersey: Prentice-Hall, 1972.

Berman, William C. *The Politics of Civil Rights in the Truman Administration.* Columbus: Ohio State University Press, 1970.

Bohlen, Charles E. *Witness to History, 1929–1969.* New York: Norton, 1973.

Byrnes, James F. *All in One Lifetime.* New York: Harper, 1958.

Cochran, Bert. *Harry Truman and the Crisis Presidency.* New York: Funk & Wagnalls, 1973.

Daniels, Jonathan. *The Man of Independence.* Philadelphia: J.B. Lippincott Company, 1950.

Donovan, Robert J. *Conflict and Crisis: The Presidency of Harry S. Truman, 1945–1948.* New York: Norton, 1977.

Eisenhower, Dwight D. *Mandate for Change, The White House Years: 1953–1956.* Garden City, New York: Doubleday, 1963.

Farley, James A. *Jim Farley's Story: The Roosevelt Years.* New York: Whittlesey House, 1948.

Ferrell, Robert H., ed. *Off the Record: The Private Papers of Harry S. Truman.* New York: Harper & Row, 1980.

Goldman, Eric F. *The Crucial Decade: America, 1945–1955.* New York: Knopf, 1950.

Gosnell, Harold F. *Truman's Crises: A Political Biography of Harry S. Truman.* Westport, Connecticut: Greenwood Press, 1980.

Goulden, Joseph C. *The Superlawyers.* New York: Weybright and Talley, 1971.

Hamby, Alonzo L. *Beyond the New Deal: Harry S. Truman and American Liberalism.* New York: Columbia University Press, 1973.

Hartmann, Susan M. *Truman and the 80th Congress.* Columbia: University of Missouri Press, 1971.

Heller, Francis H., ed. *The Truman White House.* Lawrence: The Regents Press of Kansas, 1980.

Henry, Laurin L. *Presidential Transitions.* Washington, D.C.: The Brookings Institution, 1960.

Hersey, John. *Aspects of the Presidency.* New Haven and New York: Ticknor and Fields, 1980.

Hess, Stephen. *Organizing the Presidency.* Washington, D.C.: The Brookings Institution, 1976.

Hillman, William, ed. *Mr. President.* New York: Farrar, Straus, and Young, 1952.

Huthmacher, J. Joseph, ed. *The Truman Years.* Hinsdale, Illinois: Holt, 1972.

Kirkendall, Richard S. *The Truman Period as a Research Field: A Reappraisal, 1972.* Columbia: University of Missouri Press, 1974.

Koenig, Louis, ed. *The Truman Administration: Its Principles and Practice.* New York: New York University Press, 1956.

Leahy, William D. *I Was There*. New York: Whittlesey House, 1960.

Lee, R. Alton. *Truman and Taft-Hartley*. Lexington: University of Kentucky Press, 1956.

Lilienthal, David E. *The Journals of David E. Lilienthal: The Atomic Energy Years, 1945–1950*. New York: Harper & Row, 1964.

Manchester, William. *American Caesar: Douglas MacArthur, 1880–1964*. Boston: Little, Brown, 1968.

McCoy, Donald, and Knetten, Richard T. *Quest and Response: Minority Rights and the Truman Administration*. Lawrence: University Press of Kansas, 1973.

Miller, Merle. *Plain Speaking: An Oral Biography of Harry S. Truman*. New York: G.P. Putnam's Sons, 1973.

Millis, Walter, ed. *The Forrestal Diaries*. New York: Viking, 1951.

Morris, Newbold. *Let the Chips Fall*. New York: Appleton, 1955.

Murphy, Robert. *Diplomat Among Warriors*. Garden City, New York: Doubleday, 1964.

Neustadt, Richard E. *Presidential Power: The Politics of Leadership*. New York: John Wiley & Sons, 1960.

Parks, Lillian. *My Thirty Years Backstairs at the White House*. New York: Fleet, 1961.

Phillips, Cabell. *The Truman Presidency*. New York: Macmillan, 1966.

Poen, Monte M., ed. *Strictly Personal and Confidential: The Letters Harry Truman Never Mailed*. Boston: Little, Brown, 1982.

Pollard, James E. *The President and the Press*. Washington, D.C.: Public Affairs Press, 1964.

Price, Harry Bayard. *The Marshall Plan and Its Meaning*. Ithaca, New York: Cornell University Press, 1955.

Redding, John M. *Inside the Democratic Party*. Indianapolis: Bobbs-Merrill, 1958.

Rigdon, William M. *White House Sailor*. Garden City, New York: Doubleday, 1962.

Rosenman, Samuel I. *Working with Roosevelt*. New York: Harper, 1952.

———, and Rosenman, Dorothy. *Presidential Style: Some Giants and a Pygmy in the White House*. New York: Harper & Row, 1976.

Ross, Irwin. *The Loneliest Campaign: The Truman Victory of 1948*. New York: New American Library, 1968.

Rovere, Richard H., and Schlesinger, Arthur M., Jr. *The General and the President*. New York: Farrar, Straus and Young, 1951.

Sandburg, Carl. *Abraham Lincoln: The War Years*, Vol. 1. New York: Harcourt, Brace, 1939.

Sawyer, Charles. *Concerns of a Conservative Democrat*. Carbondale: Southern Illinois University Press, 1968.

Sherwood, Robert E. *Roosevelt and Hopkins*. New York: Harper, 1948.

Snetsinger, John T. *The Jewish Vote and Creation of Israel*. Stanford, California: Hoover Institution Press, 1974.

Smith, A. Robert. *The Tiger in the Senate: The Biography of Wayne Morse*. Garden City, New York: Doubleday, 1962.

Steinberg, Alfred. *The Man from Missouri: The Life and Times of Harry S. Truman*. New York: G.P. Putnam's Sons, 1962.

Truman, Harry S. *Memoirs: Vol. 1, Years of Decision; Vol. 2, Years of Trial and Hope*. Garden City, New York: Doubleday, 1955–1956.

———. *Mr. Citizen*. New York: Geis Associates, Random House, 1960.

———. *Truman Speaks*. New York: Columbia University Press, 1960.

Truman, Margaret. *Harry S. Truman*. New York: Morrow, 1973.

———. *Letters from Father*. New York: Arbor House, 1981.

———. *Souvenir: Margaret Truman's Own Story*. New York: McGraw-Hill, 1956.

Underhill, Robert. *Truman Persuasions*. Ames: The Iowa State University Press, 1981.

U.S. National Archives and Records Service. *Public Papers of the Presidents: Harry S. Truman*, 1945–1953 volumes. Washington, D.C.: Government Printing Office, 1961–1966.

West, J.V., with Kotz, Mary Linn. *Upstairs at the White House: My Life with the First Ladies.* New York: Coward, McCann & Geoghegan, 1973.

Newspapers

Altoona Mirror, Altoona, Pennsylvania.
The Atlanta Constitution, Atlanta.
The Boston Globe, Boston.
Buffalo Evening News, Buffalo.
The Cedar Rapids Gazette, Cedar Rapids, Iowa.
The Charleston Gazette, Charleston, West Virginia.
Chicago News, Chicago.
Chicago Sun-Times, Chicago.
Chicago Tribune, Chicago.
The Christian Science Monitor, Boston.
The Cincinnati Post, Cincinnati.
The Clarksburg Exponent, Clarksburg, West Virginia.
Cleveland Plain Dealer, Cleveland.
The Columbus Citizen, Columbus.
The Courier Journal, Louisville.
The Daily Courier, Connellsville, Pennsylvania.
The Daily Times, Davenport, Iowa.
The Evening Bulletin, Philadelphia.
Evening Star, Washington.
The Evening Tribune, Lawrence, Massachusetts.
The Fairmont Times, Fairmont, West Virginia.
The Fargo Forum, Fargo, North Dakota.
The Grafton News, Grafton, West Virginia.
Grafton Sentinel, Grafton, West Virginia.
The Grand Rapids Press, Grand Rapids, Michigan.
The Herald-Dispatch, Huntington, West Virginia.
The Idaho Statesman, Boise.
Kansas City Star, Kansas City.
The Lima News, Lima, Ohio.
Lincoln Night Journal, Lincoln, Nebraska.
The Litchfield News-Herald, Litchfield, Illinois.
Los Angeles Times, Los Angeles.
The Lowell Sun, Lowell, Massachusetts.
The Milwaukee Journal, Milwaukee.
Minneapolis Tribune, Minneapolis.
Morning World-Herald, Omaha.
The Muskegon Chronicle, Muskegon, Michigan.
News-Register, Wheeling, West Virginia.
New York Herald Tribune, New York.
New York Daily News, New York.
The New York Times, New York.
The Parkersburg News, Parkersburg, West Virginia.
The Parkersburg Sentinel, Parkersburg, West Virginia.
Perth Amboy Evening News, Perth Amboy, New Jersey.
Philadelphia Daily News, Philadelphia.
The Philadelphia Inquirer, Philadelphia.

Pittsburgh Post-Gazette, Pittsburgh.
The Pittsburgh Press, Pittsburgh.
Pittsburgh Sun-Telegraph, Pittsburgh.
The Pontiac Daily Press, Pontiac, Michigan.
Pottsville Republican, Pottsville, Pennsylvania.
Quincy Patriot Ledger, Quincy, Massachusetts.
The Rock Island Argus, Rock Island, Illinois.
St. Louis Globe-Democrat, St. Louis.
St. Paul Pioneer Press, St. Paul.
San Francisco Chronicle, San Francisco.
Seattle Post-Intelligencer, Seattle.
The Sidney Daily News, Sidney, Ohio.
The Spokesman-Review, Spokane.
State Journal, Lansing, Michigan.
The Sun, Baltimore.
Syracuse Herald-Journal, Syracuse.
The Terre Haute Tribune, Terre Haute.
Times-Herald, Washington.
Troy Daily News, Troy, Ohio.
The Washington Post, Washington.

Periodicals

The American Political Science Review, Menasha, Wisconsin.
The Atlantic, Boston.
Business Week, New York.
Collier's, Springfield, Ohio.
Congressional Quarterly, Washington.
Editor and Publisher, New York.
Foreign Affairs, New York.
Fortune, New York.
Harper's, New York.
Journal of American History, Bloomington, Indiana.
Journalism Quarterly, Iowa City, Iowa.
Life, New York.
Midwest Journal of Political Science, Detroit.
Nation, New York.
New Republic, New York.
Newsweek, New York.
The New Yorker, New York.
Ohio History, Columbus.
Political Science Quarterly, New York.
Public Policy, Cambridge, Massachusetts.
Reader's Digest, Pleasantville, New York.
The Saturday Evening Post, Philadelphia.
Saturday Review, New York.
Time, New York.
U.S. News and World Report, Washington.

Articles and Monographs

Albright, Robert C. "Truman Has Crowds Eating Out of His Hand Again." *The Washington Post,* May 14, 1950, Sec. II, p. 12.

Commager, Henry Steele. "A Few Kind Words for Harry Truman." *Look,* August 28, 1951, pp. 63–66.

"Corruption and the Campaign." *New Republic,* September 24, 1951, p. 5.

Daniels, Jonathan. "How Truman Writes Those Letters." *Collier's,* February 24, 1951, pp. 13–15.

Davies, Richard O. "Whistle-Stopping Through Ohio." *Ohio History,* July 1962, pp. 113–123.

Davis, Richard. "Last Whistle Stop." *Newsweek,* November 10, 1952, p. 28.

Dunar, Andrew J. "All Honorable Men: The Truman Scandals and the Politics of Morality." Ph.D. dissertation, University of Southern California, 1981.

Franklin, Jay (John Franklin Carter). "Harry Truman's Foreign Policy." *Life,* January 10, 1949, pp. 28–29.

———. "Inside Strategy of the Campaign." *Life,* November 15, 1948, pp. 48–49.

Hamby, Alonzo L. "The Liberals, Truman and FDR as Symbol and Myth." *Journal of American History,* March 1970, pp. 859–867.

"Harry Says Goodbye: Truman Record." *Nation,* January 24, 1953, p. 6.

Hassett, William D. "President Was His Boss." *The Saturday Evening Post,* October 10, 1953, pp. 19–21; November 28, 1953, pp. 38–39.

Henry, David R. "Decision-Making in the Truman Administration." Ph.D. dissertation, Indiana University, 1976.

"Hired Man." *Time,* May 22, 1950, pp. 19–21.

Hopkins, John E. "An Investigation of the Speech and Statement Preparation Process During the Presidential Administration of Harry S. Truman, 1945–1953." Ph.D. dissertation, Ohio University, 1970.

"H.S.T. Hits Road to Work Miracles." *Newsweek,* May 15, 1950, pp. 23–24.

"I Am Your Hired Man." *Business Week,* May 20, 1950, p. 20.

La Cossitt, Henry. "He Takes the President on Tour." *The Saturday Evening Post,* June 16, 1951, p. 162.

Larkin, Al. "The Campaign and the Presidency." *The Boston Globe Magazine,* November 2, 1980, p. 1.

Leviero, Anthony. "Files Show General Expected Quick Victory." *The New York Times,* April 21, 1951, p. 1.

———. "How the President Makes Decisions." *The New York Times Magazine,* October 8, 1950, pp. 14–15.

———. "Press and President: No Holds Barred." *The New York Times Magazine,* August 21, 1949, p. 10.

"Look Out Neighbor." *Time,* October 6, 1952, p. 26.

Lorenz, A.L. "Truman and the Press Conference." *Journalism Quarterly,* Winter 1966, pp. 671–679, 708.

Lubell, Sam. "What You Don't Know About Truman." *The Saturday Evening Post,* March 15, 1952, pp. 19–21.

Neustadt, Richard E. "Congress and the Fair Deal: A Legislative Balance Sheet." *Public Policy,* 1954, pp. 349–381.

———. "Presidency and Legislation: The Growth of Central Clearance." *The American Political Science Review,* September 1954, pp. 641–671.

———. "Presidency and Legislation: Planning the President's Program." *The American Political Science Review,* December 1955, pp. 980–1021.

Phillips, Cabell. "How the President Does His Job." *The New York Times Magazine*, January 4, 1948, p. 9.

———. " 'The Inner Circle' at the White House." *The New York Times Magazine*, February 24, 1946, p. 10.

"Pomp and Politics; Truman's Non-political Tour." *Life*, May 29, 1950, pp. 22–23.

"Pouring It On." *Time*, October 27, 1952, p. 23.

Rovere, Richard H. "Letter from Washington." *The New Yorker*, May 10, 1952, pp. 119–124.

———. "Our Far-Flung Correspondents—Truman at Key West." *The New Yorker*, December 15, 1951, pp. 75–78.

"Truman's ADA Speech." *Nation*, May 24, 1952, pp. 8–9.

"Truman Train." *New Republic*, October 13, 1952, p. 8.

Walton, William. "Only Superman Could Do It; Men Who Helped Truman." *New Republic*, February 7, 1949, pp. 11–14.

"Whistle-Stop Harry Rides Again." *Newsweek*, May 23, 1950, pp. 19–20.

"Whistle Stopping Again." *Newsweek*, November 3, 1952, pp. 28–29.

Index